What a captivating achievement! In a family memoir based upon primary sources, the author has given a gripping account of his grandfather's life in the Philippines in an adventure covering exactly the period of America's hegemony in those islands. More than just the story of an entrepreneur and a leader among his compatriots, the tale is an immensely valuable addition to an understanding of American colonialism in the first half of the twentieth century.

Rich in the details of everyday life, the history contains enough thick description to warrant the attention of anthropologists, and at the same time, while lovingly recalling the feats of his grandfather as well as American contributions to Philippine society, there is more than enough violence and heartbreak to make the story ultimately a tragic one.

Henry Copeland, Ph.D.
Professor of History & President Emeritus,
The College of Wooster

This is a warm, enlightening, and deeply moving account of one family's remarkable adventures through significant trials and challenges associated with WW II. It is decidedly more than that, however. It is an important contribution to our understanding of what it means to be an American citizen in our complex world today.

Richard Ray, Ph.D.
Managing Director & Senior Editor,
John Knox Press

Beautifully composed, thoroughly researched, captivatingly told, this labor of love is worthy of the heroics and achievements of the Frank family in that Pacific islands nation from the Spanish-American War until—well—not so very long ago. Russell Frank establishes himself through this manuscript as one from that pretty impressive clan that dates back to the last couple of years of the 19th century. As for the history of the family itself, there is almost no comparable American family story related to the Philippines, and surely not too many that parallel it with reference to any American overseas dealings. Also, not incidentally, a valuable piece of scholarly work for serious historical research.

Samuel S. Hill, Ph.D.
Professor Emeritus of Religion,
University of Florida

In his poignant memoir of two generation in the Philippine Islands, Russell Frank masterfully juxtaposes a deeply moving family story with both the historical Japanese takeover of the islands in WW II and the formation of the Philippines as an independent country.

Marrion W. Ward, Ed.D.
Professor of Intercultural Studies,
Montreat College

ON THE ROAD HOME: AN AMERICAN STORY

A Memoir of Triumph and Tragedy
on a
Forgotten Frontier

JOHN RUSSELL FRANK, PH.D.

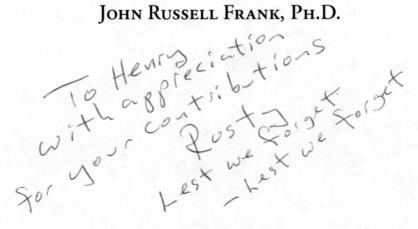

To Henry
with appreciation
for your contributions
Rost☐
Lest we forget
—Lest we forget

iUniverse, Inc.
New York   Bloomington

On the Road Home: An American Story
A Memoir of Triumph and Tragedy on a Forgotten Frontier

iUniverse books may be ordered through booksellers or by contacting:

iUniverse
1663 Liberty Drive
Bloomington, IN 47403
www.iuniverse.com
1-800-Authors (1-800-288-4677)

ISBN: 978-1-4401-9374-3 (pbk)
ISBN: 978-1-4401-9376-7 (cloth)
ISBN: 978-1-4401-9375-0 (ebook)

Library of Congress Control Number: 2009912945

Printed in the United States of America

iUniverse rev. date: 12/21/09

DEDICATION

To my wife, Peggy Ann, and daughters Cheairs, Susan,
Margaret and their families who keep me going.

And in loving memory of my parents,
Frances Anderson Russell and Samuel Boone Frank,
both of whom gave me so much.

Epigraph

The Gospel of Zamboanga

Away back in the memory of every America-born lad, there was a time when a misty-haze of romance penetrated and engraved itself upon his mind. It may have been the oriental splendor of barbarian trappings; lost treasures of gold plate, sunken chests of rare old Spanish coins; or only that uncertain "something-we-have-never-seen;" but it was there when we first sailed westward from the Golden Gate. The majority of us, on reaching our destination, were in time convinced of our delusion; but a few there were who drifted down toward the equator to the islands called the Moro group, and there found paradise.

"Moro Province Mindanao: The Pioneer's Paradise,"
Philippine Magazine (October 1908) pg. 82

CONTENTS

Epigraph vii
Introduction..xiii
Prologue.. xvii

Part 1
Accidental Arrival
1898 to 1902
"I am glad I am a soldier"

1. "I am proud I am of an age and in this thing"...........................3
2. "They did not think we could shoot so well...
   but they got fooled" 13
3. "I for one do not want any more war" 17
4. "...hence her love for the chap who wore Uncle's duds"...........23

Part 2
The Pioneer Frontier
1902 to 1908
"So watch as we get a gait on"

5. "Success or failure she has remained the same".......................33
6. "I came here to Zamboanga"...39
7. "Mr. Frank has named his plantation Frankfort".....................45
8. "It seems that Old Fate has marked out my path" 53

Part 3
Gas Lights, Transportation, and Invention
1908 to 1920
"Fate has made it my home, and I love it"

9. "The world is my home" 63
10. "If you know a bright enterprising young man..." 69
11. "Following her recovery, Okio was looking for a job"..............79
12. "When death became inevitable, Laura was not denied" 88
13. "Mr. Frank is taking his hemp stripping machine to exhibit" ...93

Part 4
The Manila Years
1920 to 1931
"Bud Boss had an opportunity to send Sam and sent him and that is all there is to it"

14. "I'm sending the boys to that great country
    I've told them about"...105
15. "I have to build and deliver ten hemp machines
    which I have sold, and it's some job".............................108
16. "I'll not ship any package off to the university
    unless I know its contents"...114
17. "I'm a little scared—new land, new people" 117

Part 5
The Jolo and Davao Years
1931 to 1940
"If anybody can light anything I can"

18. "Our boat got in at three o'clock and how excited I was" 127
19. "I'm in a daze—absolutely—totally gone" 136
20. "You know what a big 'fraidy-cat' I usually am" 150
21. "So many things have happened to me"..................153

Part 6
The War Years
1941 to 1945
"Today I don't know if you are alive or dead and perhaps until this war is over"

22. "Don't worry about the Japanese trouble".............169
23. "Frances Children Leaving End March Proceed Tucker"........175
24. "Those were Japanese planes bombing our airfield"................187
25. "Situation Normal All Well Love Sam" 196
26. "How helpless and forsaken we felt" 202
27. "We surrendered at the club" 206
28. "We volunteered to go beyond the Japanese lines" 210
29. "Somehow I have made myself believe you are still alive".......215

30. "Lt. Hosaka advised that the internees would be used for labor" 224

31. "They shot him in the back of the head..." 229

32. "Fourteen men were driven to the former Happy Life Blues Cabaret" 236

33. "We boarded the **Shinsei Maru** on Christmas Eve" 247

34. "Santo Tomas looked like a summer resortbut it didn't last long" 250

35. "The boys smashed through and what a day it was" 259

36. "Rejoice—it won't be long now" 272

37. "I found the family all well after some trying years" 276

Part 7
Return to the Philippines
1946 to 1950
"With them passes an era"

38. "I know how to start from scratch. That's about all I do know" 283

39. "I built castles in the air...but it all came tumbling down".....290

40. "A special favor I would ask of you..." 298

Epilogue..303

Acknowledgements...307

Glossary 311

Selected Bibliography 313

Reference Works..323

End Notes...325

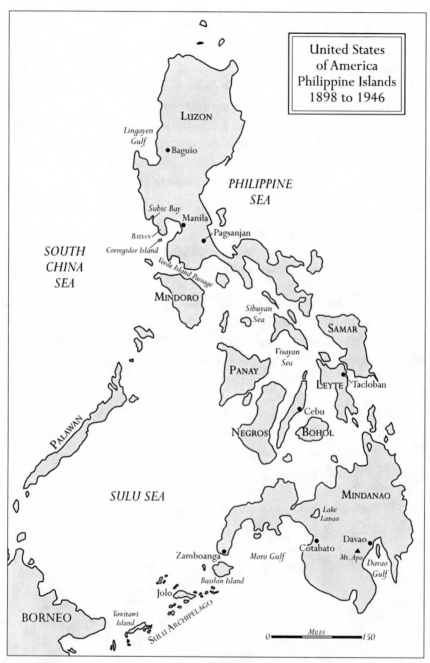

United States of America Philippine Islands Map

INTRODUCTION

"It is something in the air of this country that makes me love it, it is ours just as America is, I would fight for it just the same as America, it is one of our stars"

Patrick Henry Frank, November 5, 1905

Most Americans have forgotten, or never knew, that the Philippine Islands was a United States possession for forty-eight years and a dramatic and important outpost in the American chronicle. The event that brought the United States to the Philippines was the outbreak of the Spanish-American War in 1898, vaulting the nation into the first war beyond its continental borders. In addition, the event transformed the United States into a global power. During its half-century of colonialism in these islands from 1898 to 1946, America's tutelage brought agricultural reform, education, a common language, roads, bridges, electric utilities, public health, and democratic institutions. Filipinos and Americans defended the islands against the Japanese in World War II, fought side by side on Corregidor and Bataan, and died together on the merciless Bataan Death March. Those not killed or captured reassembled into guerrilla bands and together resisted Japanese occupation. Additionally, the Japanese interned five-thousand American civilians—children, women and men—who survived in no small measure through the kindness extended by Filipinos and, in my family's case, Japanese nationals. There was a darker side, an aggressive missionary impulse to carry the American way of life to others whether they liked it or not. The Philippine Insurrection (Philippine-American War) and the Moro Campaigns were bloody affairs, among the most gruesome in American military history. In addition, there was the story of the American colonialists themselves who arrived as soldiers and decided to stay. The balance of their influence, strength, and resolve to remain in the Philippines swung widely depending on the commitment of various American administrations to the islands during this time.

My grandfather, Patrick Henry (P.H.) Frank, was one such colonialist. He and his family lived through this important period of American history in its entirety from 1898 to 1946. Thematically this book is an epic story about his family's triumph and tragedy in a strange land, a story of how they came to absorb and become a part of another culture, and a story of what it meant for them to be Americans.

The narrative flows from a substantial amount of intimate archival material: historically rich letters, war diaries, photographs, memoirs, and oral and video histories from the family's experiences in the Philippines. In 2004, Emory University permanently housed the collection in its Manuscript, Archives, and Rare Books Library. Lewis Gleeck, Curator of the American Historical Collection in Manila, considered the collection one of the most historically rich troves of primary material from that era: "Patrick Henry Frank is the only American whose presence can be documented over the entire period of American sovereignty in the Philippines. Including both private and public accounts, there are few gaps in the record at any point in the fifty-year life of the family in the islands ... You are to be congratulated on preserving an important part of Americana in the Philippines." Gleeck was kind enough to place in his *Journal of the American Historical Collection* several features that I coauthored with historian D. Michael Parker. The 1907 photograph of my grandparents and their two children, which appears in this book, was Lewis Gleek's choice for the *Journal*'s photo of the year in 1992.[1]

In addition to the extensive collection at Emory, my research led me to a wide variety of primary sources in various collections at the U.S. Army Military Institute at Carlyle Barracks, the American Historical Collection in Manila, Duke, the University of Chicago, the Douglas MacArthur archives in Norfolk, the Library of Congress, and the National Archives. Also accessioned were records of the U.S.

Patent Office, the Philippine Supreme Court, and the historical sections of the U.S. Passport Office and the Veterans Administration. Unpublished works by contemporaries of P.H. Frank and my parents in the Philippines were also significant sources, as well as an extensive bibliography of secondary sources, which provided important background and chronology.

I wrote this book because I wanted to share a way of life and a time-period unknown or forgotten to the present generation and to record a poignant human story that might otherwise be lost, not only to my children and grandchildren, but also to others who might have an interest in these pivotal years of America's past. I could not allow the experiences and voices of my grandparents, aunt and uncle, and my parents to be the etceteras of history. My own children are now three generations away from the Spanish-American War and World War II, the events that that began and ended the history of our family in the Islands. Family stories usually last three generations, but because the fourth generation does not hear them directly from their ancestors, the reality of the stories is often lost. It is important to preserve the essence of those chronicles before they are forgotten.

The entirety of this project awaked in me a deep respect and appreciation for the adversities and accomplishments of my grandparents, parents, and aunt and uncle. They experienced life on the Philippine frontier with more intensity than most lives, including my own. Their lives remind all of us that we are what we were and give us an irreplaceable new perspective on the impact of history on our lives.

PROLOGUE

Zamboanga, 1996

I grew up believing that my grandfather was an officer in the United States Army that invaded the Philippine Islands in 1898, and that my grandmother was the daughter of the admiral of the Spanish fleet that fought Dewey at the Battle of Manila Bay. But that was a childhood fantasy, cognitive wiring of a young brain picking up bits and pieces and making something whole, super heroic, and not really the case. My grandfather was Patrick Henry Frank, a private. My great-grandfather was a Spanish engineering officer, not an admiral. My Filipino grandmother, a quarter Muslim Moro, a quarter Chinese and half Spanish, was born to a thirteen-year-old native girl. Her mother, my father's grandmother, was listed in the baptismal records of the Catholic Church in Cotabato, Philippines as "Mora Vi, Infidel."

My plane landed in Zamboanga on the island of Mindanao in the Philippine Islands, not long before dusk, in June 1996. Evening was still early enough to glimpse a tropical sunset spreading red and orange as the driver and I sped along a highway overlooking the Moro Gulf, stretching west toward Basilan Island and the Sulu archipelago. There was little traffic on the picturesque roads and bridges, parts of which I knew followed over old native trails of the Spanish and American periods of Philippine history. The American embassy had issued travel advisories for the southern islands of the Philippines warning of the dangers of Abu Serif uprisings and bandits, but I felt mystically protected by the Mohammedan Moro genetic pool that runs in my American blood. My grandfather, Private P.H. Frank, had come to the Philippines aboard the troopship *Colon* two years short of a century earlier. I had made manifest his prediction that his grandchildren would cross the ocean to the islands in "flying ships of the air."[1]

I was in Zamboanga looking for my grandfather's tread, my father's beginning, my mother's arrival, my own spring, the substance of which stretches back to 1875. I had clamored for a keener sense of how I came to be where I grew up in the shaded Druid Hills neighborhood near Emory University in the post-war Atlanta of 1946, as well as a glimpse of my world behind five decades of American colonialism in the Philippines.

I was on my return to the United States, finishing a sabbatical leave that released me from my teaching responsibilities at a small college in Georgia to lecture for a semester in China at Yantai University. My topic was human development over the life span. I was born in the Philippine Islands beneath a tin roofed, mission hospital in Davao on July 4, 1940. I left in my mother's arms six months before Pearl Harbor, her intuitions of war with Japan accurate. We left behind my father, uncle, and grandfather who were captured and interned by the Japanese army. When people ask me where I am from, I typically tell them only about historic Druid Hills close by Emory University in Atlanta. It was there, when I was six, that my family concluded its emigration following my father's rescue from Japanese prison camps, repatriation, and reunion with his family in St. Louis at the conclusion of World War II. It is rare that I open myself to the longer version.

§

Standing on the terrace of the Lantaca Hotel, I looked out over the Moro Gulf. The number of islands strewn across Southeast Asia—the region from the eastern edge of India to the western and northern edges of Australia and New Guinea—is astonishing. In the Philippines alone, there are over 7,000 islands with diverse geological histories and speciation, the result of endemic fauna and flora fostered by sea barriers. Given the difficulty of movement between islands, virtually every human habitat has a distinct culture. On larger islands like Mindanao, mountain peaks and swaths of lowlands and plateaus encouraged cultural diversity and prevented gene flow. West of where I stood, I could see dozens of smaller islands—Sangbay, Dassalan, Pilas, Tamuk—clustered about the larger Basilan Island thirty miles distant. Behind me to the east, mountain ranges ascended into the clouds. I could easily see that diversity in the Philippines is determined by combinations of geologic and climatic variation that have led to the profusion of life unique to a great number of small areas of habitat. The story of plant life, animal life, and human life and culture in the Philippines is representative of unique places, each with its own tale to tell. America's history in these islands was short. My family history in this place is long, stretching millennia before the American arrival.

§

The finish of the sunset developed. Below me, Moro Sea Gypsies lighted charcoal braziers tucked in their *vintas*. Later, I watched as they lifted *nipa* mats above their families to sleep the night, their small oil lamps reflecting in the water.

A narrow path led to a knee-high storm wall rebuffing gently lapping waves from encroaching further up the beach. Bougainvillea raised itself along both sides of the path. Orchids climbed through the branches dripping with flowers that scented the way.

I walked the path to the edge of the Moro Sea. There was a slack tide, those few suspended moments between ebb and flow. An ancient Spanish canon, a *lantaca*, mounted on the patio aimed back over my shoulder toward Basilan Island. The stars hung just out of reach, like vibrant jewels on the black velvet gown of the sky. Coconut palms rustled in the light breeze. The moon was up full but my shadow was not the only one beside me; my shallow heart was not the only one beating. On the borderline of the mind's edge where I was walking, my grandfather spoke to me.

Part 1
Accidental Arrival
1898 to 1902

"I am glad I am a soldier"

Private Patrick Henry Frank, June 2, 1898

CHAPTER 1

"I am proud I am of an age and in this thing"

Private Patrick Henry Frank, June 2, 1898

There was a subtle revolution developing in America as Patrick Henry Frank approached young adulthood in the 1890's. The close of the American frontier, and the ramifications which the "end" of the frontier would have upon American culture, were the subject of historians such as Frederick Jackson Turner as early as 1893, who noted that the frontier had often driven American development. It certainly drove many Americans of earlier times to migrate further and further west seeking a new start and greener grass. At times, Americans cloaked their wandering and conquest of new territory in quasi-mystical language, as in the eighteen-forties when writers began to proclaim the country's "manifest destiny" to conquer the American continent. With the proclamation by the federal government after the census of 1890 that there were no unsettled lands left in the United States, it appeared that individuals seeking to start fresh in an unspoiled land of opportunity would have to go to greater lengths than their predecessors had done.[1]

Patrick Henry's parents, Felix Frank and Martha McGuire, were married in Old Mulberry Church near Winona, Mississippi, on October 31, 1862. He was nineteen, she eighteen. They married over the objections of her father, the descendent of Irish Orangemen, an abolitionist who hired free Negroes and opposed the marriage of his daughter to a slave owner's son. Soon after, Felix joined the 33rd

Regiment of Mississippi Volunteers, riding to battle on a yellow mule. Pursued by Union troops following the battle of Corinth, he went into hiding, lying down with cows in a pasture until the Yankees stopped looking for him. He returned from the war erratic and temperamental. Martha suffered the loss of her three oldest brothers in the war.

Hard times after the war and a desire to leave defeat and family tragedy drove Felix and Martha to east Texas, where Felix could try his luck as a farmer. Felix, Martha, and three young children took the train to New Orleans and then continued to Texas by wagon. Along the difficult journey, another child was born and named Texanna (Deuce). It was there in East Texas, Tyler County, on March 19, 1875, that Patrick Henry (P.H.) Frank was born. Five more children, all girls, were born to Martha, the last two being twins. P.H.'s birth order was midway of the ten siblings.

Generally, farmers from Texas to the Dakotas in that era knew little but hard times. In Trinity County, where the Frank family lived during P.H.'s youth, conditions were especially trying. A large number of the county's citizens were outlaws, and the popularity of saloons posed a barrier to any attempts to reform the community. Public drunkenness and fighting were so common as to appear community norms. Women and children avoided the county seat of Groveton on Saturdays. Poverty accompanied anarchy; at Christmas time, the merchants bought no toys for the children because there were no purchasers. Such a thing as a Christmas tree was unknown in Groveton. A Texas Ranger observed that in Groveton, "...they had only two law respecting officers—the district clerk and the county attorney, and the county attorney they killed. Good citizens were so completely in the minority they were helpless."[2]

The frustrations of making a living for a large family contributed to the frequent doses of harsh discipline Felix dealt his children. His daughter Cora remembered use of a large leather strap in whippings she described as brutal. Eventually, Martha left Felix in fear because of his growing irresponsibility, but she never divorced him. Felix finally went to Louisiana where he was employed as a sawmill hand in Lake Charles. He died of sepsis at New Orleans Charity Hospital in 1907, the result of a fight involving a Bowie knife. Martha moved to Groveton where she maintained a small boarding house. There she lost two daughters and her granddaughter only two days apart in 1900 to measles and pneumonia. A year later, her uninsured home burned to the ground.

Corporal punishment, hard farm labor, erratic behavior and emotional instability of his father, competition that usually accompanies the dynamics of large families, and the wild-west milieu of Trinity County helped to forge a forceful temper and steely determination in Patrick Henry Frank. By his teen years, after his older brothers and father had gone, his seven sisters, five younger and two not much older than he, nicknamed him "Boss."

Two accounts of P.H. are particularly revealing of the child as father of the man. "Boss," in his teens, had got to gambling with a gang of boys and one day came home broke. His mother had a five-dollar bill. He asked for it just to show the boys he could quit with money still in his pockets. Over the fierce objections of his sister Texanna, his mother gave him the five dollars, explaining that it was not a bad idea for him to do what he said and then bring the money back to her. He took the money, wound up in a game, and lost it.

On another occasion while weighing in cotton at a local gin, "Boss," only about fourteen, insisted that all the hands bring in their sacks at the same time so he could get the weighing done and over with. Some were not ready. One big hand proceeded to take over the weighing. "Boss" grabbed a yoke and hit him over the head, knocking the man out. Thinking he had killed him, P.H. ran away for three days. The man had a sore head for some time, but did not die.

But Patrick Henry Frank was more than just a scapegrace. P.H. took up the heavy chores and mending around the farm. He earned extra money for his mother and sisters. He excelled in the limited schooling he received through sixth grade. Nevertheless, measure for measure he was largely molded out of his faults and, for the most part, considered himself the better for being a little bad in his youthful years.

P.H. left home about 1893 at the age of eighteen, determined, like so many Americans, to make his fortune on hard work and wits. But his hard headedness and willingness to fight followed him as the American economy sank into a severe depression. As was typical of young men from large farming families of the period, P.H. left home seeking that better future in the city. In Houston, he lived with an uncle who arranged for him a job as a motorman on a streetcar. He proceeded to see how fast it would go, burned up the motor, ran off the track, and found himself fired. P.H.'s strong temper also got him into difficulty shortly afterward, when he argued with a supervisor, struck him aside the head with a timber, and left him for dead.

It was this last episode, followed by three stints as a farm hand over the previous six months, which took twenty-one year old P.H. Frank into the army on July 6, 1896. In the town of Dallas, he joined the 23rd Regiment of Regular Infantry for a three-year enlistment. He must have been a sight. His medical examination revealed a quarter-inch scar four inches above his left eye, a half-inch scar over his right eyebrow, and his second incisor and upper jaw broken. When asked if his parents knew of his intention to enlist, "My father doesn't, my mother does," was his reply. When asked what his object was in enlisting, he replied, "I want steady employment, and I think I would like the military life." [3]

At twenty-one years old, P.H. Frank was 5'6 ¼" tall with dark brown hair and blue eyes. His features were handsome, his skin ruddy, his shoulders and neck densely freckled. A solid frame carried his one-hundred-forty-two pounds. He was square-shouldered and very straight. He was ambidextrous; he wrote with his right hand, but chopped wood and hit a baseball like a lefty.

Private Frank's tenure as an enlisted man was, according to family accounts and army records, honorable but tumultuous. He wrote home, sent money, and visited when he could. He was literate, improved his education in the army, and throughout his life he read and studied a wide variety of topics. He was a trusted soldier, hard working, and determined. He was brave, prideful, sure of his confidence. But his temper appears to have kept him from promotion, as he quarreled repeatedly and ended up in the rear ranks. However, the army provided an unexpected opportunity for promotion of a different sort—or rather the nation did. For in April 1898, the United States went to war with Spain.

§

Long before P.H.'s birth, American expansionists had hoped to acquire Cuba. Annexation fever dwindled following the Civil War, but Spanish misrule, continuous uprisings in the 1870's, and finally a depression made conditions worse. In 1895, a full-scale revolution took place that appeared to go on forever. The Spanish forces were not powerful enough to put down the insurrection and the rebels were not strong enough to win.

American newspapers, especially the "yellow press" of William Randolph Hearst and Joseph Pulitzer, printed sensational accounts of Spanish oppression and carried seriously exaggerated reports that a quarter of the population had died. Many Americans regarded conditions in Cuba as intolerable and began to demand that the United States intervene. A few felt that the United States should also acquire naval and military bases and become an imperial power. In November 1897, President McKinley pressured Spain into granting Cuba limited self-government within the Spanish empire. The rebels wanted nothing less than independence and continued to fight. Meanwhile, pro-Spanish mobs in Havana rioted in protest against self-government. To protect Americans from the rioters, the battleship *Maine* arrived in Havana harbor January 25, 1898. On February 15, an explosion blew up the ship and killed two-hundred-sixty sailors, marines, and Cuban civilians. An outraged American public instantly blamed Spain.

"Remember the Maine" became a popular slogan, but forces already in motion did more to bring about actual war. In March, President McKinley sent three notes to Spain demanding full independence for Cuba. Spain granted an armistice. On April 19, Congress overwhelmingly passed a joint resolution asserting that Cuba was independent. The resolution also disavowed any American intention to acquire the island and authorized the use of the army and navy to force Spanish withdrawal. On April 25, 1898, the United States formally declared that a state of war existed with Spain.

§

For nearly two years, the army had stationed Private Frank and several companies of the 23rd at isolated posts along the Texas-Mexico border. Regimental records place him most of that time at Camp Eagle Pass, a wood and adobe fort nestled on the Rio Grande. Most of his soldiering involved chasing down smugglers crossing the border and engaging in long training marches across the dry, rugged landscape. Now the regiment was going to Cuba to fight the Spanish. P.H. soon found himself bivouacked next to his troop train outside New Orleans waiting, as is often the case when armies are on the move.[4]

America's "splendid little war" with Spain provided the country with the imperial adventure that had so enthralled other nations in the last half of the nineteenth century. At first Cuba was the primary interest of the government and the public. Nevertheless, concerns of American policy-makers to negate Spanish naval power would lead to an almost "accidental imperialism" in a place eight thousand miles from California in an island archipelago about which few Americans had ever heard. [5]

On February 25, 1898, Assistant Secretary of the Navy Theodore Roosevelt cabled the commander of the small Asiatic Squadron, Commodore George Dewey. Dewey was to see that the Spanish squadron did not leave Asian waters and then to commence offensive operations in the Philippine Islands. The result of Dewey's battle group arriving in Manila Bay on May 1 was the complete destruction of the Spanish fleet. Dewey's "You may fire when ready, Gridley" pumped up newspaper headlines, and his rout of the Spanish presented a delighted President William McKinley with the problem of what to do with the Philippines, which was still under Spanish colonial administration under siege by a Filipino revolutionary army. On May 2, McKinley ordered an American army expeditionary force, commanded by Major General Wesley Merritt, to the Philippines. When Merritt asked whether his mission was to occupy just Manila or all Spanish territories in the islands, he discovered the president yet had no definite plans.

Merritt had a rather low-profile post as commander of the eastern military district and at age sixty-one was delighted with a final opportunity for battlefield service. However, Merritt believed his expeditionary force would have to fight not only the Spanish but Filipinos as well and threatened to resign his command if his largely volunteer force did not include experienced regular troops. Indeed, on May 17 the *San Francisco Chronicle* reported that Merritt might not be going to the Philippines at all: "I have made up my mind that I do not care to take charge of such a command as they propose to me." The force assigned to Merritt, made up largely of untrained and undisciplined volunteers from state militias, he believed to be inadequate "to the task to be performed, and inadequate to my rank in the Army." The president, who admired Merritt, gave in and assigned to his force a number of regular regiments. One of those regiments was P.H. Frank's 23rd Infantry in New Orleans, a band of men who thought themselves on the way to Cuba.[6]

§

The 23rd Regulars, seen to be composed of a "wiry lot of seasoned men" by the *San Francisco Chronicle,* reversed direction of its troop train and made its way west through Texas, New Mexico, Arizona, and into California. Along the route, P.H. wrote excitedly to his family describing the way people treated the soldiers, "I wrote to Ma yesterday and I told her about how we were treated along the road…but that was not the half of it. When we finished eating in Losangelos, the buglers began to sound their trumpets to notify us we had five minutes to get to the cars. And such handshaking you never saw. Old women and young girls and everyone seized our hands and there was no getting away from there and such a parting never was witnessed before, I know." He added that some in the crowds laughed, others cried, and some of the young girls gave their addresses and demanded a letter as soon as the soldiers reached the islands.[7]

Thus inspired, Private Frank, anticipating his journey and first taste of battle wrote to his sister from Camp Merritt, "That is what makes a man brave. We want to show these people the real meaning of the word soldier." He added, "Oh, I am proud that I am of an age and in this thing…I'll tell you Sister it gives a man courage. He knows there is something to fight for and it makes him braver and better. All I hate is that they will be too easy whipped and I will not be able to shoot any of them. But God help them if the Old 23rd ever gets a chance at them. There are a lot of Texas boys in the 23rd and they will make a few pages of history if we ever get a whack at them. We will make them remember the Maine."[8]

§

The fifteen thousand men of Merritt's force assembled in rapid fashion in San Francisco during May and June 1898. Both the American government and the city were unprepared for America's first overseas war, but enthusiasm and patriotic fervor helped to fill the obvious gaps in logistics. The expeditionary force camped at the Presidio, overlooking Golden Gate Bay. The Spanish, who had claimed sovereignty over California a hundred years earlier, first built the garrison. The place had seen little improvement over the years since the United States won the Southwest from Mexico. Winds constantly blew dust and dirt across the hillsides and regimental and company streets turned to quagmire in the rains. None of that affected P.H.'s enthusiasm.

There, in a tent set up by the YMCA, P.H. wrote letters to his family in Groveton, Texas, and spent "lots of time reading the papers and the good book," before departing for the Philippines. The news of his departure for the orient was apparently difficult for his family to accept. "I am sorrow you are all taking it so hard about me going to the Philippines. It is better than going to Cuba. Of course it is a long way to go but it is a healthy country and we will not be very likely to have any fighting to do there for they are already captured," he wrote. Private Frank, like most Americans including President McKinley, knew little of the Philippines. P.H. reassured his anxious family, "We will all receive $31.40 before we leave…we have good clothes and blankets and we will not have to buy anything for the trip or while we are gone" and noted, "They have religious services every night. I attend regular."[9]

Private Frank was exempt from the onerous duty of drilling. The 23rd's veteran officers were busy organizing into companies the thousands of ill-equipped, poorly trained volunteers streaming in from around the country and instructing them in the rudiments of soldiering. With time on his hands, P.H. wandered from his camp in the block west of the Minnesota volunteers and south of the Pennsylvanians and noted, "Soldiers are the only people here now. Everything is free to soldiers."[10]

The Christian Endeavourers and the Ladies' Red Cross had large tents by the camp that P.H. entered. It was in a YMCA tent that he wrote his letters home. Also near the site of his company billet was a row of saloons with enticing names—The Regular's Home, The U.S. Army Exchange, and The Maine—providing a cheap brand of stimulant. P.H. Frank stood in the midst of that assemblage and heard the jingle of cash registers presaging future events.

§

P.H. Frank spent a sleepless night in an unceasingly stirring encampment that broke to a misty California coast the early morning of Tuesday, June 14, 1898. He gathered for coffee with his fellow soldiers around smoggy charcoal fires long before buglers by the dozens sounded reveille up and down the rows of regimental billets. "Boots and Saddles" sounded, troops fell in, a woman's auxiliary handed out fortifying food baskets, and a several-mile march to the docks began. Regimental bands blasted patriotic melodies. Cheers and applause roared up and down the roads, and the admiring crowds joined in singing "Dixie." P.H. and the troops marched six abreast, their officers on horseback. Pretty girls waved white handkerchiefs and showered kisses from a distance. In the bay, signals passed between the side-wheelers and tugs. Barges moved rapidly to unload provisioning. Sailors in the rigging sported red stripes and blue polka dots on their seaman's blouses and hats. Pennants and bunting decorated the boats of yachters tipping and dipping around the periphery, their decks filled with hundreds of sightseers. Frederic Remington set up his easel and painted the scene.

It was lunchtime attested by a savory smell of frying steak and onions blowing over the water when Private Frank and his comrades passed the transports *Zealandia, Senator,* and *China* and boarded the *Colon.* The regimental band, serenading the men as they ate, drowned out the clatter of innumerable cups and tins. The playing of "Hot Time in the Old Town Tonight" brought P.H. and his comrades to their feet cheering and set them half-wild for a moment. The ship was jam-packed with just under 700 soldiers of his regiment, plus the 18th Regiment, Battery A of the Utah Volunteers, and personal gear, and supplies. In addition, there were sixteen head of cattle slated for slaughter during the voyage, and butchered meat stored in the ship's refrigerator, a new technology.

To these sights and sounds, the *Colon,* together with her sister ships, the *Zealandia* and *Senator,* slipped away from the docks and moved out into the bay. It was not a bright day of blue and gold. It was a gray day. A bank of fog soon obscured outlines of the transport ships from the eyes of observers, but neither observers nor departing troops appeared to be downcast. Tardy soldiers arrived and took to rowboats. No one wanted to miss the grand adventure. Then the ship's canon discharged.

The booming echoed. There was one last faint shout growing smaller in the offing, faintly resounding off the wispy white shrouded escarpment of the Golden Gates. Private Patrick Henry Frank said good-bye to the low profile of San Francisco.[11]

Forty-eight years later, P.H. Frank would once again pass into that bay. This time he would sail under a bridge spanning those hills of the Golden Gates and would be buried in a national cemetery located on the same ground upon which he encamped those days in May and June, 1898. But for now, Private Frank and America savored the moment his transport pulled out of San Francisco for the Orient, with no realistic notion of the difficulties that lay ahead. At that moment, he and his country were seeking their manifest destiny further west than his ancestors and America had ever moved.

Chapter 2

"They did not think we could shoot so well...but they got fooled"

Private P.H. Frank, September 18, 1898

Aboard the *Colon*, the patriotic sendoff of General Merritt's expeditionary force quickly died off to the realities of life for enlisted men on board the transport. Bunks were stacked four high, and the men were rolled in groups of six bodies to a bunk tier. The ship heaved and pitched, and the straw mattresses were soon soaked in sweat and vomit. The hurriedly installed ship's refrigerators gave out, and fresh meat spoiled almost as quickly as the cattle were slaughtered. Conditions were wretched, and P.H. became seriously ill. Isolated in the windowless hold, P.H. grabbed a doctor's arm, told him he would die if not moved from this place. His grip tightened, and he refused to let go until he heard orders for an orderly to take him above deck. There he recuperated in the fresh air and sunshine between Hawaii, which the fleet bypassed in its hurry to get to the Philippines, and Midway Island, where they took on coal. [1]

During June and July, 1898, American forces arrived in Manila Bay and disembarked at Cavite. The 23rd moved some ten miles toward Manila to Camp Dewey created in a flat peanut field. P.H. and his comrades attempted to drill and dig trenches, which was made extremely difficult by the incessant downpour of the rainy season. P.H. escaped the outbreaks of disease, especially measles, but also dysentery, malaria, and cholera, which burdened the troops. What he could not escape was the interminable rain that fell steadily, filling the trenches and soaking uniforms and personal belongings. A *Harper's* correspondent described soldiers casting aside their drenched uniforms and drilling in their underwear. As P.H. dealt with these miseries, his commanders and the Spanish authorities danced a delicate *pas de deux* aimed at Spanish surrender with honor.[2]

The Spanish were aware of the impossibility of their position. Defeats in the Philippines and in the Caribbean had insured the end of their colonial regime; they had no intention, however, of losing sight of two final objectives: surrender with honor, which would necessitate a semblance of combat and surrender to whites only, as the contemplation of coming under the authority of the natives was both dishonorable and dreadful.

Without American intervention, native autonomy was a real possibility. Many Filipinos had taken Dewey's victory as opportunity for a final independence drive, a revolutionary movement against Spain they had waged for many years. The arrival of Merritt's forces made these objectives feasible. In May and June, Filipino forces under General Emilio Aguinaldo had made considerable progress in creating the government and military for their new republic. About thirteen thousand of these troops had besieged the Spanish in Manila before the American arrival.

§

The Philippines had a history of resistance to the Spanish for over three hundred years. The latest revolutionary movement paralleled that in Cuba, which the American press was covering, and around which American sympathies had closed.

The same week P.H. joined the army in Dallas in 1896, the Spanish authorities in Manila had executed Jose Rizal, a local leader of the Philippine revolution. Rizal's death was a hero's execution that flamed Filipino anger and ensured the revolution's permanence. Cavite, the province next to Manila, gradually emerged as the revolutionary hotbed. A string of victories against the Spanish by the young nationalist General Emilio Aguinaldo eventually settled the revolution's leadership.

The start of the Spanish-American War could not have been more opportune for the Philippine revolutionaries. Within three months of Commodore George Dewey's sailing to Manila on April 25, 1898, and sinking the Spanish fleet, General Aguinaldo's forces had almost all the archipelago islands under his Filipino troops, had surrounded Manila with thirteen-thousand troops, and was moving to form a government. Outside Aguinaldo's home in Cavite, the Philippine flag flew, and a band played the new national anthem. By the time Private Frank landed at Cavite, the *Republica Filipina* (First Philippine Republic) was established and Aguinaldo was President. However, American troops blocked Aguinaldo's forces from entering Manila and seizing the reins of government.

§

General Merritt and Admiral Dewey, unsure of their government's intentions toward the Philippines, had handled the Filipinos with some distance and detachment, but by late July, General Merritt was convinced that he could and should take the capital. On July 30, several of his units moved into Filipino trenches south of Manila. The local Filipino commander, General Noriel, tricked by Merritt into vacating his position in return for several cannons, never received the artillery pieces. The Spanish, after discerning that the Americans were relocating and strengthening their positions, began harassing fire culminating during the evening of July 31 in the Battle of the Rain. The 10th Regiment of Pennsylvania Volunteers believed the Spanish were attacking in an attempt to turn their right flank. In the darkness and confusion of the evening downpour, artillery and rifle fire took ten American lives, the first casualties of the campaign.

Three days later, P.H., garrisoned at Cavite Arsenal, moved out for Camp Dewey with his regiment. There, on the evening of August 5, he received his first baptism of fire during a tour of duty in the trenches. On that Friday night, the firing began at seven-thirty and lasted until ten. The Americans, believing that the Spanish were once again attempting to turn their flank, fired 20,000 rounds into the darkness. The *Groveton* (Texas) *Herald* printed the prideful words P.H. wrote to his mother, "It was Companies D, E, and F of the 23rd that did it all. We were right in front and were the only ones allowed to fire. The Spanish tried to take our camp that night and if we had not fought like we did they would have carried out their plans." The engagement, he observed, cost three American dead and several wounded. The Spanish dead counted 147 and 183 wounded. "They did not think we could shoot so well at night but they got fooled," he added.[3]

After incidents such as these, the American commanders presented the Spanish Governor General Fermin Jaudenes with an ultimatum that gave him forty-eight hours to surrender—later lengthened to five days. During that time, the Americans negotiated with Jaudenes and agreed upon a scheme to allow the Spanish to surrender with honor and without sacrifice of life. On August 13, Admiral Dewey's force in the bay would fire a few token shells at the Intramuros, the ancient walled portion of Manila, and Fort San Antonio Abad. After a decent interval, the Spanish would surrender the city to the Americans. General Merritt believed that the charade would take only a few hours, with no loss of life on either side.

§

The Americans approached the city from the south where the Spanish had placed their defensive positions. Anchoring their west flank was Fort San Antonio Abad overlooking Manila Bay. Blockhouse 14 adjacent to dense swamps anchored the Spanish east flank. Between the fort and blockhouse lay mile-long entrenchments. The 23rd constituted the right flank of the American advance. P.H.'s Company F positioned itself approximately two-hundred-fifty yards in front of Blockhouse 14. As the time of advance drew near, P.H. gathered his courage. He knew nothing of Merritt and Dewey's arrangements with General Jaudenes. Feeling the steady lashing of a tropical monsoon, he crouched in a muddy trench and prepared himself for a hard battle. He carried his Krag-Jorgenson rifle, 200 rounds of ammunition, two days supply of rations, and an entrenching tool. His intestines roiled with fear.[4]

CHAPTER 3

"I for one do not want any more war"

Private Patrick Henry Frank, September 18, 1898

At 9:35 on the morning of August 13, Dewey's squadron joined by artillery of the Utah Battery opened fire. On the left flank, the 1st Colorado Volunteers moved into Fort San Antonio Abad and raised the American flag without resistance, just as the Spanish and American commanders had negotiated. On the right flank, however, the presence of Filipino troops provoked Spanish response. Under a shower of bullets, P.H. advanced at 10:30 as American artillery peppered Blockhouse 14 and the Spanish defenders with shells from 3.2-inch guns from the Utah Battery. For a hotheaded young man all too willing to fight, P.H. came face to face with the deepest horrors of war. He wrote: "I waded in mud and water for two miles into Manila on the 13th. I saw men shot down. I saw men carried back on stretchers, and when we reached the Spanish lines, I will never forget the awful sight. There laying in a few feet of each other were five dead Spaniards all torn to pieces. One of Dewey's shells did the work, and in a blockhouse nearby lay sixteen more killed the same way." Such carnage left P.H. wondering at the tactics of his leaders, "I sometimes think that if 'Brave Old Admiral Dewey' could see the awful destruction one of his shells was going to cause before he fired it he would have changed its course and just aimed it near enough to the enemy to scare them." That was actually the plan, of course, but it was unknown to Private Frank.[1]

Advancing another 1,200 yards to Singalong, P.H. crouched in the shadows of the barrio church where Spanish defenders had taken up positions in their hasty retreat toward Manila. Private August Tholien pushed ahead of P.H. as the two headed toward the door of the church. Rifle fire spitting from the windows cut down Tholien as P.H. and the remaining members of Company F took prisoners of the surrendering Spaniards. At that moment, the Americans turned to block entry of the Filipino troops into Manila. With units disposed to control Aguinaldo's troops, the rest of the Americans, including Private Frank, resumed their advance through two miles of mud and water and entered the city.

Before the sun set on August 13, 1898, Private Frank served on a color guard, lowering the Spanish flag and raising the American flag over the Intramuros—the citadel surrounding the Old City—thus ushering in American sovereignty over the archipelago.

Drenched from the morning monsoon, troopers dried off in the late afternoon baking sun, sweating profusely, reeking of the remnants of fear smells and waste. P.H. stood with Company F, while high above him on the wall of the fort, Nebraska Volunteers lowered the Spanish flag and raised the American flag. P.H. stood exhausted in the ranks of soldiers, Krag rifles at parade-rest, attired in sweat stained blue shirts and khaki pants, slouch campaign hats, hefty ammunition belts cinched at the waist, and mid-calf boots caked with dried mud. Buglers sounded order arms; the high fort walls echoed the chords of "Retreat the Colors" through the Old City.

Pompey and Caesar's troops, like Napoleon's, left their graffiti upon the Pyramids. P.H. and his comrades in the 23rd left their names carved on the walls of Blockhouse 14. That night at Malate Barracks, P.H. felt little exultation. Surveying the prospects of fighting the thousands of Filipino troops still under arms, he wrote, "I, for one, do not want any more war." Unfortunately, the war was just beginning. Like Vietnam and Iraq, the Philippine wars killed tens of thousands and split the nation in contentious debate.[2]

§

Over the next few months, as American diplomats and politicians debated the fate of the Philippines, P.H. and his comrades settled into the chores of occupation. The 23rd was one of two regiments assigned to the provost guard in Manila, a military police detail of soldiers under the authority of the provost marshal. As P.H. put it, "The policemen are the soldiers." However, sometimes the soldier becomes the prisoner. P.H. was placed in confinement for twenty-six days from August 17 – September 12, according to regimental records, for the offense of punching out a sergeant. As he later told his family, his hotheadedness resulted in recklessness, a tendency that was difficult for him to modulate once provoked.[3]

America had "boots on the ground," and Private Frank filled one pair. He emerged from his confinement an exemplar of the tendencies and possibilities of turn-of-the-century American life played out on America's frontier in the Philippine Islands. But first, America had to decide what to do with the Philippines

§

After residing in the Spanish surrendered Malate Barracks, the 23rd moved into the walls of the Intramuros, taking quarters in the old Spanish arsenal. From December 1898 – April 1899, P.H.'s company provided guard of the Customs House, the hub of Manila business, which meant a big slice of commerce in the orient. Duties and taxes were collected and all manner of collateral businesses operated from docking wharfs and *bodegas* (warehouses) to inter-island transshipment. There were also offices, restaurants, and bars where business ties were forged and deals made. His company also guarded the Malacanang Palace, the seat of government, and the Treasury, both important locales for greasing business.[4]

P.H informed his family he was rapidly learning Spanish and made the wondering observation that "there is a great rush of business here," both early indications that he, like other colonialists, was already weighing options, considering opportunities, and preparing himself. Just as back in Camp Merritt, he heard the cash registers jingle, he now took in the orient busily trading.[5]

P.H. was also sizing up the people who he described as "way behind the times, they are awful friendly, even the Spanish are friendly, especially the Spanish soldiers" who were allowed considerable freedom of the Intramuros, wherein he noted they were permitted to roam at will for several hours a day. "I have talked with a good many of the Spanish soldiers that were in the battle and they say it was awful," he wrote, adding that the Spanish prisoners were getting fat "since they now get plenty of Uncle Sam's pork and beans and good fresh beef." As soldiers usually do, P.H. lamented the profiteering of the civilian populace. He wrote, "One of our dollars is worth two of the Spanish, but they charge us double price for anything we get in the stores. Eggs are five cents a piece. If a soldier gets any extras, it costs like thunder."[6]

Still, P.H. observed, he and his fellow troops were doing fine. Their camp was located near the beach and had a continuously refreshing breeze. Having some time on their hands, the soldiers watched the recovery of Spanish ships in Manila harbor. "The Spanish sunk two of their torpedo boats in the Pasig River and threw a lot of guns overboard, but they have all been recovered and the boats raised and 'Old Glory' run up on them. We could set up on the walls and see the work going on." One of the Spanish gunboats cleared from the murky water was the *Pampanga*.[7]

The 23rd escaped diseases that vexed other units. Indeed, P.H. reassured his family he was getting as fat as a pig. Beef arrived regularly from Australia. "The finest I have ever seen," said this boy from Texas. "We have lots of good soup and coffee, plenty of biscuits, beef-steak, onions, and potatoes, and in fact, we have everything a man should want to eat. We have plenty of rice, and rice is said to be a very healthy diet here. We don't eat much fruit. The native fruit is not healthy and American fruit is scarce" P.H. had never tasted bananas, mango, and papaya. Continuing his wonderings about opportunities on this side of the world, he scribbled, "We get all our potatoes and onions from Australia and they are awful fine. I may go by Australia when I come home."[8]

Those tendencies, opportunities, and possibilities P.H. Frank was already sensing—business, wealth, social mobility, a vision of the world as his home—would evolve out of the American decision to annex the Philippines.

§

The fall of Manila for all practical purposes brought about the end of the Spanish-American War but sparked another war. A strong feeling was spreading over America in favor of colonial expansion. Imperialists like Senator Henry Cabot Lodge concluded, "We must on no account let the islands go...we hold the other side of the Pacific, and the value to this country is almost beyond imagination." Other motives surfaced around Lodge's theme. Christian evangelists intoned. Businessmen portrayed Manila as the gateway to China, and patriotic groups envisioned joining the European colonial empires, albeit late. Soon a strong feeling of colonial expansion drowned out the warnings of the Anti Imperialist League, among who were steel magnate Andrew Carnegie, textile manufacturer Edward Atkinson, lawyer-orator William Jennings Bryan, and author Mark Twain. The whole thing was a curious blend of idealism, racism, power, and evangelism.[9]

After a great deal of anguished deliberation, President McKinley, as he informed a delegation of Methodist missionaries, decided to keep the islands in order "to educate the Filipinos, and uplift and Christianize them, and by God's grace do the very best we could by them, as our fellow men for whom Christ died." These humanitarian objectives cost America a $20 million payment to the Spanish and nearly four years of armed struggle with Filipinos who vigorously resisted the attentions of Americans determined to take up "The White Man's Burden," as Rudyard Kipling phrased it, with all the vigor and optimism that turn-of-the-century Americans could evidence.[10]

Peace protocols between Spain and the United States ceded the rights of Spain to the United States. Aguinaldo and his followers, angered at U.S. control in the Philippines, turned against their former allies. Six months later in February 1899, fighting broke out between Aquinaldo and U.S. forces in what became known as the Second Battle of Manila. This skirmish began what the American government called the Philippine Insurrection, and the Nationalist Filipinos called the Philippine-American War.

American troops were soon waging war against Emilio Aguinaldo and his Filipino troops. P.H. referred to Aguinaldo's army as the "insurrectionists," which was what the American government was calling those Filipinos who resisted American annexation. For several months, P.H. remained on provost duty in Manila while major elements of the 23rd commenced operations in the northern islands. However, P.H. was not left long in Manila. As operations in the north began, several companies of the 23rd, including Private Frank, moved south on May 17, 1899, aboard the *S.S. Leon*, a former Spanish vessel, and arrived offshore Jolo Island three days later. P.H. had the satisfaction of relieving the last Spanish sentry of the Jolo garrison. At two o'clock in the afternoon, the Spanish flag on the masonry fort, situated at the end of a long rock wharf on the seashore, was hauled down, and Private Frank unfurled to the breeze the Stars and Stripes. P.H.'s compatriot, Private Needom Freeman, Company H, described the scene, "The Spanish seemed very much grieved, the officers wept, the Americans were jubilant." President McKinley marked the occasion saying, "The authorities of the Sulu Islands have accepted the succession of the United States to the rights of Spain, and our flag floats over their territory." However, that was not really the case and it was not going to be that easy.[11]

"...hence her love for the chap who wore Uncle's duds"

P.H. Frank, November 5, 1905

The Sulu Islands were the southern most chain of the Philippine archipelago, meandering to within thirty miles of Borneo. Jolo is the largest island, and Jolo Town is where P.H. landed and took up garrison outside the town's fortress walls. Jolo was a beautiful island, the prettiest P.H. had seen in the Philippines, but a very different world from Manila. This had been Spain's frontier in the Philippines and was now America's frontier. One hundred sixty thousand Muslims and 4,000 non-Muslims, mostly Catholic Christians, inhabited Sulu in 1899. Malay in race, the Muslim Filipinos were virtually indistinguishable physically from the Christian Filipinos. During the late fourteenth century, the arrival of Arab missionaries initiated the conversion of the native population to the Islamic faith. The phrase "Christian Filipino" was an island term used to distinguish between such peoples as the Tagalogs and Visayans, on the one hand, and the Mohammedan Moros and pagan tribes on the other.

In the fifteenth century, the Spanish limited their colonization of these southern islands to a few fortified coastal towns. Catholic conversions to Christianity were limited to the areas where the army offered protection to the Jesuits. The Spanish called the natives "Moros" after the Moors of Spain. Anthropologists today stress that except for Filipinos of Chinese or *Negrito* stock, the Filipinos are racially one people. But ethnically and culturally, the Moros developed independently, though with highly varying sub-groups. On Jolo, P.H. was meeting the Tausug Moros ruled by the Sultan of Sulu. He would meet additional Moro groups shortly and learn to distinguish their cultures and languages.

The native Moros believed they had a right to resist the American rule just as they had resisted Spanish rule for three hundred years. They claimed that the transfer of sovereignty from Spain to the United States was a mockery of the facts. In their view, the Spanish had no real sovereignty over their land. Moreover, the so-called "transfer" was affected without consulting the Moro civil and religious leaders who regarded the affair as an attack upon Islam. Serious disturbances began, and P.H. found himself in the middle of it. The 23rd soon fell into sanguinary conflicts with Moros. Fifty days later, on July 6, 1899, P.H. re-enlisted for another three years. However, P.H. apparently entertained grave doubts—doubts about conflict with the Moros ending soon and doubts because of being homesick. Despite a promised $500 bonus from an army now strapped for soldiers in a hostile foreign land, part of his deciding included flipping a coin on the pier at Jolo. "Heads." He stayed.

For the next two years, P.H. served with Company C of the 23rd in garrison at Jolo, Zamboanga, and Cotabato. All combat soldiers found terrifying moments among the hours and days of seemingly interminable boredom. On one occasion, P.H.'s unit was patrolling on a jungle trail, along which Moros had laid bamboo pipe to carry water to their village. As P.H. reached down to move the pipe off the trail, a Moro jumped out of the bush raising his *kris*, a frightening thirty-inch, wavy-bladed sword of tempered steel. P.H. froze at the sight but at once felt the muzzle of a Krag laid across his shoulder and a mutter, "Don't move, Frank. I've got a bead on him." P.H. survived, shaking, near senseless and deaf from the rifle burst; the fate of the Moro just as certainly death. On another occasion his company accompanied the 23rd band to "show the flag" believed by American officers to be a way of demonstrating dominion at a *barrio* named Maraquina. The resulting skirmish left ten troopers painfully wounded, slashed and laid open to deadly tropical infections.[1]

Most Americans thought of Mindanao and Sulu as places of bloody conflicts with fanatical Moros and populated by wild men from the hills. That was the view of many Americans who read about the bloody, barbarous cruelty on all sides that came to be known as the Moro Wars, which lasted until 1912. It is difficult to know if P.H. agreed with this assessment. Certainly, he may have in the beginning. But time and experience in the culture on Mindanao and Sulu modulated, toned down, and wised him up to the stereotypes. And fate also intervened in a softening, personal way.

§

In April 1900, P.H. boarded the transport *Zealandia* with his infantry company at Zamboanga. The ship moved around the tip of the Zambo peninsula and entered the Moro Gulf. As the ship plowed east, P.H. felt near heaven when the sky turned hazy gray in the afterglow of the closing day. Behind him in the west, the distant land turned mauve, the peaks of the mountains flaming like volcanoes from the hidden sun. Then the big stars came out and left a comet-like trail upon the dancing water. The Southern Cross lay low on the horizon of the darkening sky behind him. Private Frank's destination and destiny was Cotabato, a night's steam across the Moro Gulf.[2]

P.H. awoke as the *Zealandia* moved quietly up the Pulangi River, called by the Spanish the *Rio Grande de Mindanao*, the longest river on the island of Mindanao, which, together with its tributaries, forms the chief means of transportation for conveying people and produce up and down the stream to the coast. Along the banks and the broad river valley lived the peaceful Moro group, the Maguindanao, "People of the Flood Plain." Their name derives from the fact that the river, affected by the tide for more than ten miles inland, regularly overflows its banks, inundating the adjacent plain. The soldiers watched as these peaceful Moros began the day, where high above the river they stirred from their homes built on sturdy stilts connected by overhead bamboo walkways, which led into a tight community of fishers, farmers, and traders. P.H. saw greening rice paddies and small boats polled and pushed to the fields. In the boats, heaps of rice plants awaited their addition to the crop, hand placed by the children, women, and men who laughed, sang, and conversed as they wadded through the freshwater lowland waters fed by the Pulangi.

The troopers disembarked the *Zealandia* onto the smaller, shallow draft, Spanish gunboat *Pampanga* that proceeded twelve miles upstream to Cotabato town, meaning "stone fort," built by the Spanish two hundred years earlier in order to safeguard the area for trading and a Catholic mission.

On April 17, 1900, Company C set up garrison in Cotabato at the stone fort. P.H. walked through the markets where another community of Maguindanao manufactured brassware making beautiful trays, urns, and gongs sold alongside the produce and cloth vendors. The majority of the Maguindano were Moros, who lived peacefully among the many Chinese who were traders and storeowners, and the Christian Filipinos, who migrated into the Cotabato region, all under the protection of the Spanish and now the Americans. Historically, after the coming of Islam, the region divided into several Moro political provinces, each with its own *datu* leadership within a Sultanate that encompassed the entire southwest portion of Mindanao.

Four days later, two dozen Buayan Moros from Malabang under Datu Udasan raided Callalanuan, a *barrio* of Cotabato, looting property, killing local officials, and carrying away a number of women as slaves. Slaving was an important economic institution in traditional Muslim Mindanao and Sulu. Slaves could be bought and sold at will. Some were exchanged for debts or given as part of a bride-gift. There were degrees of slavery and a distinction was made between *olipon* slaves and *baniaga* slaves. *Olipon* bond slaves were those enslaved for limited periods in payment of debts, fines, or punishment for serious offenses. *Baniaga* were chattel slaves, regarded as property of their masters, with no standing. *Baniaga* performed menial household tasks and sometimes became concubines of their masters. It was unlikely that an enslaved person would remain so permanently. Patronage, kindly masters, or remarkable ability freed most slaves who, with their descendents, blended into general Moro society through marriage, adoption or fleeing to another area where they became commoners under the protection of another *datu* hostile to their original masters. Lieutenant Bret, commanding Private Frank's encampment at Parang-

Parang, leading a force of twenty-five soldiers, boarded the *Pampanga* and gave chase to the marauders.[3]

§

Beyond Cotabato, the region turned to a vast swampland crossed by sluggish, muddy streams. Twenty miles inland from the coast, the river forked into north and south branches. Guided by friendly Moros, the *Pampanga* made its way up the north branch, further and further away from the floodplain's mangrove and bamboo forests. Slowly the boat entered the lowland rain forests of mahogany. There Liana and other vines reached from the ground to the canopy, providing a natural highway on which monkeys, squirrels, civet cats, and lizards moved from the dark quiet of the forest floor to the sunlight far above.

Lt. Brett disembarked his troopers at a dilapidated village pier and headed inland along ancient trading trails. It was a terrain where extensive limestone outcrops covered boundless areas. Natural erosion gave rise to a sublime karst landscape dominated by white cliffs and ridges riddled by small caves, where rainwater quickly drained away, leaving behind parched conditions where only a few small molave trees prospered. The rugged mountain rose quickly. Deeper shades of green revealed themselves as P.H. struggled up the narrow trail. The wide diversity of frogs, lizards, bats, birds, trees, orchids like none he had ever seen before, comprised an isolated set of animal and plant species. Two soldiers on point hurried back to report the Moro party occupying a cave. Brett sent P.H. ahead with additional scouts to secure the approach. Disquietly P.H. took a position as the Lieutenant reconnoitered, returning to whisper orders that the men should disperse in a semicircle around the cavern and fire on his orders.

P.H. sweated profusely in the tropical heat. The palms of his hands laid runny wet prints on the butt of his rifle. Salt from perspiration burned his eyes. He took aim.

The Moros congregated in front of the grotto, opening and divvying up loot from the raid. The women, kept back in the cave, had been allotted earlier in the day. The crack of Lt. Bret's pistol was answered by twenty-four 1899 Krag Constabulary carbines opening fire simultaneously. All fourteen Moros fell. There were no survivors—a typical outcome of such conflicts.

P.H. entered the cave. Dim light illuminated the faces of the frightened women. One, a girl of sixteen years in a white Spanish dress stained with muddy goop, looked up. She was of olive-brown complexion. Her deep brown eyes caught P.H.'s blue eyes. She was scared, shaking; perspiration turned jungle dirt to flowing mud on her face and arms. Her black hair hung jostled in long lengths below her shoulders. He knelt down, extended a comforting hand to her elbow, and helped her to her feet. She knew no English, but although P.H. was speaking Spanish, it took no particular language to understand she was safe.

Thus it was that P.H. met his bride-to-be, Viudo de Eugenia Garcia. As he later wrote his sister Texanna, "Eugenia thinks the Americans are the only people. She has a good right to her opinion, as she had her life saved by the timely arrival of the American soldiers in Cotabato, hence her love for the chap who wore Uncle's duds."[4]

§

Eugenia was born in Cotabato July 10, 1884, to Don Fermin Garcia and Donna Andrea Magno and was educated at a Catholic convent in Cotabato run by Spanish nuns, where she learned music, art, embroidering, and the graces of Spanish colonial life.

Her younger brother Antonio was ten years old. Her father was the Spanish naval officer second in command on the gunboat *Pampanga* at the Battle of Manila Bay. He survived the war, returned to Cotabato, and turned to earning his livelihood in the world of inter-island trade and commerce, living in the Spanish colonial style. Eugenia's mother Andrea was Chinese-Mestiza. At Andrea's baptism in 1870, the Catholic Church listed her mother as "Mora Vi, Infidel."

Eugenia and Private Frank began to see one another under the strictest Spanish colonial chaperoning. P.H.'s attraction to Eugenia Garcia and the various encouragements offered by the U.S. government to those who might stay and develop the Philippines helped convince him to transfer out of the 23rd as it prepared to depart for the United States. On October 4, 1901, he joined Company A, 17th Infantry, as it took up its duties in Cotabato.[5]

Private Frank was not alone, as there were hundreds of similar transfers into the 17th as the 23rd departed. P.H. could have gone home with the 23rd, as he had eight months left on his enlistment. His Regiment was going home by way of the Suez Canal, and the attraction of being among the first American regiments to circumnavigate the globe must have been a powerful incentive. It was an enticement, however, overcome by romance for Eugenia. The 23rd shipped westward in September 1901, through the Suez Canal to New York, and P.H., still a private, began soldiering with the 17th.

Six months later, P.H. was among 1,200 American soldiers participating in battles against Maranao Moros around Lake Lanao. The scene was composed of malarial swamps, darkened jungle trails corduroyed with logs, and mules hauling heavy artillery pieces on their backs. Together with a muleteer friend, Kentuckian Ned Duckworth, who served in the Lake Lanao campaign with him, they managed the exhausting labor of getting the artillery pieces through the high elevation mossy jungle to the lake.[6]

Major General Adna Chafee sent a letter to the *datus* on April 13, 1902, informing them, "Under the Treaty of Paris between Spain and the United States, executed in the year 1899, the Philippine Islands, including the island of Mindanao, were ceded by Spain to the United States, together with all the rights and responsibilities of complete sovereignty..." Chafee sincerely intended friendship and called only for justice in the letter's balance. However, the tone seemed arrogant to the Lanao *datus* who had never heard of Paris. Besides, these Moros had defeated Spain in all attempts at conquest and could not have possibly ceded the Maranao country to some other foreign nation.[7]

The Moros fought mainly from earthen and bamboo *cotas*—fortress homes—with brass *lantakas*—cannon. The campaign was tough and bloody. Murderous assaults on the *cotas* left close to four hundred Moro fighters dead. There were twelve American casualties in the slaughter.[8]

P.H. wrote his family that campaigns against the Moros at Lake Lanao in May, 1902, helped him decide that more of the military life was not for him, "I had just about all the soldiering I wanted, and decided if Uncle Sam would dispense with my services, that I would endeavor to turn to other trades." In June 1902, the 17th left the Philippines, and P.H. transferred into the 10th Infantry to serve out the month remaining in his enlistment.[9]

Homesickness and a longing to see his family were in competition with his courtship of Eugenia Garcia and the enticements of making money in the Philippines. To his sister Texanna he wrote, "…the desire to go home gnawed at my heart continuously." Love and opportunity, it might be said, and a landscape more beautiful than east Texas, kept him in the Philippines. On the frontier of America's newest marchland, he wrote home, "I had a little money, and a strong desire to make more before returning to God's country." He was thinking of what his future held for him. He was looking for something better than another round of days in east Texas.[10]

With a character rating of "excellent", the army released P.H. Frank from service on July 6, 1902. He was free to make manifest his own destiny on America's newest frontier.

Part 2
The Pioneer Frontier
1902 to 1908

"So watch as we get a gait on"

Fourth of July Bulletin, Zamboanga, July 4, 1903

CHAPTER 5

"Success or failure she has remained the same"
P.H. Frank, November 5, 1905

The civilian world P.H. Frank entered July 5, 1902, was as different from his army service as were the cultural differences between Cotabato, Philippine Islands, where he mustered out of the army, and Groveton, Texas, United States of America, where he had spent part of his growing up years prior to joining the 23rd Infantry in 1896. Private Frank had found himself in the Philippines not by plan or even army design. He arrived in what was to be his frontier because of General Wesley Merritt's intentions and attitude brought about by President William McKinley's response to the drumbeat of war and a country yearning to join its global neighbors in imperial adventure. P.H. was a part of the milieu, and he loved it.

Cotabato, located on a swampy delta island where the Cotabato River enters the Moro Gulf, was a small garrison town on the island of Mindanao, the second largest island in the Philippine Archipelago, containing a vast wealth of agricultural, forestry and mineral resources. In the twenty-first century, much of Mindanao continues to be part the nation's pioneer frontier. P.H. had served in the U.S. Army Department of Mindanao and Sulu and detached from the army in that geographical locale because that was where political and military decisions and the flip of a coin put him. His letters revealed a man emotionally aware of his "frontier." His formal education was limited, and he had dirt under his fingernails. He disregarded conventions, had unbridled optimism, and saw opportunity for himself.

Mindanao was "an enormously large land with a vast body of wealth without American proprietors," to paraphrase Frederick Jackson Turner. Turner was writing about the American West. He could have been writing about America's newest frontier. Iron, copper, and gold deposits proliferated. Land covered with tropical forests produced mahogany reaching 180 to 200 feet high. Trees in canyon floors reached for sunlight, attaining 250 feet in height. Rattan vines used for making furniture were in abundance. Mangrove trees produced cutch, a chemical used for tanning. The forests teemed with woods of rare beauty such as ebony streaked with pink, purple and black. Fisheries and pearling abounded. Editors of the new American newspapers in Manila, urging colonization, named Mindanao the "New Promised Land." They said it was to the other islands what the West was to the United States seventy-five years earlier. P.H. Frank knew all of this, and more—the wild tribes that prowled the hills and jungles, hunting with spears, eating bats, and taking fish by throwing intoxicating weeds into pools, lizards that flew, vicious wild boars in battle with huge pythons, and man-eating crocodiles. And the most vivid South Sea fiction tales are no more exciting than the bald history of Mindanao. Its Moro lands included the musically named islands of Basilan, Jolo, and Tawi-Tawi, which strung out toward Borneo. Pirates, pearls, and Moro spearmen locked in mortal hand-to-hand battles had made Mindanao known from Arabia to South China even before Columbus sailed west.[1]

From P.H.'s point of view, the Philippines was distinctive in place and time, much as his ancestors saw the American frontier. He saw it as the last American frontier and he, the heroic pioneer. His migration was the fruit of an old prophecy of Manifest Destiny. He was aware that he was a member of a recent immigrant group among many well-established groups. In addition, the tropical islands were beautiful. Private Frank the warrior gave way to P.H. Frank (sometimes "Boss"), the entrepreneur.

§

P.H.'s first business sign in Cotabato read "Pool, Billiard Hall and Restaurant." His clientele were the 10th Regulars of the U.S. Army now engaged in steady combat with the Moros. Such a business required capital, and he had a small amount of cash saved from previous reenlistment bonuses. He also had connections with the quartermasters of the units returning to the States who provided him with pool and billiard tables "on the cheap," and he was up and running. "I made money fast, and began making other deals" utilizing income from his establishment for additional investments guided by Eugenia Garcia's father.[2]

Eugenia and P.H. were seeing more and more of each other. Eugenia's father, Don Fermin, had solid connections to the Spanish community. The young entrepreneur valued Fermin's business savvy and greatly admired the man, whom he described as "a very high type, plain, honest, and square." In his letters home P.H. recalled that Fermin had a good head on his shoulders, and he admired Fermin's kind face and wonderful dark eyes. P.H. and Fermin Garcia were both heirs to a tradition of setting out in search of a better chance than the one they had been born to—Don Fermin from roots in Galicia, Spain and P.H. from his roots in east Texas and his mother's roots in Ireland. Both had a long history of poverty and emigration. Upon the retreat of Spain at the end of its 300-year colonial occupation in the Philippines and America's entry to the islands, it seemed appropriate that the two men would mutually respect one another. "I never met a better man," P.H. wrote.

Fermin Garcia knew the Spanish and Mexican officers and government officials who, with the United States now firmly in control of the Philippines, were returning to Spain and Mexico, selling or leasing their homes and businesses. Following Fermin's advice, P.H. used his accumulating profits to buy up leases on homes and buildings in Cotabato, and sublease them to the American government. He brought in considerable money, but his string of luck was not to continue.[3]

In November 1902, P.H. invested his trove in a herd of cattle. The American government wanted live cattle for their troops stationed in Cotabato—"beef for the soldiers," he wrote, "and they gave me a contract." He scoured the countryside for cattle and found and bought a large herd about twenty miles from town. However, the ensuing transaction was not really a "purchase;" it was a classic investment in "futures." He gave the owner of the cattle a down payment on the future delivery of cattle at $16.50 per head and simultaneously made a deal with the government to pay him $27.00 per head. All went well as he made his profit from the first delivery of thirty-two bovine. Taking his profit and spreading the proceeds over a larger herd, he held his delivery to the government in hopes of a rise in price. He gambled. "I took other peoples' advice, and decided to keep them several months for a raise. The raise came, but when it did, I had neither cattle or money, for on Christmas day, 1902, they began dying with the rinderpest, which is a dread disease here among cattle, and few escape it." P.H. had only one cow left which he gave to an old Spaniard who had helped him try to save the herd. Patrick Henry Frank was out of beef and out of money. His first rise and fall had lasted one year.[4]

Alone, disheartened, with no one to help him, P.H. received the emotional support he needed from Eugenia Garcia. She and P.H. had courted before and after his discharge, but she refused marriage because of her doubts about his remaining in the Philippines. "And to tell the truth," P.H. wrote, "I was very much so in doubt, but kept it to myself." Eugenia had seen plenty of Filipino girls left holding babies at the wharf when their units returned to the United States. She was not going to be involved in that kind of "benevolent assimilation."[5]

"Well you can imagine how disheartened I was," P.H. wrote his sister, "and right at this critical moment, with no one to go to for aid or to tell my troubles to, I learned for the first time in my life, and learning, appreciated the pure love of a pure girl. When I went broke she was the first one to come to my aid, and it soon dawned upon me that there were far greater and better things to seek in this world, than gold."[6]

§

Spanish intermarriage with Filipinos was established for 300 years before the American arrival. A Chinese pattern of *mestizo* intermarriage also developed throughout the islands. Over time, lighter complexions became highly prized, and Spanish and Chinese *mestizos* came to occupy a place in Philippine society superior to the native Filipino. In Philippine culture, both Chinese and Spanish *mestizos* constituted and dominated the middle and upper class. Among some of these *mestizos*, wealth accumulated over the generations; these Spanish mestizos became known as the *illustrados*, a landed, and business elite from which business and political leadership emerged. Eugenia represented both forms of "mixed blood." Although not of the *illustrado* class, her social occupations would have been largely within the relatively privileged Spanish-Chinese *mestizo* ethnic group, enjoying middle class, Spanish colonial life.

Don Fermin Garcia had worked himself up to the rank of a Spanish naval officer, while P.H. Frank came from a long line of yeoman class farmers, blacksmiths, and trades people. He also had particles of a redneck view of the world that he had to overcome if he were going to succeed in his courtship of Eugenia. He was going to have to make some compromises in the rougher hues of his east Texas upbringing. He would also have to modulate his beliefs about the superiority of Western European culture and, hence, the American culture derived from it. Eugenia was from a tradition that favored Spanish *mestizo* culture. She was insistent that they communicate with one another in Spanish. She also made it clear that their progeny would be raised in the Catholic Church.

Nevertheless, Eugenia also saw P.H.'s entrepreneurial bent, his capacity for hard work, and his sharp eye for opportunity, prototypically the idealized American virtues of his time. He had those virtues, to be sure, but their value was greatly enhanced in a culture where few others did in the backwaters of the Spanish colonial frontier of Cotabato. P.H. had neither money nor education. His "Americanness" was his edge, as it would be for any American who had the "right stuff" in him. This is an idea that suffuses his early letters.

It is probably impossible to be a colonialist without a belief in the superiority of your own people, however you define that superiority. If P.H. seemed to acquiesce to the Spanish and Catholic influences of Eugenia, it is perhaps because he thought it all harmlessly domestic or perhaps because of his respect for Don Fermin. He saw it all as culturally attractive, maybe even distinguished. He may even have felt that to some degree he was going to marry above himself in marrying an officer's daughter.[7]

P.H. Frank and Eugenia Garcia married by Catholic ceremony in the home of her parents in the *barrio* of Pollok, Cotabato on April 22, 1903; he was 27, the bride 18. Eugenia's childhood priest in the

Mision de Cotabato arranged for dispensation by the Catholic Church for her to marry a protestant. P.H.'s friend Henry Hubbell, like himself a private in the 23rd and now an American pioneer, served as one witness. Eugenia's brother Antonio served as a second witness. In the busy years ahead, she provided a stable center for the hurrying entrepreneur, "Success or failure she has remained the same, she is all the word wife implies, and more, too." The couple looked for a place to live that had the promise of new beginning, Eugenia working quietly behind the scenes as her husband's cultural attaché.[8]

CHAPTER 6

"I came here to Zamboanga"

P.H. Frank, November 5, 1905

Fortified by marriage, P.H. and Eugenia moved west across the vast Moro Gulf from Cotabato to Zamboanga at the southern tip of a curving peninsula distinctive for its fertile coastal plains which rose sharply to high mountains just inland from the ocean. The town had at one time been a native village upon which the Spanish founded a settlement in 1635, erecting Ft. Pillar for the protection of Christian Filipino settlers against Moro pirates. The name "Zamboanga" was derived from the Malay "*jambangan*," meaning "a place of flowers;" the term is an apt description for the preponderance of beautiful bougainvillea, orchids, and lush tropical flowers within which were nestled homes and buildings of Spanish-style architecture. Nearby Muslim villages were built on stilts over the water slowly moving through the lowlands into the Basilan Straight. Seeking fish, coral, and shells, these Banju—"Sea Gypsies"—sailed small boats, *vintas*, with multicolored sails. Besides the small Spanish community and even smaller American community, native Tau, Sugs, Samals, and Yakans lived together in a narrow coastal strip on the Basilan Strait with a mountainous backdrop. The area was known for a cooler and less humid climate than Manila, which was 550 miles from Zamboanga, a three-day journey by boat. Commercially, Zamboanga was a center for agricultural products, fishing, timber, and

Moro brass and bronze-ware. It was also a collection point for shells, exported or used locally for button and jewelry manufacture.

By 1903, American troops had defeated the insurrection led by Emilio Aguinaldo in the northern islands of the Philippines and turned its attention to Mindanao and Sulu, with the full intention of bringing those areas fully into American hegemony. Thus, Zamboanga became the center for American troops engaged in the Moro Campaigns intended to subdue Muslim Filipinos who were as unwilling to accept American rule, as they had been to subjugate themselves to Spanish rule or even to the brief assertion of sovereignty by the insurrectionary government of Emilio Aquinaldo. By 1904, the American military was engaged in full-scale campaigns and major battles against the Moros. Zamboanga was the headquarters of the American effort to administer the Moro Province under the aegis of a civil-military government.

P.H. began his second commercial enterprise in Zamboanga investing all he had, "which was not much, in a building and lot near the soldiers' barracks in a line strictly confined to the American trade." P.H. knew the saloons of his childhood in Groveton, Texas. He heard the jingle of money going into the cash registers of Camp Merritt groggeries in San Francisco. He witnessed the busy comings and goings around the customs house in Manila and the business of commerce exchanged in the nearby waterfront pubs. His first commercial enterprise in Zamboanga also had a uniquely American character and outcome to it which was tied to P.H.'s past. Following his earlier business failure in Cotabato, he named his new enterprise The First and Last Chance after a similarly named saloon of his childhood in Groveton, Texas. He identified his clientele as the American troops freed from fighting in Luzon against Aguinaldo and now engaged in the Moro Campaigns. He located the business smack dab next to the headquarters of the American army. For P.H. Frank, the First and Last Chance was an honest-to-god house for the public, a created sanctuary, a place where soldiers from Pettit Barracks could savor a feeling of safety and return, a place where they could relieve the scourges of boredom that often accompanied army life.[1]

The increasing number of American troops stationed in what became known as the "Moro Province" together with supporting contingents of teachers, engineers, and civil servants sent to the province to carry out the American mandate in the Philippines, played a significant role in the early business, civic, and family life of P.H. Frank.

Pettit Barracks, by another name, had been the Spanish Army headquarters around Fort Pillar in Zamboanga. In the days of the Moro Campaigns from 1903 to 1912, the barracks were headquarters for the American troops in Mindanao and Sulu, and in the years ahead Pettit Barracks was considered a desirable assignment for ambitious officers and their families. American troops barracked in several camps on Mindanao and Sulu, but the largest number remained stationed at Pettit. Whereas American soldiers drank, few Filipinos imbibed, and the Moros were Muslim with strong prohibitions against alcohol. There were also men in Zamboanga who, like P.H., left the army and stayed in the islands taking up their own ventures. Increasingly, there were the newcomers—American government employees, teachers, engineers, lawyers, and Joseph Conrad characters straight off a tramp steamer who had come to make their fortune. P.H. noted that he "made money fast" and reported a profit of "$2,000 the first year."[2]

It was not long before P.H. was importing 340 barrels of Moerlein Beer a month, brewed in Cincinnati, Ohio, which, according to the local *Mindanao Herald*, "would seem to indicate that famous beverage is not wanting in popularity." For his place and time, P.H. had the product and he had location. A man named Dick Thrasher tended P.H.'s early bars. Thrasher was a big man, a veteran, smart and comfortable with himself. When a skylarker turned rowdy, Thrasher handled any roughhousing firmly.[3]

Eugenia and P.H. made their home in the *barrio* of Santa Maria about two miles from P.H.'s businesses in Zamboanga. On March 29, 1904, the couple became a family with the addition of a son, "the best baby I ever saw...and a chip from the old block," he wrote his mother. Samuel Boone Frank, P.H. proudly added, "never cried at night." The nursery was a small corner room with two windows providing cross ventilation. Silk mosquito netting hung loosely above the crib to which curious lizards migrated for a look. Sam started his life bilingual as Eugenia spoke only Spanish and insisted on its use at home. Eugenia had a gentle way of handling children. Two or three times a week P.H. hitched a small Filipino pony to his modest carriage and took Eugenia and Sam for an evening ride, conversing with his son in English and his wife in Spanish.

Eugenia and P.H.'s home was of typical Spanish middle-class style suitable for a tropical climate. It was two-storied, and more generous with space than the native homes. The house design afforded opportunity to catch every breeze through the tall shading mango, banana, and coconut trees providing their fruits year round. The ceilings were ten feet high. The roof was made of foot thick *nipa*, a thatch made from a Malay palm. The gutters were half-round bamboo. The ground floor held rooms for the houseboy, the cook, and the *lavandera* who washed the clothes. An *amah*, a nursemaid, moved in when Sam was born. This plenteous number of servants was common among the Spanish, Filipino, European, and American business classes.

Eugenia maintained flower and vegetable gardens, and her hanging baskets, which overflowed with orchids, hung from the porch rafters. In her softly crenulated dress, Eugenia moved quietly, and restrained among the plants she maintained, and she responded to her children with gentleness and a tranquilizing touch. Eugenia also played the melodeon, a small reed organ. The smooth, sweet flow of sound filled their home in the evenings and spilled over the Santa Maria roadway.

The couple furnished their home with simple furniture—bookcases, tables, rattan chairs and other items. One table was reserved for the couple's new music player, a gramophone with a tall, wrap-around horn and branded with the picture of a white, cock-eared dog. Beds were made of *bejuco* or woven rattan sleeping surfaces upon which a thin mat—*petate*—was placed. Mosquito netting hung from the bed frames. This type of bed was hard, for it had neither mattress nor springs, but it was cool. Mattresses invited all manner of tropical critters as did hollow stud walls covered on both sides, so walls were built one board thick. Kerosene lanterns provided light.

They bathed in the Malay style by ladling water from a big clay jar with a half-coconut shell until P.H. devised a shower connected to a rooftop tank, which he filled by hand pumping from a well dug in the back yard. After a day in the tropical sun, the water was comfortably warm. Used water fell to the ground through spaces in the open bamboo floor. Next to the bathroom, P.H. gimmicked together a toilet. The contraption worked by pulling a chain which let a flush down a pipe from the roof tank and thence down a drainpipe to a septic tank. It was a Zamboanga potty house premiere heralded from household to household.

The kitchen was an extension off the opposite end of the back porch from the shower and toilet facilities. A charcoal fire in a low, open, clay cook stove was replaced within a few years with a cast iron stove from America. The pantry was self-standing like the old Hoosier cabinets built in Indiana, its four legs in half-filled sardine cans of kerosene to drown the bugs. Long strings of flypaper hung from the rafters. There was no ice and no refrigeration. Food spoiled within hours, so daily marketing for local produce was routine. Anything imported came in cans or bottles. Fresh eggs made it safely into a bucket of thick limewater. Sometimes Eugenia pickled their eggs in vinegar. The dining room table was six feet in diameter, constructed from a single slice of a giant mahogany tree. [4]

§

Even in these early years of the American enterprise in South East Asia, world events were foreshadowing the Frank family experience in the Philippines. The European nations with colonial interests in the region included Great Britain, the Netherlands, France, and Germany. These powers, together with the United States, were concerned about Russian designs and the Czar's intentions of expanding into South East Asia. The editor of the *Mindanao Herald* did not trust the Russians and was fearful they would take over control of Asiatic ports. He denigrated any Americans and Europeans in the Philippines who worried more about the Japanese "yellow peril" than the "Russian bear."

Any Russian superposition also threatened Japan, which began strengthening itself with British-built battleships, Krupp guns built in Germany, and loans floated in the United States and Britain. The Russian-Japanese War in 1904 was a bloody naval engagement that left Japan standing at the end of the last round and the few survivors of the Russian fleet limping into Manila. A few months later, the Japanese defeated the Russian land armies in Manchuria. These events marked the emergence of the Japanese island nation from feudalism to a modern nation state. P.H. was not alone among Zamboanga Americans in his admiration of Japan's victories, particularly their decisive naval blow at Port Arthur. In this sweep of the Russian navy, the duel ended in true *samurai* fashion—a blinding, decisive first blow. Indeed, P.H. had a favorite dog that he named Togo after the Japanese Vice-Admiral, Heihachiro Togo.

CHAPTER 7

"Mr. Frank has named his plantation Frankfort"

Mindanao Herald, June 30, 1906

In October 1905, James H. Ankrom, owner of the Elite Cafe which advertised Moerlein Beer as the "Best in the Orient," approached P.H. Frank. Ankrom was impressed with P.H.'s success, his work ethic, frugal habits, knowledge of the local languages, and connections. Ankrom invited him to go into the wholesale beer and liquor business with him.

Ankrom had a fine place in the best location in town. The "Red House," as the building was known in Zamboanga, was a large building owned by the government during Spanish days, located on Calle Madrid overlooking the ocean and adjacent to the Custom House and pier. Ankrom was a man of fifty, experienced, and a careful and shrewd businessman. P.H. and Ankrom each put $2,000 into the wholesale business, maintaining their retail operations separately. The two men announced the formation of "Ankrom & Frank, Wholesale Liquor Dealers and General Importers and Exhorters." The first order of business was the acquisition of some large shipments of various liquors from Europe and America. "We have the sole agency for Moerlein Beer, Cincinnati, Ohio, U.S.A. and are doing a flourishing trade," P.H. wrote home. He had linked up with a man who could be his mentor.[1]

P.H. and Ankrom were importing beer and booze directly from the producers. This meant that P.H. was now acting in partnership with

Ankrom as wholesaler not only to his own retail outlets but also to the other bars in Zamboanga, vastly enlarging his business reach. That arrangement provided P.H. a slice of everything his competitors sold. American liquor laws today do not permit a wholesaler to engage in both ends of the business, but the wholesale-retail arrangement was not prohibited in early twentieth century Mindanao.

P.H. moved his First and Last Chance to the ground level of the Red House, renaming his former location the Old Kentucky Bar, which he soon shortened to the OK Bar. The former private knew that a business like his must become the preferred shelter of his customers from their military duties—a sanctuary. The saloon occasioned people seeking a quiet break, putting together a business deal, savoring time with companions, meeting new faces and, for a few, there was time for marinating in regrets. The First and Last Chance became the most egalitarian of all American gathering places in Zamboanga. His was a place where Americans and Europeans, far from home, could find their own community. In the upstairs of the Red House, Ankrom maintained his Elite Café, a gentleman's bar and restaurant, a classier place where officers from Ft. Pettit, American civil servants, engineers, and a dressier crowd could enjoy themselves.

P.H. Frank was not a businessman who suffered forever his accounts receivable. On one occasion, R.M. Dennison, owner of the Palace Saloon, advertised as "a gentleman's resort, cleanly, quiet and respectable," owed Ankrom & Frank for supplies. However, he refused to pay even though P.H. had staked him to get started. P.H. with Dick Thrasher, neither man a hugger-mugger, went over to Dennison's place, got into his storeroom, and rolled out the unpaid barrels of Moerlein Cincinnati Beer onto the street. The two men rolled the heavy wooden barrels all the way back to P.H.'s storeroom at the Red House. Soldiers passing along the Zamboanga streets guffawed, Spaniards engaged in dignified glances, Christian Filipinos covered discrete smiles, and Moros stood about in wonderment.[2]

The move to the Calle Madrid waterfront location opened up additional clientele. British ships in the Borneo-Sandakan-Zamboanga run would come to Zambo, dock, unload, and pick up cargo and passengers while the officers, crew, and some of the passengers came ashore. It was pleasant for them to walk into a cool bar and restaurant for a cold drink. German ships on the China-Manila-Australia run did the same. The prime, spacious, Calle Madrid location became headquarters of P.H.'s many business interests and enterprises for the next seventeen years.[3]

§

Now a flourishing booze merchant, P.H. turned his attention to civic activities. November 16, 1905, was a day of celebration in Zamboanga, for it was on that day in 1899 that the first American troops landed and took possession of Mindanao in the name of the United States. The *Herald* noted the celebration that year was on a very elaborate scale. Private Frank, along with thirty-one other veterans who had served in various units in the Spanish-American War, represented the "Fighting 23rd" in the parade. The 20th Infantry Band stationed at Pettit Barracks and a Zamboanga native band supplied the martial strains. An American infantry unit from Pettit Barracks and an honor guard of Moros, under command of Datu Mandi, escorted the veteran soldiers.

Following the parade, veterans repaired for refreshments and patriotic speeches. Captain William J. White, Superintendent of the San Ramon Penal Colony and the parade Grand Marshall, formed a committee to arrange for a permanent veterans' organization. A fund was raised to defray the expenses of the celebration to which P.H. was a contributor of 50 pesos. The ensuing organization institutionalized within a month with former Private Frank elected second vice-president of the United Veteran Defenders of the Flag.[4]

P.H. also organized and managed the Zamboanga Athletic Club, began a baseball team, arranged sparring bouts, and did a little of any and everything to have a little sport. The local newspaper noted that the newly organized baseball team made its first appearance against a scrub team from Pettit Barracks. The paper reported that P.H.'s team, the "Mindanaos," played a very fine game, the score being six to one in their favor at the close. The number of teams grew as Filipinos quickly took up the game unknown in the islands before the Americans were there. Soon there were seventeen teams competing for "ringers" recruited from every American naval vessel making the Zamboanga port. During this time, P.H. also became a Mason, rose to the thirty-second degree of Masonry, and served as secretary of the Mt. Apo Lodge.

On April 17, 1906, P.H. and Eugenia delighted fully in the birth of their daughter Laura. The young family had grown to four and the number of *amahs* to two.

§

P.H. Frank's early successes in Zamboanga did not constitute a monopoly on his entrepreneurial spirit. In June 1906, P.H. took up land along the Dago River fronting the Davao Gulf in eastern Mindanao and named his stake "Frankfort," a 2,530-acre tract of jungle he intended to turn into a hemp plantation. The reason for the government land opening was to encourage economic growth. American agricultural experts had discovered that the volcanically rich soils and moderate climate around the gulf were outstanding for the production of abaca plants from which were derived hemp fibers used to manufacture rope. Actually, Spanish-American War veterans had already jumped the gun and taken up land on the Davao Gulf between 1901 and 1905, creating the town of Davao. They cleared land and planted hemp while awaiting the "official" opening of public lands by the government. The scene was reminiscent of the American land rushes of the 1870s and 1880s, but these American settlers found their promise across the Pacific rather than on the plains. They saw profits in the hemp business and were willing to work hard and risk their lives for it. The native Tagacaolo, Bagabos, and other Moro and pagan groups were encouraged to take up land, but few did at the beginning. After all, the forests were already theirs.[5]

As a partnership, Ankrom & Frank was eligible for 2,530 acres though Ankrom never took an active interest in P.H.'s venture. Under the rules of the Philippine Commission, a lease ran for twenty-five years, renewable for an additional twenty-five years. The lease rate was not to be less than 10 cents per acre yearly, the rate for the second twenty-five years could not exceed 60 cents per acre, and the government exempted taxes the start-up year. It was a sweet deal in any language.[6]

Like homesteading everywhere, life clearing the jungle and constantly fighting back the Cogan grasses was difficult. One never got used to the crocodile danger, snakes, including the deadly green tree vipers, and big centipedes. Before dressing, P.H. habitually shook his shoes to rid them of lurking scorpions. Monkeys were incessant raiders in his camp and sometimes moved in packs of a hundred or more. Enlisting labor from among the native groups was difficult. The government encouraged the native inhabitants to move to the coast near the plantations, but there were few takers in the beginning. To start, P.H. brought a few Christian Filipinos, then their wives and children, from Cotabato and Zamboanga. After awhile a couple of dozen families were working his place. The pay was attractive, one-dollar gold a day, which meant plenty of eager hands. Glorious orchids painting brilliant patterns against solid forest greens were compensation to the soul, and digging and returning them to Zamboanga was a profitable side business for the workers.

As a young boy, Bagaka, a Sangir Moro, helped out around P.H.'s *vinta*, a small sailboat that made trips from the plantation to Davao for supplies. The Sangir were the dominant Moro group in the Davao region. Bakaka was short, powerfully built with handsome Malay-Polynesian features that eventually won him two wives. He walked barefoot, wore tight silk draw-stringed pants pulled above the calves and a similarly tight, collarless, silk pullover. His green vest, cut several inches above the waist, sported fourteen shinny brass buttons. A tri-colored scarf tied about his waist held a sharkskin sheathed *bolo*. He revealed a betel nut stained smile when recalling his failures to do things the way P.H. wanted them done. On such occasions, he recalled P.H. scolding, "Got damn it, Bakaka, Got damn it, Bakaka," always twice and with pronounced body language.[7]

Naturally, there were indigenous natives groups who resisted. The pagan Bagobo tribesmen were fierce swordsmen who obtained their blades from the Moros. Rumors circulated of a conspiracy between the Bagobo and Moros to engage in assassination of American government officials and the general robbery and slaughter of the Christian planters. A force of the American planters moved into position to interdict the raid, and that brought the Davao District Governor, Edward Bolton, to the scene on a peacekeeping mission. Bolton and a planter emissary, Benjamin Christian, were murdered, "killed by bolo cuts to the top of their heads, the weapons penetrating the brain and evidently causing instant death." Upon receipt of the news of the murders, Davao planters and businessmen "armed with every conceivable kind of firearm, started immediately for the scene" with plans to "remain in the field until order has been restored." It was P.H. Frank aboard the coast guard cutter *Negros* who brought word of the murders to Zamboanga, which resulted in the expedition of "100 picked men from the 6th Infantry led by Captain George Langhorn." The perpetrators of the crime were never brought to justice, at least not in a court of law. The *Herald* noted that, "a number of the outlaws were killed and the Bagobo leader shot to death while being arrested." Two months later, the planters raised funds for a 10,000 peso clubhouse in which Governor Bolton's pistol would be enshrined. Both the resulting Davao Club and the relic would take on significance for the Frank family three decades in the future.

The native uprising was short lived. The ability to earn cash, the much-improved roads, and the steady development of the muddy Davao crossroad into a shipping port for the agricultural products of the new plantations soon brought the Bagobo and Moros into the emerging economy sporting silver centavos for buttons on their vests.

§

From the beginning of serious hemp production around Davao, P.H. took an active interest in finding a mechanical means of stripping the hemp for its fiber. The abaca plant reached a height of about twenty feet, the leaves growing directly from the plant's trunk without branching. A tough sheath, a petiole, covered the bases of the leaves. These sheaths, called *tuxie*, contained strong, hard fiber that made Manila Hemp, as it was known world wide, the preferred element in cordage when long, hard usage was expected.

Growers harvested abaca fields two to four times a year by cutting the mature plants, and allowing the roots to remain in the ground to produce new plants. Stripping the leaf sheaths into ribbon-like fiber strands was backbreaking work, which required that the *tuxie* be hand-pulled through platform-mounted stripping knives in one motion, resulting, as a rule, in a hernia of some sort to the laborer. The job also required a large labor force. Within a year of the official opening of the lands around Davao, there were forty-one plantations engaged in hemp production, several of them exceeding 100,000 plants. The want of labor to strip the fiber became the principal obstacle. While some planters had enough labor, the workers suffered severely, and often, hemp remained rotting on the ground for lack of workers to strip it. To solve the problem of a labor shortage, the Davao planters brought in Japanese workers, but they too suffered severely using the torturous stripping methods. However, the Japanese were used for agricultural labor because they were hardy, and dependable. They were also a communal people interested in developing mutual supporting institutions like schools and hospitals. In just a few years, their numbers grew to 6,000 with a trajectory reaching 20,000 within three decades, the largest population of Japanese in the Philippines.

P.H.'s stint of plantation life was short lived. On January 15, 1907, Ankrom's wife became ill, and he decided to return to the States. P.H. purchased his partner's share in the wholesale business, the Red House, and his upstairs Elite Café for $2,742. His first order of business was to reserve a half-page in the *Mindanao Herald*, advertising his First and Last Chance as "Where the Jolly People Meet," and the upstairs Elite as the "Gentleman's Café."

With Ankrom gone and P.H.'s expanding businesses and family in Zamboanga, there was little time now for his stewardship of "Frankfort." Filipino families working on the plantation required supervision, and given P.H.'s abundant responsibilities in Zamboanga, he sold out to another tough soul. However, he maintained a fondness for the place and people. Long after he had sold the plantation, he continued to maintain visits with Bagaka when he was in Davao for business. P.H. may have been out of the plantation business, but hemp continued to interest him, especially finding a mechanical means of stripping hemp fiber from the 250-300 pound *tuxie*.

§

By late 1907, P.H. Frank could survey his recent past with justifiable pride. He had left the farming country of east Texas in order to find his place and his fortune on the other side of the world. With the proud spirit of a pioneer, he wrote to his sister in Texas that the Philippines needed more enterprising, hard workers, "the kind that went west in the good old days and made America what she is today." To P.H., Mindanao was virgin territory, ripe for development, and offering "more inducements of Americans than the rest of the islands combined." As a Texas boy might, he took note of the vast acreage. He believed the Philippines needed "rail-splitters, genuine settlers, farmers, and the kind that settled the early west." To him the islands were American territory, "one of our stars," as "good old American blood was spilled" for the islands. He declared he loved the islands as much as he loved Texas, "fate has made it my home, and I love it." He added, "you can say the same for America, the roar of cannon and musket, and the shedding of blood made her what she is today, the greatest, grandest, and noblest nation on the earth. Why my dear sister one in America does not realize what it is to be an American, like one out here does, where one can meet people from all over the globe, there is a lot of consolation in the words, I AM AN AMERICAN."[8]

CHAPTER 8

"It seems that Old Fate has marked out my path"

Patrick Henry Frank. June 5, 1905

Two events in early 1907 linked P.H. Frank to the development of technology aimed at overcoming the labor shortage and backbreaking work of stripping hemp. The first was the opening next door to the Zamboanga Cold Storage Company of an up-to-date machine shop fitted throughout with the latest American machinery. James Wilson was head of the new enterprise and prepared to handle any work likely to be demanded at Zamboanga for some time in the future. The second was the opening of the first Zamboanga Agricultural and Industrial Fair. One of the exhibits included a session on the practical working of hemp stripping machines. Two machines were demonstrated, one by the Manila Hemp Machine Company and the other by the Padre Atienza Hemp Stripping Company. However, neither hemp-stripper evoked enthusiasm among the Davao planters who were seeking a workable machine.

P.H. was still fresh from his plantation venture, had many friends among the Davao planters, and recognized that if a machine could be developed to strip the hemp grown in Davao, then Davao could deal a fatal blow to the position of Manila in world hemp export. It also helped that P.H. knew that the Philippine Assembly was offering a 50,000 peso ($25,000) prize to the person who could develop a workable hemp-stripping machine.

That was big money and a worthy goal, and P.H. entered the race, as did many others. He and Wilson began experimenting in the machine shop and developed a fast friendship that would last their lifetimes. Shortly the two made a connection with an English engineer, C.G. McLane, working on a stripper for the J.G. White Company at Cebu. Taking a room at P.H. and Eugenia's home and supported with P.H.'s financial sponsorship, McLane began experiments with a hemp-stripping machine at Wilson's shop. McLane developed one prototype, but it failed when tested on the plantations, and he soon dropped out of the scene. Over the next decade, P.H. tinkered with different ideas in his backyard shed and at his friend James Wilson's machine shop, but inventing was difficult and frustrating. The hemp would break or some other failure would occur, but P.H. sustained his interest and kept his eye on the 50,000 peso prize. His children had the benefit of playing with some of his toy-size models. Nevertheless, the hemp plantations around Davao that were growing rapidly needed such a device, and P.H., once he had made up his mind to do something, was resolute.

§

P.H.'s civic and business associations continued to enlarge. The Commercial Club that formed in June 1907 was the first club in Zamboanga with Filipino business members "open to all." Racial integration had opposition in the American community, but P.H. had the future of his mestizo children in the forefront of his mind as well as good business sense and moral sensitivities provided him by his mother. He supported John Hackett, editor of the *Mindanao Herald*, who rallied supporters. P.H. was a member of the first board of directors, and his Elite Café at the Red House hosted Commercial Club meetings.[1]

P.H. also called together a gathering of retail liquor dealers of the Moro Province for organizing an "association for their mutual benefit" which he then headed. A week later, P.H. attended an organizational meeting of the Manila-Davao Planter's Association in Manila which was to lobby effectively a short time later for government-subsidized shipment of hemp from Davao to Zamboanga. This was another early indication of his interest in hemp fiber production for the world rope trade. It also showed his republican view of monopolies and government subsidizes to businesses when he had a financial interest in them. [2]

P.H. was doing well. By early 1908, he owned at least five retail saloons, eating establishments, and his wholesale business supplying his retail outlets and scores of his retail competitors. He had also remodeled the Red House to accommodate a twelve-bedroom hostel upstairs above his First and Last Chance Saloon that he named the Mindanao Hotel. The hotel catered to planters, business people, and government officials who lived in other areas of the Moro Province and came to Zamboanga for business, shopping, or relaxation. The second floor also contained a fancy *salle a manger* and P.H.'s Elite Café with a screened area overlooking the Basilan Straights and Moro Gulf.

Sam Frank recalled his childhood memories of the meals and ambiance at the Red House, "I remember having meals in a large cool room by the sea, screened to avoid flies by day and mosquitoes by night. It was a family-style single entree meal prepared by Chinese cooks and served by Filipino waiters. The favorite fare was American chop suey. The spacious upstairs *sala* served a dressier clientele. Every night there would be ten or more tables with fresh white tablecloths and napkins and with meals elegantly served by the Filipino waiters who spoke a fair amount of English. The menu was the same in both places, but there were elegant and well-dressed women and men in whites at one contrasting with boisterous camaraderie and men wearing khakis in the downstairs saloon." Sam observed of his father's dress, "Dad always wore whites. I never saw him in khakis."[3]

§

In 1908, ten years since his arrival in the Spanish-American War, P.H. Frank, undoubtedly financially successful, made plans for a trip home to Texas. His itinerary included circumnavigating the globe. He was not forgetful of his words written in 1905 to his sister, Texanna, "Well sister, you can see how from time to time, circumstances have kept me from going home. It seems that old fate has marked out my path, and steps in every once and awhile and says, you can not go yet, but I think he will let me off by and by."

A rousing send off by the members of the Bolton Post Veteran Defenders of the Flag marked the beginning of P.H.'s return to the States. Joining P.H. were Dr. D.C. Beebe, a contract army physician and Basilan lumber dealer, and C.F. Vance, a government engineer in the provincial office. The veteran's band struck up a chord as the group prepared to cast off from the Zamboanga pier aboard a motor launch to their liner's deep-water anchorage. Eugenia gave her husband a smile that both encouraged his leaving and assured him that she and the children would be fine. Two-year-old Laura took in the hustle and bustle of the wharf with her short arms wrapped within as much of her mother's skirt as she could enfold. Four-year-old Sam stood transfixed as his father leaned down to whisper in his ear, only responding to his father with an assuring nod.

P.H. knew that Eugenia was with child and would be cared for through her pregnancy and birth by her mother Andrea who was now living in the Frank's Santa Maria home following her husband's death in 1904. During the couple's courtship and engagement year, Eugenia had worried that her intended might return to America, and justifiably so. However, Eugenia loved her husband, and knew he had made a permanent nest in the islands with her. She was a mother now and understood that Martha McGuire, now 60 years old, missed her son.

P.H. Frank, Eugenia Garcia, Sam (3 years), and Laura (baby), circa 1907. *(Courtesy of Emory University MARBL, Frank Family Collection)*

P.H. and Eugenia Frank's home in Zamboanga, circa 1907. *(Courtesy of Emory University MARBL, Frank Family Papers)*

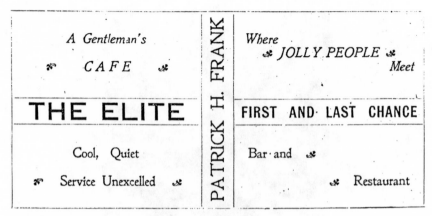

P.H. Frank ad in the *MindanaoHerald*, circa 1906. *(Courtesy of Emory University MARBL, Frank Family Papers)*

P.H. Frank and R.M. Dennison compete for business in the *Mindanao Herald*, circa1906. *(Courtesy of Emory University MARBL, Frank Family Collection)*

Pettit Barracks was headquarters of the American army in the Moro Province. *(Courtesy of Emory University MARBL, Frank Family Collection)*

The provincial government building for the Department of Mindanao and Sulu, Zamboanga, circa 1909. *(Courtesy of Emory University, MARBL, Frank Family Papers)*

For the greater part of the period 1903 to 1913, the Moro Province was governed by a military Department of Mindanao and Sulu with headquarters at Pettit Barracks in Zamboanga. *(letter head, Committee on Exhibits, Moro Province Fair at Zamboanga, 1910. From the author's collection)*

Part 3
Gas Lights, Transportation, and Invention
1908 to 1920

"Fate has made it my home, and I love it"

P.H. Frank November 5, 1905

CHAPTER 9

"The world is my home"

P.H. Frank, June 20, 1920

In 1908 travel by ship was so expensive and time-consuming that the only people to use it were the idle rich for recreational purposes, colonial power military and civil officials, and immigrants who were changing countries, and usually placed in lower class berthing. For a thirty-three year old from places like Groveton, Texas, and Zamboanga, Philippines, the idea of being able to circumnavigate the globe was enormous. P.H. had lived in the Philippines for ten years, far from family and old friends. That he could afford such an undertaking is testament to his financial successes. Dr. D.C. Beebe, a contract army physician, and C.F. Vance, a government engineer in the provincial office, were civil servants, and had paid leaves coming. The two coordinated their plans with P.H. in the Elite Café, working their itinerary by using a 1906 *Baedeker Guidebook*. The adventurers left Zamboanga on February 22, 1908, aboard the *Bremerhaven*, a German liner of the Norddeutscher Lloyd Company, routed from Australian ports to Hong Kong and west to Singapore through the Mediterranean to Hamburg. The men's bookings were first class aboard one of the biggest and most resplendent of European ships.

Gliding into the mountain-encircled harbor of Hong Kong the men marveled at President Theodore Roosevelt's Great White Fleet flying the American flag in anchorage below the Victoria Heights. The fleet was composed of sixteen steam-powered, steel battleships arranged in four squadrons with their crews of 14,000 sailors and marines smartly manning the rails, the ships painted solid white. The United States had shown an increasing interest in the Pacific since acquiring the Philippines; Hawaii was annexed the day before Private Frank forged into Manila in 1898 and was established as a territory in 1900, followed by Guam and parts of Samoa. Though Roosevelt intended the voyage of the fleet to be of a friendly nature, he also meant it to be a demonstration of American strength and resolve in the face of increasing Japanese naval power following the Russian-Japanese War—a part of his "big stick" diplomacy. It was a naval deployment the scale of which had never been seen before. To P.H., the Great White Fleet was indeed a show of strength. The United States Navy was now on a par with the German navy and second only to Great Britain. A British newspaper quoted Admiral Togo who said if the ships reach Japan, "We will greet the men as friends."

§

The British controlled their calling ports along the route as far as the Mediterranean. With the British Empire at its height, the Union Jack flew around the world. In British Hong Kong and the Crown Colony of Singapore, P.H. observed many differences from America's colonial approach to the Philippines. The British had arrived much later on the Southeast Asian scene than had the Spanish. Rather than dispersing as the Spanish and Americans like himself had done in the Philippines, the British created an exclusive cantonment. White troops were conveniently close in order to guard the European population and the institutions of a transplanted England which included the Anglican Church, the cricket ground, the Government House, government office buildings, the sports club, racetrack, and residences.

The style in which Europeans, and already some wealthy Chinese, lived in tree-shaded enclaves, impressed P.H. Their arresting tile-roofed homes with high ceilings and broad porches had an air of colonial permanence that was lacking in the Philippines. The British had come to stay, and they were making themselves as comfortable as possible; in contrast, most Americans seemed only to be camping out in the Philippines, as evidenced by houses like his own Santa Maria *nipa-*

roofed home with attached Zambo potty house. What interested him most were new technologies: electricity, telephones, automobiles, cranes, and innovative machinery. British management skills and their efficient colonial bureaucracy impressed him. He was also in the company of other successful entrepreneurs, and from their conversations, P.H. gleaned new ideas of organization and management as well as the advantages of incorporation.

Penang in Indonesia was the next port of call. In transit he spent time in the ship's engine rooms studying the great Krupp generators producing the ship's electricity. If only he could get electricity to Mindanao, he thought. Then it was across the Indian Ocean to Ceylon (now Sri Lanka) where P.H. got a look at coconuts grown on British plantations and processed into desiccated confectionary used on cakes and candies. The machinery intrigued him, and the whiteness of the processed coconut was superior to any he had seen in the Philippines. But the real money in coconuts was coconut oil. The oil, with a high concentration of glycerin, was used in the manufacture of gunpowder in munitions when countries went to war.

P.H. spent time in Europe and England. There he saw even more automobiles than he had seen in Manila, Hong Kong, and Singapore. In Paris he attended an automobile rally and visited art museums where he was taken with the first impressionist paintings he had seen. He took trips into the Alps and was fascinated with the dykes of Holland. In London he ordered a new suit, pants, and shirts custom made for him on Savile Row and picked them up after returning from sojourns to Scotland and Ireland.

On the Cunard liner *Mauretania*, P.H. crossed the Atlantic to New York where he took a railroad ride through a new tunnel under the Hudson River and stayed in the fashionable Fifth Avenue Plaza Hotel, which was lighted by innumerable electric chandeliers and considered one of the prettiest in the city. At Madison Avenue and 24th Street, he watched concluding construction of the 50-story Metropolitan Life Insurance Building, the largest office building in the world. He then rode one of Pullman's fine new train cars to Chicago to the world fair where he studied the technology of a new electric gas light. In Detroit the Model T was not yet in full production but ready to roll and in Cincinnati he met with his Moerlein Beer suppliers. He saw for the first time other marvels such as telegraph-transmitted pictures that had not yet reached Zamboanga. Everywhere there was electricity, and he thirsted to know more about its physics and production.

§

Sojourning solo to see their families, P.H., Beebe, and Vance split up in St. Louis, which was preparing for its own world exposition. In Dallas, P.H. bought a horse and buggy and took to the forty miles of hot, dusty roads to Iredell, Texas, where his mother was now living with her second-oldest son. There on the Bosque River at a place called Sadler Crossing, between Iredell and Walnut Springs, the Franks and McGuires gathered in picnic and reunion, celebrating the first of their own to be an around-the-world traveler.

It was a warm, dry, June day. The Bosque at that inland spot was a small stream, and the dry weather afforded an easy crossing of the buggies at the ford. None of the thirty-eight Franks and McGuires arrived by automobile. All came by buggy and wagon, farm worn and utilitarian. P.H., with his twin sisters Cora and Nora and his older sister Texanna sat on the thick, drooping branch of an oak tree and admired the new buggy with a folding top that P.H had brought as a gift for their mother. Young girls and children wadded barefoot in the stream. The women wore long sleeved, full-length dresses, and ruffled bonnets covered their heads. Little girls were dressed in three-quarter sleeve dresses. The men and boys were in long pants and white long-sleeved shirts; some had wide belts with large buckles. Many of the clothes were cut from the same bolt of cloth. A few blouses were made from printed flour-sack. The oldest and youngest gravitated for rest on the small folding camp chairs and wooden benches that dotted the gathering place. Two young teen boys admiring a hatband leaned in straight back chairs; two lazy hounds, one a black and white, the other a tan lolled at their feet. Large hamper baskets held ample picnic foods. Floppy cowboy hats lay on the ground. The contrast between Bosque River-English language versus Moro Gulf mixtures of eighty-seven languages and dialects and homespun versus exotic dress, was dramatic.

P.H. was wearing his white, long sleeved, Savile Row shirt, suspenders, armbands, and a tie. He had anticipated relating his experiences and accomplishments in the Philippines. However, his stories of strange lands and peoples elicited no more than perfunctory interest. Eyes quickly glazed over. This was a reunion of two families whose members rarely saw one another, the kind of time when opportunity to talk was maintained briefly while folks moved from individuals to small clusters. And for P.H. there were new relationships to forge with his sisters, now in young adulthood. One sister and her daughter were dead from Yellow Fever. His mother was no longer the picture of strength that had buffered him growing up. P.H. and his family were so far away in place and time that they, at first, seemed almost irrelevant to one another. They did not realize how much he had changed in his ten years away; he did not fully appreciate that they had lived different lives than the one he had been experiencing.[1]

P.H. and his family soon turned the conversation from his adventures in the exotically different Philippines and around the world to subjects that they both understood, such as sports and domestic politics that interested both the women and men. His mother noted news of a small demonstration by a group called "suffragists" trying to open the way for women to vote. Then there was enthusiasm for Jack Johnson, a Negro heavyweight fighter from Galveston with a string of knockouts, who might go against world champion Tommy Burns in Australia. The Populist Party had offered up Tom Watson for president in April. In July the Republicans just might nominate Howard Taft and come August the Democrats could put forth William Jennings Bryan. A mob lynched six Negroes for an alleged murder plot a week earlier in Houston.

P. H. Frank left his home and childhood in Texas for the second time, knowing this time he could not really return. Now P.H. considered himself bigger than Texas saying, "While I love old Texas and the names and deeds of the men who put her on the map, I have seen so much of the world that I have lost my state pride. The world is my home, but I am still 100% American"[2]

§

P.H. stood nostalgically by the railing of the Japanese liner *S.S. Ten-Yo Maru* as the ship glided out of San Francisco on the final leg of his journey. The hills of the Golden Gates rose clear in the blue sky above him; dense fog had obscured the heights of their cliffs during his egress from the bay ten years earlier. Behind him, the city was in a building frenzy due to an earthquake and fire two years earlier that reduced the bayside town to ashes and left thousands dead. His stops included Hawaii which his *Colon* bypassed in 1898 in its hurry to deposit him in Manila. The ship took on coal at a tiny island called Midway and there were a few days in Nagasaki, Japan, before coasting by Formosa with its great mountains dipping into the sea.

On August 13, 1908, the tenth anniversary of the Battle of Manila, P.H. entered Zamboanga waters. Small, flag-bedecked *vintas* met his boat with those aboard joining in cheers and greetings and falling in line behind the procession. A larger boat brought the spiffily dressed Constabulary Band which played gaily. His friends Beebe and Vance, who had preceded him by a month, accompanied the Veteran Defenders of the Flag on an even larger boat. Red and white bunting was draped along the overhanging Spanish-style balcony of the Red House, and a forty-six star flag flew in the private's honor. Next door, construction was under way on the new American Provincial Capital of the Department of Mindanao and Sulu.

CHAPTER 10

"If you know a bright enterprising young man…"
P.H. Frank, November 5, 1905

P.H. held onto the metal rail as the inter-island steamer *Darvel* bumped the Zamboanga wharf and slid into its berth. A little four-wheeled *carromatos*, drawn by two stocky Filipino ponies and driven by the Frank's native driver, drew up to the end of the pier where the twenty-five foot decking met the macadam surface of Calle Madrid. Disembarking the *Darvel*, P.H. approached the carriage where Eugenia, four-year-old Sam, and two-year-old Laura welcomed him home. In Eugenia's arms was Patrick James (Pat) Frank, now four months old. With a capable little trot, the ponies wheeled down the Santa Maria Road to home, the family's spirited Spanish and Cebuano trailing high in the palms.[1]

When P.H. Frank disembarked in Zamboanga in August 1908, he ushered in a new age of technology on the Philippine frontier. During his trip, he had witnessed unimaginable inventions that stimulated his entrepreneurial instincts, and he brought with him the new lighting system he discovered in Chicago. Immediately he installed the system in his Red House establishments and advertised in the *Mindanao Herald*, "The wonderful 'Radio' Lamp—the light of modern times." A well-placed patron wrote to the newspaper, "This light is undoubtedly the most successful in the world for all lighting purposes. Its simplicity of construction and operation, its symmetrical beauty, powerful white light, cheapness, and durability are its crowning features." The technology, in this case, was the Radio Lighting System manufactured by the Acorn Brass Manufacturing Company that he had visited in Chicago. "If any body can light anything I can," P.H. boastingly advertised. His system operated by placing gasoline under sufficient pressure to vaporize the liquid and carry it along a copper pipe in a 94% air mixture to an arc lamp. The light had a timer switch for turning automatically on or off, day or night, and friends touted the system as a great deal cheaper, cleaner and safer than kerosene.

The perceptive P.H. appealed to homemakers in his ads to "add cheer and comfort to the home," and reminded merchants that "trade is like a moth. It is attracted by a bright light." His appeal to the "City Fathers" was for "well lighted streets." The latter market received encouragement by the Commercial Club, which wrote, "The new Radio Street Lamp which is being exhibited by Mr. P.H. Frank in front of his place on Calle Madrid gives a beautiful, steady and powerful light, and its simplicity makes it an ideal street light. Our city leaders would do well to investigate the proposition of installing the Radio Light throughout the city." And so it was that the town of Zambo installed one hundred Radio Gaslights purchased through P.H., the sole agent for the Radio Gaslight in the Philippines. Orders reached his desk and skyrocketed as P.H. shifted his business focus from owning a bar to lighting a small city.

P.H. accomplished this by using the successful distributorship model he used to establish his thriving wholesale and retail beer and liquor lines. Only this time he substituted selling a gas tank and several lights to one business, which in turn would sell lights to other businesses, which would connect to the original tank. The fuel to operate his gaslights was ultra-refined "white gasoline," that he purchased wholesale from Standard Oil of New York. He stored the flammable liquid in fifty-gallon drums at the end of a pier used solely for loading and unloading gasoline, munitions, and fireworks. From there he pumped the gasoline into smaller tins for distribution.

§

During that same summer of 1908, P.H. and other Zamboanga citizens gathered at the wharf, watching the arrival of the *Romulus* and the unloading of the town's first automobile, long anticipated, with a sense of awe, wonder, and historical import. The purchase of the car by the provincial government was for inspecting roads, getting payrolls to laborers, and for transporting people on official business. The used motorcar car was a Coventry made by Humber Limited of London. New, the cost for the twelve horsepower car would have been 6,000 pesos; used the car cost 2,800 pesos.

Several days following arrival of the Coventry, J.H. Taylor, a traveling representative for the John R. Edgar Company of Manila, arrived to do business with Zamboanga merchants. Taylor was also serving as agent for the famous Tourist Automobiles, which he described as fine for Mindanao. P.H. took a great interest in this car and ordered the first private automobile on Mindanao, a two-seat Brush Roadster that he had admired on his global jaunt; his friend Dr. Short soon had his own Brush. Taylor also had a fine line of books including the new *Harvard Classics*, which P.H. ordered, becoming the backbone of his growing collection of reading.

Boarders at P.H.'s Mindanao Hotel needed transportation, and a Mitchell was the first automobile P.H. bought for that purpose. He hired one of the Filipino drivers who had been taught by the provincial government to drive its official auto. He titled the driver *chauffeur* and rented the car out by the hour. There were also many well-to-do Americans, Spaniards and Filipinos in town who desired automotive transportation. As business grew, P.H. experimented with different makes of cars. He had the Brush, he tried the Mitchell and the Reo, and then he got a Hudson Super Six. There were not any good mechanics available, so P.H. was always going from one make of car to the next looking for a more dependable automobile. Finally he got a Hupmobile and after that a couple of Dodges. Then he got a Model T Ford, which he considered an ideal car. It was easy to maintain, light, and had no difficulty on the road. He kept building his garage to accommodate more and more Fords, bringing down a trade school engineer from Manila to teach mechanics to a core of talented Filipinos and himself. P.H. advertised his business as the Mindanao Hotel Garage located on Calle Madrid not far from the hotel.

With the assistance of Frank Yeager, a Harvard educated attorney and judge of the Court of First Instance in Zamboanga, P.H saw to the incorporation of his five saloons, Mindanao Hotel, gas light franchise, and Mindanao Hotel Garage. Then P.H. hired Henry Wolff, a bookkeeper, and began a correspondence course in accounting so he would understand the reports that Wolff produced. He followed that with a course in business administration offered by the International Correspondence School. Thenceforth, P.H. Frank was president of every company he established. Soon leaving his saloons and hotel in the hands of Dick Thrasher and his gaslight distributorship to the management skills of John Gigling of the Reception Hotel in Dansalan, he continued his venture into transportation. P.H.'s enterprises began to take up fully one-third of the advertising space in the *Mindanao Herald*.

§

In 1909, Brigadier General John J. "Black Jack" Pershing succeeded Tasker Bliss as Governor of the Moro Province and Commanding General of Department of Mindanao and Sulu. Pershing had served on Mindanao in 1903 and left as a captain with a well-deserved reputation as a Moro fighter. P.H. thought well of Pershing who was a regular diner at his Elite Café. Pershing's two daughters and the Frank children were good friends, playing hide-and-seek in the general's study and schooled together at the Post School.

The southern Philippines in 1909 remained dangerous, and Pershing subscribed fully to the policy of his predecessor of maintaining strong and prepared armed forces in the province. He increased the training of Philippine Scouts—native combat troops led by American officers—and disbursed them in strong units throughout Mindanao to support the native Constabulary forces. American officers also led the Constabulary which had the major task of law enforcement and maintenance of peace. In Pershing's view, the Scouts surpassed the American soldiers as fighters of the Moros who continued to resist American hegemony. Numerous bloody encounters with Moro and pagan groups continued.

In the northeastern part of Zamboanga District, Subano pagans were aroused against the government by Moro *datus* around Lake Lanao. Several thousand took up defensive positions within 175 *cotas* armed with *bolos*, *krises* and *campilans*—head-taking knives. It took two months for the Constabulary, supported by the Scouts, to restore peace.

American troops, Philippine Scouts, and the Constabulary often cooperated in pursuing bands of Moro outlaws ranging in size from ten to forty fighters engaging in slaving raids, kidnapping for ransom, and theft. Occasionally some bands wandered into Zamboanga where fighting would flare up close to town. Steep forest-covered slopes and almost impassable lowland swamps made detection and pursuit difficult.

Of ghastly concern to American soldiers, pioneers, and Christian Filipinos was the Moro *juramentado*, which could make life in garrison towns like Zamboanga, Cotabato and Jolo a nightmare. The term *juramentado* meant swearing an oath to kill the enemies of Islam. These radical Muslims would shave their eyebrows and bind up the vulnerable parts of their bodies (including the testicles) so that they would not bleed to death, and anesthetize themselves against pain if wounded. They would then dress in white garments, go before a *pandita* or *imam*, take their oaths, and seek out infidels, usually Christian Filipinos and American soldiers and civilians. The *juramentado* attacked with his *bolo* and *kris* bringing down his victims with vicious blows and stabs. This was not an act of banditry, piracy, or kidnapping for slaves. This was a religiously sanctioned act of suicide. As a civilian, P.H. protected himself with the newest .45 caliber pistol, designed specifically for warfare in Moroland, and a nearby 12-guage pump shotgun.[2]

At Pettit Barracks in early 1909, a *juramentado* Moro attacked a captain, who fired six .38 caliber shots into him. The Moro did not stop running, cut the captain to pieces with his bolo, and started on his way rejoicing when a guard finally finished him with a .45 caliber bullet.

Eugenia's recent ancestors included Moros. P.H. was familiar and respectful of various Moro groups and their distinctive cultures. He respected Moro culture and knew that the vast majority were peaceful. As a soldier, he had respected their tenacity and bravery in battle. He employed Moros, and they were loyal. Nevertheless, P.H. knew the dangers of the *juramentado*, as did most Moros who feared them as much as the Christian Filipinos. In the crazed state of a Moro *juramentado*, few religious distinctions were made. The *juramentado* was infrequent, but a heavyweight, defensive firearm was always close at hand.

§

The United Veteran Defenders of the Flag, which P.H. had been instrumental in organizing in 1905, underwent several name changes, becoming more exclusive and, if anything, more patriotic. By 1909, the group called itself Bolton Camp No. 10, Veteran Army of the Philippines and Defenders of the Flag—V.A.P. for short. On April 16, 1909, the post held an "encampment" at San Ramon farm just up the coast from Zamboanga. A large attendance of the membership and their guests departed on the launch *Jewel* at dawn. Good cheer and enjoyment prevailed. Stepping toward the gangplank, P.H. cast a glance back over his shoulder as a dove cooed. If a native Bagobo started on a trip and a dove called over his left shoulder, he would return home at once for it was considered a bad omen. But at that very moment, an orchestral quartet made up of a gong, bagpipes, piccolo and a megaphone struck up a rendition. The *Mindanao Herald* quoted the iconoclastic P.H. as remarking that the sound reminded him of a "lost chord pursued by a Chinese band," and he winced, stepping aboard, the sounds of the band drowning out the cooing of the dove.

One of the main events of the day involved a shooting match. Comrade Griffin placed several carbines at the disposal of the Camp, and some remarkable scoring was done though there was some doubt as to the reliability of certain of the markers due to alleged monetary considerations passing between them and the would-be sharpshooters. Several of the crooks had their scores wiped off the board leaving Comrade Huber with 22 out of a possible 25 at 150 yards with a carbine and P.H. Frank second with 21. Comrade Griffith was easily the best revolver shot, with Comrade Frank a close second.

What a day it was with games of quoits and horseshoes. There was a table of chance presided over by the Detective Bureau's own Gumshoes Johnson, a culinary department under the able management of everybody present, and there was the ever-present orchestral quartet rendering exquisite music at intervals during the day and on the homeward voyage. P.H. strolled soberly behind the wavy, spirited crowd as the revelers meandered to the boat for the return to Zamboanga.

Dusk was settling over the encampment; P.H. slowed his pace and felt about him an uneasy premonition. Darkness had fallen as the *Jewel* tied up at the wharf.

P.H.'s chauffeur met him at the dock, hastily urged him home, and accelerated the Mitchell down the Santa Maria Road. P.H. found Eugenia in a fever. An angry infection swelled on her cheek at the spot where a Spanish doctor had lanced an insect bite two days before the encampment. Anthrax-carrying flies were common in the area and the doctor considered a bite from such a fly the infection's cause. Sanitation and health were improving under American administration; but the dangers of microbes persisted, and the Spanish doctors, whom Eugenia trusted above the Americans, were not as well trained or amenable to hand washing and the use of antiseptics.

P.H. called immediately for an American army doctor at Fort Pettit and set up a bed in the living room. Two Filipina nurses and the doctor did what they could. Fate had been generous to P.H. until April 23, 1909, when seven days following the encampment, Eugenia died. Her death came on her baby Pat's first birthday. It was the kind of story later told by a father to his son that could never be forgotten, that his mother had died on his birthday. The beautiful Eugenia was only twenty-five years old when she died. She and P.H. had been married for six years.

P.H. was shattered as he stepped through the sliding doors to the porch. Five-year-old Sam, peering through his tears and the translucent panels of *capis* shell, watched and listened as his father began to keen, releasing his grief to the night, unable to console his son. Alone in his bed, Sam heard the heavy, hardwood slatted shutters closed hard against the storm that came during the night, while in the *sala*, an army mortician prepared Eugenia for burial. The next morning a barefoot houseboy skated across the floor on a pair of coconut husk halves, polishing the wide mahogany planks to a mirror-like finish in preparation for the wake.

Family and friends followed the horse and wagon that carried Eugenia's coffin the half-mile to the Old Catholic Cemetery where a larger crowd of friends and acquaintances waited. Father Mario Suarez, who had blessed the marriage of Eugenia and P.H., officiated mass in the small chapel at the entrance to the cemetery. Concrete blocks enclosed the large plot that P.H. had purchased for a gravesite. A six foot high concrete cross stood in the center, Frank and Garcia inscribed on opposite sides of the pedestal. Young Sam held tightly to his father's leg as his mother was laid to rest.

§

Eugenia's mother, Andrea Magno, had been living with P.H. and Eugenia since the death of Fermin Garcia four years earlier. Taking over the household duties after Eugenia died, Andrea and P.H. soon clashed over raising his children. Andrea was devoted to raising Sam, Laura, and Pat in the social and cultural traditions of the Catholic Church in the Philippines, and called them by their baptismal names, Jose, Laora, and Emilio. P.H. left no doubt that he would have the children raised as Americans—Sam, Laura and Pat. The two fought over continuing Spanish language in the home, attending Catholic mass and school, dress, mannerisms, and Andrea Magno's place in the family. The cadence sped up, and P.H. finally had all he could take; an argument took place, and he decided she had to leave. He put her belongings in a wagon, and she went to live in a small coconut grove north of Zamboanga with Eugenia's brother Antonio. It was the last Sam, Laura, and Pat ever saw of her, except once at a distance in the market. Perhaps the scene simply revealed an inevitable gap of culture, class, and race that was once bridged by Eugenia and earlier, to some extent, by Fermin. On the other hand, maybe the bare facts spoke for themselves—a widowed father with three small children in the same house with his widowed mother-in-law who was only nine years his senior. Nowhere in the world, in any culture, were such dynamics very promising.

With Eugenia and Andrea gone, Mrs. Wolff, the wife of his accountant, helped run the household. P.H. would leave his Santa Maria home in the cool of the early morning, and was driven by his chauffeur to the Red House. Sam accompanied him to a drop-off point where an army wagon picked him and other children up for the drive to the Post School. Laura and Pat were still not old enough for school, but when they became of age all three rode the wagon.

Upon P.H.'s arrival, Filipino employees had already made the First and Last Chance ready, washed glasses from the night before, polished, and placed them on the shelf behind the long mahogany bar. A young Moro boy named Ippano skated over the thick beamed floors with coconut husks tied to his feet. Upstairs in the Elite Café, Chinese cooks made preparations for the lunch special of American Chop Suey, and workers placed starched white linens on the tables. On Calle Madrid, American-bred Morgan horses ridden by black cavalrymen, trotted at a clip toward the Fort Pettit gate, where two twelve-foot-high obelisks supported ornate steel barriers.

P.H.'s office was at the back of the first floor bar. The furnishings were simple, a wooden partner's desk, a swivel chair with rattan seat, a footrest, and a straight back chair. A wire-basket paper-holder spilled over with correspondences and invoices. Ancient plaster on the walls was chipped in places. His mother's photograph hung between a calendar and a zigzag business chart that trended upward.

P.H. ate lunch upstairs on the screened porch of the Elite, which overlooked the Basilan Straight. In the dining room, at a round table General Pershing lunched with several Filipinos, members of the Provincial Council who advised him. At two o'clock, P.H. stretched out on the corner cot in his office for a *siesta*.

P.H. made a lot of money with his companies. The businesses brought in cash, lots of it, and mostly coins—American, German, British, French, Dutch, Chinese, Japanese, Spanish, and Portuguese. By the end of the day they were piled everywhere in behemoth mounds and spilling out of his large, standing-steel safe made by Hall's Safe Company of Cincinnati. In the late afternoon, P.H. counted every coin, and he and Mr. Wolff put them in long-handled leather pouches. Two of his employees stepped out of the door of the Red House, wearing .45 caliber revolvers strapped to their waists and holding 12-gauge pump shotguns loaded with lead slugs. Two hotel chauffeurs, who holstered .45-calibers cinched to their girths, each carried two money pouches out to the street. Together the four walked to the Bank of Zamboanga two blocks away and made P.H.'s deposit.

P.H.'s employees occasionally were the brunt of his short temper. On his way home one evening, he came upon one of his drivers who had mistaken a muddy field for the road, resulting in the driver's being thrown to the ground by P.H. who then pitched a thin, woven *petate*, over the man and repeatedly stomped him.

About dusk, P.H. pulled into the backyard where a high white picket fence surrounded the household chicken and duck flocks as well as several goats. In the back corner of the yard, he maintained a shed where he kept Kate, his first little Filipino pony, who shared her quarters with the outmoded two-wheeled buggy. He was exhausted, and he missed Eugenia very much.

CHAPTER 11

"Following her recovery, Okio was looking for a job"

Samuel Boone Frank, Remembrances, 1991

In need of help to care for his young children, P.H. engaged Okio Yamagouchi to serve as *amah* for them. The events leading up to Okio's tenure in the Frank home became legend in the early American-European community of Zamboanga. [1]

Okio had been the magazine picture bride of J.H. Verment, a Hollander who entered the logging business with George Case, a native of New York State, their operations located on Basilan Island across the strait from Zamboanga. American and European men on the Philippine frontier sometimes used such arrangements for marriage.

On Christmas Eve 1907, Joloano Moros raided the Case and Verment logging camp. They severed Case's head from his body and, as he lay on the bed, dealt Verment a vicious blow across the abdomen with a barong, nearly cutting him in two. Verment, a reportedly powerful man, managed to climb to his knees before a decapitating stroke left his headless torso remaining in a crouched position. Okio escaped through a window as a Moro viciously slashed her across the back. The wound, described as deep, reached from her left shoulder diagonally down her back to the right hip.

Case's Japanese bride escaped the slaughter. A Moro grabbed her by the hair, swung at her neck with a barong, and missed his mark, cutting off her long hair at the nape. Leaving her hair clutched in the Moros hand, she fled into the dark jungle, arriving at a friendly Yakan village three miles from the logging camp. A Yakan rescue party returned to the scene and found Okio lying in the bushes some distance from the house. Made as comfortable as possible in a *vinta*, paddlers brought her to Zamboanga on Christmas, her wounds so serious that at first there was reported little chance of her recovery. She rallied, but healing and convalescence took over a year.

While Okio was being cared for by surgeons, a detachment of American troops returned the bodies of Okio's husband and Case to Zamboanga for burial in the Tumaga cemetery. This was a frontier community, and the funeral obtained considerable public attention. Tasker Bliss, the military governor, officials of the provincial government, and a large number of American residents of the city, attended services for the popular lumbermen, who were former employees of the British North Borneo Company. Several American women were present and sang that dear old hymn "Nearer My God to Thee."

To aid the government in the capture of the murderers and arrange for the care of the survivors, the citizens of Zamboanga held two rousing mass meetings at the Zamboanga Theater. P.H. Frank contributed 50 pesos to the reward fund of 1,000 pesos offered by the citizens of Zamboanga to match a similar amount put up by the provincial government.

The murders stirred the community to a sense of the dangers that attended the isolated Americans and Europeans who faced the wilderness with the spirit of the western pioneers in an effort to push a little further the bounds of their civilization. The Zamboanga citizens responded exactly as would have citizens in the old American West, by forming a posse, except that this time Bliss interceded, and soldiers rather than the posse took up the chase. The army captured a Moro named Wadja and four accomplices who went to trial and received prison terms. The sentences seemed rather lenient in light of the mores of the era and American frontier justice though harsher frontier justice might have been meted in ways unofficially recorded.

Following her recovery two years later, Okio was looking for a job. It was December 1909; Eugenia had died nine months earlier and her mother had been banished from the Frank's home. Mr. and Mrs. Wolff brought Okio out to P.H.'s Santa Maria house. She was needed badly and immediately proved helpful. She was arresting in her beauty, tranquilizing in her modesty, and composed in her carriage. She was mentally nimble and physically strong. She could not speak English well, but was learning. She and the children connected affectionately, and she looked after all three, mainly Laura, and did the housekeeping.

While *amahs* were usually considered servants, Okio was more akin to an English nanny and shortly became like an adoptive mother. She lived in the house, bathed the Frank children, and dressed every Sunday night to eat with them at a round table in the fancy public dining room at P.H.'s Mindanao Hotel where he would join them when he could. She would also picnic with the family at San Ramon and took her meals with P.H. and the children at home. Family studio portraits included Okio, and on many evenings, P.H. would hitch his Morgan, an American cavalry horse, to the buggy and take Sam, Laura, Pat and Okio for fun-filled rides around Zamboanga. Other times they used P.H.'s Brush Roadster, Okio in the front seat with Laura, and Pat and Sam standing up in the jump seat. A close and familial relationship pivoted about Okio and lasted seven years. P.H.'s grief over Eugenia's death had deadened his heart, and as the years passed, falling in love with Okio resurrected it.

§

Road building on Mindanao and Sulu was in full swing by 1911, a huge undertaking by the American government. As the roads extended into the hills from Zamboanga and Jolo, more and more people could bring goods to sell and trade in town. General Pershing made this construction one of the highest priorities of the provincial government in the early American years. Farmers would be able to get their produce to markets, purchase goods and return home, and American hegemony advanced. For their time, the roads were first-class with well-supported sub-grades, good drainage systems, and macadam surfaces of crushed white coral and shell. The government maintained the roads by the *caminero* system which assigned a man with shovel, broom, and wheelbarrow every two miles. This man's job was to fill potholes and keep the road smooth. Periodically, a steamroller would make a run.

P.H. envisioned a bus line and bought two Gramm trucks with chassis on which he had a Japanese carpenter build a simple platform. Then together they designed and cobbled seats. Because of Zamboanga's temperate climate, the affairs were open-air with no sides. There was also a driver and a conductor who would collect the money. Filipinos would scramble on the busses with chickens, goats, ducks, pigs, fruit, vegetables, and whatever else they were taking to market. At the end of the day, they boarded again with what they were taking home. He soon incorporated the business as the Zamboanga Transportation Company, sought and secured investors, and expanded.

From Zamboanga, P.H. moved into Jolo and started a bus line and auto rental under the name Jolo Garage. In connection with the garage, he incorporated the Sulu Commercial Company, sold automobiles and needed tires, tubes, gasoline, lubricants, parts, and service. A small American community led by a young schoolteacher unsuccessfully opposed his bus line, fearing it would transport a dangerous element of Moros into the town center. Nevertheless, P.H. prevailed after convincing the American authorities that peace with the Moros and social progress were tied to the Moros economic well-being, advanced by good roads and transportation. General Pershing agreed, and that was that.

In the course of running his businesses, P.H. met capable Filipinos, many of whom he employed to operate his growing enterprises. Such a young man was Venigno Viray. A former army sergeant in the 23rd had adopted Venigno and saw to his education at a technical school in Manila. The sergeant wrote P.H. upon Venigno's graduation and sent him down to Zamboanga where he turned out to be a whiz mechanic. He could keep the cars going, and he knew how to get along with people. Therefore, when P.H. was ready to move into Jolo, he sent Venigno to the island to take charge and did the same when he expanded his transportation business to Cotabato.

Two legs of P.H.'s transportation business were automobiles for hire and busses. A third leg was hauling cargo by truck. P.H. also took advantage of the growing number of private automobiles by selling parts and services out of the garages he established for his transportation company. He soon advertised a full line of automobile accessories, Ford parts of all kinds, many useful tools and devices for chauffeurs and mechanics, and Firestone tires and tubes of all sizes.

§

Operating a bus line had its dangerous and sometimes deadly moments, particularly on the island of Sulu. P.H. armed his conductors and drivers with .45 caliber revolvers and shotguns against the chance of attack by thieves or a Moro gone *juramentado*. However, sometimes the incidents were not so clear-cut as simply to lay blame on the cultural or religious zeal of Moros. On one occasion, a bus running from Jolo to Maimbung struck and killed a Moro boy. Instead of reporting the matter to the authorities, as should have been the case, both the conductor and chauffeur kept quiet about it, and the relatives of the boy, believing that no redress was coming from the authorities, took the matter into their own hands.

The Moros laid trees across the road, and when the bus stopped and both the conductor and driver alighted to remove the obstacle, they were attacked; the head of the driver was completely severed while the body of the conductor was mutilated along with the lone passenger's body. P.H. had pictures of the incident taken and posted on the walls of the garage as a reminder to his employees to immediately report all incidents to the Constabulary and remain diligent and cautious.

§

Peace and order had greatly improved in the Moro Province before General Pershing's arrival in late 1909, but Pershing considered conditions still far from satisfactory. It was widely believed in the Christian-Filipino and American communities, Pershing concurring, that full respect for the law would not occur until the Moros were disarmed. Pershing felt like complete disarmament was vital even though he believed that a general uprising or a holy war might ensue. It was time, he believed, "to teach the Moros the meaning of government." In September 1911, he issued an executive order directing a disarmament policy. The Moro reaction was predictable. The last large-scale action occurred at the battle of Bud Bagsak on Jolo Island. Government casualties were fourteen killed and thirteen wounded. Moro dead reported in official dispatches came to five hundred. American newspapers, however, quoted soldiers numbering the Moros killed in the thousands including over four hundred children and women, which created an outpouring of public outrage and Congressional investigations in the United States. All of this was happening during a presidential election pitting William Taft against Woodrow Wilson.[2]

§

The Republican Party had been in power in Washington for the first thirteen years of the American presence in the Philippines. The Democratic Party, which had opposed the American seizure of the country, had no significant part in the determination of Philippine policy. The basic elements of Republican policy under McKinley, Theodore Roosevelt, and William Taft were good government and preparation of the Filipinos for democratic self-government. In general, the Republicans favored a long period of Filipino tutelage which P.H. also supported. Legislative power was exercised through a Philippine Commission effectively dominated by Americans. On the other hand, the Democrats proposed independence for the Philippines at every opportunity and criticized the various legislation passed by the majority Republican Congress respecting Philippine government and commerce. In the United States, views ranged from isolationism to fervent imperialism. Among many Americans in the Philippines, including P.H. Frank, a go-slow approach dominated.

Woodrow Wilson was inaugurated President of the United States in March 1913, and democrats gained majorities in the congress. A change in American policy in the Philippines encouraged the acceleration of Filipino participation in their government, looking to independence at the earliest feasible time. By October 1913, Francis Burton Harrison had arrived in Manila as the new United States Governor General. In the Luneta, a large park outside the Old Walled City, he delivered Wilson's message, an American pledge of Philippine sovereignty looking ultimately toward independence. Harrison began an almost immediate implementation of "Filipinization." He gave Filipinos the majority on the Philippine Commission—five of nine positions—and he began replacing Americans with Filipinos throughout the bureaucracy. In December 1913, Frank Carpenter succeeded General Pershing as

Governor of the Moro Province, and the name of the province was changed to the Department of Mindanao and Sulu.

Frank Carpenter had held numerous civil service positions in the Philippines since 1899. He was promoted to the highest positions in the Insular Government and learned to speak both Spanish and Tagalog; many Americans in the islands respected and admired him. In Zamboanga, P.H. was pleased with Carpenter's continued development of the social, political, and material conditions of the Moros and Pagans. He was also appreciative of the government's stimulation and development of the natural resources, industry, commerce, and agriculture of Moroland, especially around Davao. It was the rapidity of the Filipinization of government personnel that grieved him.[3]

P.H. and other Americans in Zamboanga followed the news in the weekly newspaper, which published English and Spanish editions. The publisher, John Hackett, was from Louisiana and the son of a Baptist minister. He went to the Philippines in 1899 as a soldier in the aftermath of the Spanish-American War, stayed, and in 1906 bought the *Mindanao Herald* from another American. He was a Democrat, as were most white southerners of that time. He supported the ultimate independence of the Philippines, but he editorialized for slow change, favoring continuity and stability. He was concerned that the highly educated, wealthy Filipino elite, the *illustrados* who had been given power under the former Spanish administration, would not work for the benefit of the masses of Filipinos. He was also concerned with the graft and corruption that he observed among Filipino politicians as well as lower and mid level employees of government bureaus. Due to the Filipinization policy, the province was losing fine American engineers, foresters, botanists, geologists, and health officials, all trained in some of America's finest universities. The army was also being reduced faster than Hackett and P.H. wished. There was skepticism that the Moros would remain peaceful.

After fifteen years in the Philippines, P.H. Frank was not opposed to Filipinization. His wife was native, his sons mestizo, and his daughter mestiza. His own mother came from a background of emancipation and antislavery views. However, he was against quick change, especially in Moro country. He was being conservative for liberal motives. However, he was opposed to the "full speed ahead" approach as liberalization continued. He saw progress toward independence as too soon and decidedly too fast. His future business trajectory would link directly to this Filipino and American political history.

§

By 1914 Zamboanga was a much-changed town from the one it first appeared to be to the American troops in late 1899, and the community was evolving into a more domestic atmosphere. An American engineer Thomas Hanley designed roads, drainage canals lined with flowering trees, shrubs, and vines, and beautiful parks in the city and nearby. P.J. Moore, an attorney and early American resident of Zamboanga, boasted that "the gardens of Java would in no way surpass Hanley's Pasonanca Park had he lived and been supplied with even very little money."[4]

Another Hanley masterpiece was Plaza Pershing in Zamboanga's downtown "which had a bandstand and archway dripping with bougainvillea and yellow bell flowers," recalled Bessie Hackett Wilson, daughter of the *Herald* editor. She remembered the quiet, peaceful beauty of Zamboanga and the water-lily-filled canal that separated P.H.'s Red House from Hackett's home and *Herald* office by only two blocks. Sam Frank recalled the pleasant evening concerts by the Constabulary band.[5]

Isabel Anderson, a well-known travel writer of the time, wrote of her approach to Zamboanga during that period "over a sea of polished jade, which shown at night with phosphorescence like gleaming silver." She arrived to a "flotilla of native boats…with sails and canopies of such colures and combinations of colures…green, purple and orange in designs of lemon, red and magenta…" In particular, she commented on Pettit Barracks, "The post was beautiful, for it had much of the old Spanish times. The green parade had a terraced canal passing through it, and avenues of palm; the officers' quarters, smothered in flowering plants and fronting over the glittering blue sea, were large, airy, and finer than any we had seen before."[6]

§

For some in the American community in Zamboanga the élan of a good sporting event was as essential to community as parks and domesticity.

Even though prizefighting in the Philippines was outlawed at the time, what became remembered as the "great fight" was one organized by P.H. Frank. One of the community's well-known citizens was Bob McIlwain, an African-American who had left military service in the Philippines, married, and lived in a house with a large brood of children. McIlwain, known to be very likable, carried the American flag in the Fourth of July parade. He also had a tendency to boast of his numerous boxing exploits in the States and in the service. This swellheadedness aroused the curiosity of the sporting community, who wondered just how good McIlwain was. McIlwain's bragging in the First and Last Chance was a catalyst to the entrepreneurial spirit of P.H. Frank who set about organizing the local "fight of the century."

P.H. found his man in Roy Kenny, an Australian, who occasionally fought in touring groups of athletes and entertainers that traveled throughout Asia in this era. When Kenny came to Zamboanga, Frank brought him to his home and vowed not to let any unfriendly hands touch him until the great fight was over.

There was much excitement at the Frank home on the outskirts of Zamboanga where Kenny worked out on a punching bag hung to rafters beneath the house and regularly spared with a half dozen of Frank's friends. As McIlwain continued to swagger, Kenny, a quiet, somewhat taciturn man, said little. Meanwhile, fight talk and heavy wagering flew fast and furiously. At the Frank house, there was talk of how an unfortunate household cat, which interrupted Kenny's sleep, met a swift and brutal end.

The fight took place in "secret" at an old Spanish prison in the barrio of Calarian. Zamboanga's sporting establishment was not disappointed in the show which went a full fifteen rounds, but many disputed the outcome which left both fighters still standing and a decision awarded to McIlwain. It was never ascertained if short or long counts saved McIlwain or Kenny, if the judges were bought or intimidated, or if the timing of the rounds was long or short. Even the descendants of P.H. Frank are not sure on whom he placed his money or hedged. Nevertheless, Bob McIlvain, an African-American, would always be the champion of Zamboanga.[7]

CHAPTER 12

"When death became inevitable, Laura was not denied"

Samuel Boone Frank, Remembrances, 1991

In 1914 when the First World War broke out in Europe, the demand for glycerin used in the manufacture of munitions was insatiable. Copra, the dried white meat in coconuts that yielded coconut oil, contained 8-14% glycerin. As the cannons roared along the Western Front, the appetite for coconut oil skyrocketed, and the Philippines had millions of coconut trees. Coconut plantations on Mindanao expanded and flourished as freighters carried the valuable commodity to Manila where the Philippine Vegetable Oil Company had hurriedly expanded its capacity. The price of coconut oil had jumped from six cents per pound to fifty-five cents per pound and more companies had formed to extract coconut oil from copra. P.H. took note of these developments in which he would one day participate. At that time, he lacked the capital to invest in the manufacturing machinery of grinders, cookers, expellers, and filters, but he did invest in several coconut plantations.[1]

Zamboanga felt the war's reach in another way. President Wilson started recalling American troops in the Philippines to the "preparedness campaign" in the United States. The attention of the world was on Europe, but in Moroland there was a lot of heed being paid to concerns that the Sultan of Turkey, who sided with the Axis Powers against the Allies, might incite the Moros against the "Christian" government. There were still stiff encounters with Moros, particularly on Basilan and Jolo.

Slavery had not been fully eliminated. Piracy occurred occasionally. Sometimes there were small uprisings against the government. However, none of these violations and disturbances was beyond the power of the Constabulary to control. Still, it was disconcerting to Americans and Christian Filipinos who were fearful that American officers in the Scout and Constabulary units might also be withdrawn if the United States entered the war in Europe.

Governor Carpenter consulted with P.H. Frank and other American "Old Timers." No American businessman in Zamboanga had more experience in Sulu than P.H. Frank who thought of the Moros as indifferent to the War in Europe both before and after the American entry. P.H.'s predictions played out. The Moros remained loyal to America. The people of Sulu subscribed to Liberty Loans, donated to the Red Cross, and requested, though it was not granted, that a battalion of Sulu men be allowed to join the Moro Regiment of the Philippine National Guard. Governor Carpenter regarded the maintenance of comparative peace during World War I as one of his most important achievements.[2]

A not-entirely-welcomed development of World War I was Japan's alliance with Britain and the United States. Many in Japan saw Micronesia as a natural part of the Japanese Empire. Therefore, it was no surprise in 1914 that Japan sent an expeditionary force to take possession of the islands from Germany. The badly outgunned German garrisons surrendered peacefully. The United States and Britain had serious reservations about Japanese intentions in Micronesia and the Pacific generally, but after the war, following a good deal of diplomatic maneuvering, the League of Nations gave Japan a mandate to administer the islands. One of those islands, Palau, would play a significant role in the lives of the Franks.

§

Much changed in P.H.'s saloon and hotel business with fewer American soldiers. A good number of the remaining Americans in Zambo were planters who had settled down in out-of-the-way places, living hard, frugal lives with native wives. They were a society of their own with plans to live out their lives in peace and contentment right where they were. P.J. Moore opened the Plaza Hotel catering to tourists, and P.H.

was busily involved with his lucrative transportation businesses in Zamboanga, Jolo, and Cotabato. He closed his First and Last Saloon and devoted the entire Red House to his Mindanao Hotel, turning the downstairs into an attractive lobby with comfortable rattan furniture, ceiling fans, and potted miniature palms on a black and white tile floor. At the back of the lobby was a small friendly bar with a large round table for the five o'clock regulars. A small dining room of about eight tables in two rows was set on one side of the lobby. Upstairs he maintained several comfortable rooms for his guests, mostly planters come to town for business and shopping.

§

The Jones Act of 1916, also known as the Philippine Autonomy Act, established the legitimacy of "Filipinization". It was a statute announcing the intentions of the United States government to withdraw its sovereignty over the Philippine Islands as soon as a stable government could be established. One of the most significant sections of the Jones Act, which replaced the Philippine Commission with an elective Senate and with minimum property requirements, was the extension of the franchise to all literate Filipino males. The law also incorporated a bill of rights.

Provisions of the act reserved to the American appointed Governor General the power to veto any measure passed by the new Philippine legislature. However, Governor General Francis Burton Harrison rarely used this power and continued to move rapidly to appoint Filipinos in place of Americans in the civil service. Likewise, Governor Carpenter was assiduously carrying out Filipinization on Mindanao and Sulu.

§

That same year Laura was growing and maturing into a beautiful, loving youngster. At ten years of age, she had captivating long black hair that hung to her waist. When tending Laura's bath, Okio would grate fresh coconut, pour hot water over it, squeeze the milk out, and strain the liquid. She would then take down Laura's hair and rub the soft milk over the strands, letting the strained liquid remain on the hair for hours. When they were ready to wash the milk out, Okio used a Go-Go tree bark rinse, which made lather like soap. Slowly, she rinsed

Laura's hair in the Malay style and any coarseness metamorphosed to shiny silk strands.

Laura began to complain to Okio and her father about abdominal pain in early March 1916. As Laura's condition worsened, the doctor suspected an appendicitis, which in those years involved the real possibility of death. As other parents of that time, P.H.'s hope was for a successful operation, and, that if the surgery was unsuccessful, her death would be swift with no pain and with great dignity. Following an appendix operation at the Brent Hospital of the Episcopal Mission, Laura developed peritonitis. While she was in the hospital, the Frank's Santa Maria home burned to the ground, the result of hot coals carried by the breeze to the *nipa* roof of the house. The coals had come from a steamroller driven too fast down the road at quitting time. No force pump could quell the flames; all objects of memory were ashes. Laura's father, Okio, and brothers never told her about the fire.

Penicillin was over twenty years short of discovery, and the medical technology available in Zamboanga did not permit heroic interventions or resuscitations; there were no assortments of machines, tubes, and intravenous drips, and there was no fear of overusing medications to relieve suffering. Laura's father, brothers, and Okio were present when Laura's life ended in a brief morphine induced coma.

At the Old Catholic Cemetery filled with grieving Zamboanga friends, but without Laura's Grandmother Andrea, P.H. buried his daughter next to her mother's and grandfather's tombs in the Frank-Garcia plot. It was a service presided over by the town's Episcopal priest. P.H.'s grief was so great that it frightened eight-year-old Pat and twelve-year-old Sam. Okio, who stood next to them, provided some comfort.

Every life is different from any that has gone before as is every death and every grieving. P.H. was despondent, overloaded by grief. The sudden and unexpected losses of Eugenia and Laura at such young ages were devastating to him. Laura had lived long enough to have a distinct personality and place in the family, and P.H. suffered, racked by sorrow but also by powerful emotions of guilt, denial, and anger, juxtaposed against relief that she did not suffer. He desperately needed to hold Laura, look at her, find out what was hurting, and mend it. His entire instinct was to cuddle and comfort, to examine and inspect, to try to understand, and most of all to hold. Yet his beloved Laura was draped in an uncomplicated coffin covered by a plainly embroidered purple pall on a simple limestone catafalque next to her mother's tomb in the Old Catholic Cemetery. Her grave was dug chest deep, her casket lowered by friends, and the soft gray soil turned.

At Wilson's shop, P.H. fashioned a box from teak wood in which he placed the few remains of Laura's life, including a doll she had with her in the hospital and his own twelve-page remembrances of her short life.

§

Pushing out of his life those who most reminded him of what might have been, P.H. sent his sons to Hong Kong. They were accompanied by Okio who saw to their enrollment in the Diocesan School & Orphanage, part of the Church of England. The final visage the boys had of Okio was seeing her off at a busy quay. Her destination was one from which she never returned—Nagasaki, Japan.

For the boys it was a horrible, lonely year of inadequate food and lengthy intestinal illnesses in the infirmary. The loneliness was broken only by trolley rides from one end of Hong Kong to the other during which the boys could drink in the rich variety of the Chinese culture. Sam was twelve years old, and Pat was eight. The boys returned to the Philippines at the end of the school year where, on a Manila wharf, they stared at their new stepmother. This was the first inkling the boys had that their father had remarried the year they were in Hong Kong.

CHAPTER 13

"Mr. Frank is taking his hemp stripping machine to exhibit"

Mindanao Herald, January 7, 1921

Annie Pauline Simoes was the Portuguese daughter of Jose Simoes, a prosperous planter and businessman in Zamboanga, and his wife Rosa. Annie was born October 22, 1896, in Sandakan, British North Borneo, the oldest of three sisters. Her father saw to her education at a Catholic convent in Singapore. She was twenty-one and P.H. forty-two when they were married in the Simoes home on February 3, 1917, by the Reverend Father Mario Suarez, the same priest who had married P.H. and Eugenia in 1903, and conducted Eugenia's funeral in 1909. Annie was only eight years older than young Sam was.

Back in Zamboanga, Sam and Pat found that their father had decided on the Red House as their new home. He leased the downstairs to Atkins-Kroll and Company, a San Francisco importing and exporting firm. He had also reduced his hotel to four rooms which he kept for old friends on outlying plantations who wanted a place to stay when they came to town for a few days. For their home, P.H. had built an expansive addition to the Red House on the ocean side of the building with full-length picture windows facing the Basilan Straight and tropical sunsets.

Settled once again, P.H.'s sons continued their education in the public schools of Zamboanga under the tutelage of American teachers.

Annie learned stenography, handled her husband's correspondence, and built a non-familial but cordial relationship with the boys.

§

Three years earlier, in 1914, with the outbreak of World War I in Europe, German merchant ships everywhere headed for neutral ports. The United States was still neutral from 1914 to 1917, so Zamboanga was a safe port for German vessels in a part of the world dominated by British and French imperial states now at war with Germany. The Norddeutscher Lloyd steamer *Darvel* dropped anchor at Caldera Bay, a U.S. Navy coaling station which was a few miles from Zamboanga. The Chief Steward on the *Darvel*, Herr Reitzenstein, a German Jew, came to work for P.H. as hotel manager and *Maitre d'*. He greeted customers, mostly American and European, and showed them to their table. Herr Reitzenstein's erect posture, imperious demeanor, and *pince nez* glasses imparted to the Mindanao Hotel just the ambience it needed. He also took a great interest in the manners, conduct, posture, and general welfare of Sam and Pat who responded to him like a grandfather figure.

Reitzenstein was with P.H. until the United States entered the war in April 1917, at which time he was interned with other German civilians by the American government and placed in a building next door to the hotel. Sam and Pat visited their German friend every day where, as a prisoner of war, Reitzenstein continued his lessons on courteous deportment and cooked for the internees in the kitchen of the Red House. Several times a day Sam and Pat sat listening on the steps of the Red House as a German prisoner wailed the mournful sounds of his harmonica, while others joined in the melancholy ballads of sorrowful men—ballads both boys would recall in later years.

§

In November 1917, P.H. formed a new corporation, Zamboanga Autobus Company. The public notice required by the public services commission provided a glimpse of the scope of his transportation businesses and furnished some early Zamboanga automotive history.

P.J. Moore, owner of the Plaza Hotel and his own small fleet of cars, sold all of his automobiles, supplies and fixtures to P.H. Frank's new company for the sum of 17,730 pesos. Moore's inventory included seven Overlands, one Buick, and one Chalmers. On the same day, P.H. Frank sold all of the automobiles, trucks, fixtures, and supplies connected to his Mindanao Hotel Garage proprietorship to his new corporation for the sum of 84,270 pesos. Next, he sold his own inventory of twenty vehicles in his Zamboanga Transportation to the new corporation. The machinery included five Fords, three Dodge Brothers, one Hudson Super Six, one Mitchell, five 1½ ton White trucks, two 1 ton Gramm Bernstein trucks, one 3 ton White truck, and one ¾ ton Reo Motor Car truck.

P.H. then capitalized the combined companies through a stock offering and realized a personal capital gain through his sale to Zamboanga Autobus Company. He did this while maintaining a controlling number of shares in the new company. He clearly had managed a monopoly on transportation and paid himself off handsomely for his substantial efforts as a provincial motoring pioneer. He then left for a vacation. The Manila newspapers identified P.H. Frank as a "prominent provincial business man." In May 1918, following an extended trip to China and Japan, he and Annie returned to Zamboanga aboard a Japanese liner.[3]

§

Among P.H.'s surviving correspondence, there is only one indication that he was considering a return to the United States. It came in a letter to his sister Cody who, in 1920, lived in San Antonio, Texas in which he wrote, "Since last October there has not been a day on which I could state definitely what I was going to do, in fact cannot now, altho I very nearly sold out on March first, and have bitterly regretted ever since that I did not. I have sold my interests in Jolo, am making pretty good returns on my investments here, but doing my best to sell out and get something near its value, and when I do it is us for the U.S., and I think southern Cal."[4]

In large part, P.H. was fed up with the Democratic Party administration of Frank Carpenter on Mindanao and Sulu. To his mind, Filipinization was moving too rapidly. Inexperienced Filipino officials were assuming increasingly greater responsibility in the government of Moroland. P.H. claimed that these untried Filipino officials were seriously abusing their powers. He saw his destiny in the hands of "the politicos in Manila." He, along with other American businessmen, pressed for a separation of Mindanao and Sulu from the rest of the Philippines so that the southern islands would become a territory of the United States and thus offer greater inducement for development by Americans. The proposal never gained traction much less legitimacy. The Filipino national concept included keeping Moroland on the map of an independent Philippines.[5]

It is not as if P.H. was blind to the accomplishments of the Democratic administration. During the Woodrow Wilson years, P.H. saw continuing support for the extension of road building into the interior. His transportation businesses and the native population benefited from these policies. He also saw continuing improvements in health services and education. Rubber plantations were introduced on Mindanao and Sulu, and Davao was rapidly developing as a hemp center. However, the government, in his view, was giving way to Filipino inefficiency and corruption.

Dispirited and fed up, P.H. sold his interest in the Jolo Garage and Sulu Commercial Company to Henry Hasemeyer, an associate of Frank in his Jolo businesses as well as a principal in the Lapac Plantation and Sulu Lumber Company. Providing some idea of the return he had made on his soldier's bonus about which he had written home in 1898, P.H. stated in a letter to his sister, Cody, "I hope to reach the U.S. with about $50,000. Do you think I could make a living without working very hard? I am getting tired and want a rest and give the young generation a chance." Simultaneously, the letter also instructed his sister to locate a school for Sam. He suggested that she reconnoiter the schools of California partly because she "might see something in schools better than you have in Texas," and partly because "I would for you to see California, because I plan to go there and would like for you to join me in case I do." Whether or not P.H. returned to the States, he wanted to find good schools for his sons. P.H. did not believe the public high schools in Zamboanga were adequate, leaning more to native schooling, and private education for Sam and Pat was limited in the islands.[6]

§

The Brent School in Baguio was a boarding school similar to schools in New England. However, it denied admission to native and *mestizo* boys like Sam and Pat Frank. There were limited options for the very wealthy *illustrado* children of mixed Spanish and Chinese ancestry, but in 1920, the school operated in an atmosphere of segregated, private education. The Silliman School was viewed as a native school, operated as an agricultural and technical boarding school, but P.H. did not consider it a viable option.

P.H. despised racism but understood the Manila social system. He wanted his mestizo sons, born and raised on the Philippine frontier of Mindanao, to be Americans, know America, and wished them to become fully immersed in American culture. There could be no better location than Texas and no better tutor than his sister Cody. To this end, P.H. crossed out Sam's baptismal name "Jose" and scrawled across the official document needed for his transit papers: "Samuel Boone Frank—American." Then, without consulting his sister, P.H. put sixteen-year-old Sam aboard the Japanese liner *Shinyo Maru* with the name and address of his aunt in San Antonio and a letter of introduction to all Masons asking that they render assistance to his son should it be required. At some point in Sam's trans-Pacific journey, Cody received a letter from her brother announcing that his son was on the way and "overjoyed at the prospects of going to the great country I have told him about." She immediately wrote her sister Texanna that "Bud Boss... had an opportunity to send Sam and sent him and that is all there is to it. We will do the very best with the material we get, which I am inclined to believe is the very best that can be had." Once again, Sam knew what it was to be lonely and displaced.

Cody's husband Charles Riley, an Englishman and successful builder in San Antonio, rushed to San Diego just in time to meet Sam's boat on July 15, 1920. Cody, who worked for American Railroad Express, stayed home to find a school for her nephew and fix up a room for him in their cottage. A month later, Sam enrolled at San Antonio Academy, an Episcopal military school.

Just over a month following these words, P.H. Frank sold his controlling interest in the Zamboanga Transportation Company to Ignacio de Longa, a wealthy Spanish sugar planter of Bais. The sale netted P.H. 86,500 pesos for his 33,440 shares.

In United States dollars of the time, P.H had sold his transportation business for $43,250 and held onto a minority interest to see if the new managers could improve on the value of his remaining stock. It was his second sale and capital gain on his transportation company within three years. It looked like P.H. would make his move to Southern California, but his tinkering with a hemp-stripping machine that had occupied his spare time for the previous ten years took a dramatic turn. In 1920, he determined to make a life-changing move based on the product of his ingenuity that resulted in a revolutionary change in hemp manufacturing and the lives of those Filipinos who toiled in its labor.

§

On Christmas Eve, 1920, P.H. Frank left Zamboanga for a short business trip to Basilan on the *Islas Filipinas*. The Masonic dinner dance scheduled at the Overseas Club that night was the highly anticipated annual gala involving 120 persons. And P.H., being a Mason and secretary of the Mt. Apo Lodge would normally have attended. The big question in Zamboanga was what it meant that P.H. was forgoing this festivity with his hasty trip to Basilan?

Three months earlier, P.H. had written excitedly to his sister that everything was going on smoothly and that he would have his hemp-stripping machine finished within a month. P.H. had managed a breakthrough in the design of his apparatus. He had figured out a way of taking off the butt of the petiole before passing it through the stripping knives that harvested the hemp fiber. On June 5, 1920, shortly after seeing Sam off to the United States, P.H. had filed for a patent with the U.S. Patent Office and shipped several prototypes to Dr. J.W. Strong's Basilan Island plantation for final testing. Six months later Strong had sent word to P.H. that the newest machine modifications tested in Strong's abaca fields were working. The new system was ingenious, and P.H. had additionally perfected an automatic system of feeding and carrying off the stripped fiber. He had done all of this himself, a result of his tinkering and with no training at all in mechanical engineering.

On January 7, 1921, P.H. and Annie departed on the Japanese liner *Aki Maru*. They were going to Manila to attend the agricultural and industrial trade show taking and with them his hemp-stripping machine for exhibition. There among crowds of planters and potential investors, P.H.'s hemp stripping machine was judged a success, and he held in his hands the 50,000 peso national prize he had dreamed of since 1907. The Manila newspapers and the Philippine Chamber of Commerce trumpeted his machine as capable of saving forty percent labor on present hand-stripping methods and declared P.H.'s invention first rate.[7]

P.H. began to line up manufacturing capability and financing in Manila while Annie returned to Zamboanga. They were moving to Manila. Her advertisement in the *Herald* announced, "Furniture for Sale; Beds, bedding, chairs, tables, bureaus with and without mirrors, clocks, lamps, and other such items; Call any time at 14 Calle Madrid, upstairs on seashore."[8]

§

Less than one inch from Annie's ad, an editorial declared that the election of President Warren G. Harding "will mark one of the most important historical and economical events in the United States for many years." Many Americans in the Philippines understood that in the event of a Republican victory in November 1920, the United States and the Philippines would have a businessman's administration. With the election of Harding, P.H. foresaw a pro-business era for his enterprises.

Financially girded by the proceeds of his sale of Zamboanga Transportation Company, situated in Manila with its financial and manufacturing base, with the political expectation of a more stable business climate, and a Republican urge to stay in the Philippines, P.H. Frank at forty-six years of age entered his third decade in the Philippines.

P.H. Frank lights Zamboanga—*Mindanao Herald* ad, circa 1909.
(Courtesy of Emory University MARBL, Frank Family Collection)

Okio Yamaguchi, *amah* to the Frank children, Zamboanga, 1909 to 1916. *(Courtesy of Emory University MARBL, Frank Family Collection)*

P.H. Frank's earliest Zamboanga Transportation Company bus was built by Japanese carpenters on the chassis of a Gramm truck, circa 1912. circa 1912. *(Courtesy of Emory University MARBL, Frank Family Collection)*

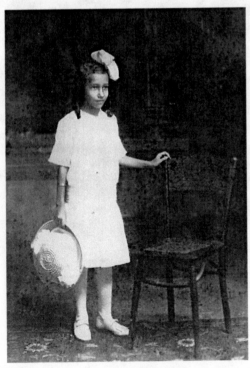

Laura Frank, 1906 to 1916. *(Courtesy of Emory University, Frank Family Collection)*

P.H. Frank and his second wife Annie Simoes, circa 1917. *(Courtesy of Emory University MARBL, Frank Family Collection)*

Part 4
The Manila Years
1920 to 1931

"Bud Boss had an opportunity to send Sam and sent him and that is all there is to it"

Cody Frank Riley, June 29, 1920

CHAPTER 14

"I'm sending the boys to that great country I've told them about"

P.H. Frank, June 20, 1920

Already a successful businessman, P.H. Frank arrived in Manila with a special opportunity to produce a hemp-stripping machine. It would take capital and manufacturing capability that could only be marshaled in Manila. P.H. had a vision of investing in the development of his machine and a more abundant life from that investment. The cultural fauna of the Manila community of Americans was decidedly different from that of Zamboanga. For many of the newcomers to Manila, places like Mindanao, Sulu, Zamboanga and Davao were in the provinces. Nevertheless, P.H., the former army private, was at home with the men who could help make his dream become a reality.

Many among the Spanish American War veterans had done well in the Philippines and now lived in Manila. Privates, corporals, and sergeants had become capitalists and bank presidents and had money, property, and influence. N.H. Duckworth, who had been a teamster in the 23rd Infantry, owned Benguet Mining Company. Bill Shaw, a friend from the old days, headed Atlantic, Gulf & Pacific, the largest construction business in the Philippines. Emil Bachrach was in transportation. Julius Reese had the Ford franchise and Manila Trading Company, while Pete Grimm headed Luzon Stevedoring. These men influenced the early institutions of the American community in Manila and welcomed the former Private Frank. All became investors in P.H.'s hemp machine.

P.H. was spending most of his time in Manila procuring manufacturing facilities for his hemp-stripping machine. He was also looking for a home on Santa Mesa and investors from among his friends.

During this same time, an old friend of P.H.'s, Emil Bachrach, contacted him about the demise of P.H.'s former Zamboanga Auto Bus Company, which after just a year was about to be run into the ground by the new owners. When P.H. sold out in 1920, the Catholic Church in Zamboanga had financed the sale, but Bachrach held the mortgage notes on the GMC buses, automobiles, and trucks.

Known as a tough businessperson, Bachrach had the reputation of never parting painlessly from any of his earnings. He and P.H. worked out an arrangement for P.H. to repossess the bankrupt Zamboanga Auto Bus. P.H. knew the possibilities, hired his own loyal managers in Zamboanga and Jolo and again began operating the company despite its long distance from Manila.

§

It was also in the summer of 1921 that P.H. faced the same schooling issue for Pat as he had with Sam. The public Manila Central School was open to *mestizo* children, but the newly established American School which catered to the American community and prepared their children for United States universities was not. In addition, Brent School in Baguio remained as closed to Pat as it had to Sam. This slight of his sons had to have stung, but P.H. was nimble in a multicultural world. He joined the Manila Polo Club, the single most important social club patronized by Americans. When the predominantly American membership turned down a prominent Filipino for membership, P.H. quietly joined other Americans and Filipinos who established the Tamaraw Club, the result was an integrated and flourishing second polo-playing club. His friend Bill Shaw, who was investing in the hemp-stripper, established the cosmopolitan Whak-Whak Country Club as an anti-segregationist response in defiance of the segregated sentiment of the Manila Golf and Country Club; P.H. also joined in, maintaining his membership in all four clubs.

For his son Pat, P.H. chose Mt. Tamalpais Military Academy in San Rafael, California, near San Francisco. Just as he had done with Sam, P.H. marked through Pat's baptismal name, Emilio, and scrawled across the official document needed for his transit papers: "Patrick James Frank—American." Pat enrolled at Mt. Tamalpais in the fall term of 1921. At the age of thirteen, Pat experienced a disastrous first semester. Cody brought Pat to her home to join his brother at San Antonio Academy where he enrolled for the balance of the 1921-22 school year. Pat flourished under the warm guidance of Cody and Charles, putting his excess energy into athletics. His grades improved.

For the next half-decade, Cody saw to her nephews' assimilation into the extended Texas family of aunts, uncles, and cousins. She introduced the boys to San Antonio social life, and saw to dancing lessons and cotillion invitations; she bought them tuxedos and made sure that they kept their hair length to academy and social standards. San Antonio had a large number of wealthy, established families of Mexican descent, who enrolled their children at San Antonio Academy, and Cody, an Episcopalian, had been a Texan since her parents arrived following the Civil War. The brothers never experienced any form of racism while living with their aunt or while attending the school.

CHAPTER 15

"I have to build and deliver ten hemp machines which I have sold, and it's some job"

Patrick Henry Frank, June 26, 1922

In a Manila manufacturing facility along the Pasig River, P.H. was fabricating machines as fast as he could and shipping them to Davao, the largest hemp region in the Philippines. The hemp-stripper was a success, cutting the petiole first and then stripping the tuxie of its thin fiber in one motion. Finally, the machine bundled together the long strands of filament for drying. But there was a shortcoming. The machine was too heavy for transport into the abaca fields. Making it lighter to carry was an innovation that would save even more labor, and a task P.H. was sweating over. He was selling the machines but just enough to cover his overhead. Continuing to try to perfect a lighter machine, he and a Davao planter named Billy Gohn jointly filed for a patent on a second machine in 1923. The less cumbersome model was an immediate success, light and durable enough for direct use in the fields, and capable of stripping a great quantity of hemp at a time. Under the name The Universal Hemp Machine Company, P.H. was soon manufacturing hundreds of the hemp machines in Manila and shipping them to Davao where Gohn sold the strippers, engines, lubricants, and replacement parts under yet another Frank company, Mindanao Sales and Services. Eventually their sales reached into the thousands at 800 pesos for each machine.[1]

Billy Gohn had come to the Philippines in 1903, one of the early Americans seeing the hemp potential on the vast lands around the Davao Gulf. He, along with American soldiers and their successors, was beguiled by both the adventure and profits, which seemed to await those bold enough to wrest the riches of plantation crops from the fertile soil and excellent weather conditions east of Mt. Apo along the Davao River. P.H. had struck out for the area establishing his plantation, Frankfort, in 1905, but soon gave it up and sold out to another foolhardy soul willing to brave the dangers of hostile tribes, trackless, steaming jungles, and unknown diseases. Gohn held on and by 1907 there were forty-one American plantations with 100,000 hemp-bearing plants in the Davao area. The shortage of labor was acute. There were flirtations with the idea of imported Chinese labor as the British had done in Malaya as well as efforts to tap the stream of Old World immigration with eighteen Armenians. By 1910, Billy Gohn was such an advocate of the hemp possibilities of Davao that the *Manila Times* anniversary issue warned that "those wishing to invest money in hemp should stay away from him as he would have you staking a claim on the land and toiling on a plantation after listening to him."[2]

The Japanese were also beginning to put their stamp on Davao. Japan stayed mostly on the sidelines in World War I. But with a nod from Britain, Japan had occupied German possessions in China and the central Pacific. Japan also provided naval escort to the allies. Neither of these actions was decisive in the outcome of World War I, but they kept Japan friendly rather than hostile. Following World War I, with a mandate from the League of Nations, Japan inherited the former German Caroline Islands just 550 miles west of Davao. A status quo in the Pacific went into effect heading off a British-Japanese-American naval race. One of those islands, Palau, would play a significant role in the future of the Franks.

But curtailment of Japanese economic expansion was not on the table. In 1914, K. S. Ohta, a young Japanese merchant in Manila, gathered a band of a hundred Okinawa men employed on the construction of mining roads and led them to Davao. There, with the encouragement of established American planters, he founded the Ohata Development Company and entered the plantation business while at the same time continuing and expanding his merchandising business. By 1918 Ohta had established a ninety-bed hospital staffed by a Filipino doctor and Japanese nurses. He had also established an experimental farm, which studied seed selection and methods of cultivation. Japanese schools, teaching both Japanese and English, were established. Well-financed Japanese-owned plantations and businesses were fully established around Davao by the late 1920's, and by 1930 Davao had a Japanese population of 10,000 and over 300 Japanese corporations.

The strength of the Japanese was in their efficiency of organization. Large Japanese companies financed their plantations and other businesses, and there was active Japanese government participation through a diplomatic Consul who organized roads, schools, and hospital facilities. The Consul also saw to acquiring monopoly trading permits and other valuable concessions. The technical advisors, many of whom were Americans, were the best procurable.

Many of the American planters sold out during this period. Some were getting old and looked toward a deserved retirement. For others, the interest load to commercial banks was too heavy a burden. These planters turned to Japanese companies which offered financing at lower rates. The American and Filipino plantation owners formed corporations holding sixty percent of the stock, the Japanese holding forty percent. With majority ownership by Filipinos or Americans, the arrangement was legal under laws governing foreign ownership in the Philippines. Following this transaction, another Japanese company would immediately finance the new corporation, which entered a large credit on its books. The new company demanded all the stock as security as well as full authority in administration of the plantation. The newly minted company had no chance to get out of debt in this arrangement and essentially belonged to the Japanese. The same arrangements gave Japanese control of timber cutting and exporting logs to Japan. By 1930, with the exception of three American plantation companies including International Harvester and Del Monte, the Americans had bowed out. Still some of the American planters stayed on as managers of the Japanese-controlled plantations and prospered.

§

On the Ohta experimental farm outside Davao, the Japanese had been working on a hemp-stripping machine since at least 1918. The demonstrations and sales of P.H.'s 1920 machine and his improved 1923 machine drew the attention of the Japanese engineers who purchased both P.H.'s 1920 and 1923 models and took them apart. Once they figured out how it worked, they added the patented features to their own machines. The collusive nature and corporate interrelationships of the Japanese-controlled plantations assured the sale of their own machines manufactured at nearby Bago. [3]

P.H.'s Universal Hemp Stripping Company was endangered. P.H. engaged engineers and attorneys to defend his patents and won in the Davao Court of First Instance in 1924. The Japanese appealed to the Philippine Supreme Court which affirmed the first ruling in 1925. Undeterred, the Japanese at Ohta made a modification and resumed production. P.H. filed again in the Court of First Instance. This time the legal process dragged on for several years.

§

Ever looking for a fresh economic venture, P.H. had another developing interest during this period—electric power generation. Now based in Manila where he was close to business information, he was aware that the government was dissatisfied with the management and development of electricity in the outlying provinces and had taken over the power plant at Jolo. P.H. was intimately aware that the generators were antiquated, left over from American military occupation, subject to breakdowns, and unsuitable for expanding service. Investing another portion of his remaining capital, P.H. bought up the municipal franchise in Jolo from the government. If he could get the utility up and running and meet all the requirements of the Public Service Commission within five years, then the government would award him a fifty-year legislative franchise. He had no knowledge of electricity and even less about how to operate a power plant. What he did have was capital with access to more, knowledge of Jolo and Mindanao, and a vision of the possibilities. His notion of the "right stuff" matured considerably as he rose in the world and his horizons expanded. A sharp eye on the cash register and the competition down the block were fine for the Zamboanga saloon keeper, but a light and power entrepreneur would have to have bigger thoughts. He had always seen Mindanao as the Promised Land and had confidence in himself to make this new enterprise work. The first thing he needed was engines.

§

Count Shizmarov was an officer in the Russian navy. He fled to the Philippines after the Russian Revolution with contacts in the German industrial giant, Krupp, which supplied the Russian navy with their powerful engines. Shizmarov looked at the old generators at Jolo and told P.H. to put in Krupp engines. P.H. gave Shizmarov funds and paid his way to Germany where he bought the machinery. The Count then went on a drunk and ended up in Switzerland. To his everlasting credit, Shizmarov did not go on his binge until he completed the purchase and shipping arrangements. P.H. cabled him money to get back. Count Shizmarov was an educated man, knowledgeable, tall, erect, always dressed properly, and dependable when not drunk. He admiringly addressed P.H. as "Mr. Frank," while other business contacts addressed him as "P.H." The Count remained in P.H.'s employ until his death several years later.

The second item P.H. needed was generators to go with the Krupp engines. While Shizmarov was in Germany, an electrical engineering professor at the University of the Philippines, Harry Leo Reich, an Englishman from Hong Kong, was trying to sell P.H. on the idea of buying Westinghouse dynamos. Unable to understand what Reich was talking about, P.H. employed Reich to teach him for several months. At the end of that time, P.H. had a good education in electric utilities and had bought himself some fine American Westinghouse generators to go with his German Krupp engines.

Finally, P.H. needed someone to put it all together in Jolo and manage the utility. He had met a Spanish engineer, Francisco Suche, in Manila when Suche was trying to develop a knotting machine that would tie hemp fibers together. Recognizing the utility of such an invention, P.H. let him experiment in the machine shop where he was manufacturing his hemp machines. He got to know Suche well and asked him to go to Jolo with his family to get things started on the Jolo electric plant. Soon after, P.H. received a municipal franchise for the broken down electric utility in Davao that was in about the same shape as what he had first found in Jolo.

§

At length, yet another opportunity came P.H.'s way, one that he had seen in 1914 with the start of World War I when he had watched while fortunes were made in the coconut oil business as glycerin was extracted for use in the manufacture of munitions. However, in 1918, with the end of World War I, the price of glycerin held for a couple of years at fifty-five cents per pound; but one day in 1921, without warning, it dropped to the pre-war price of six cents per pound. The smaller coconut oil producers were out of business. In 1922 the American congress, responding to protectionist lobbying, established a tariff on Ceylonese desiccated coconut, a confectionary used in baking. British Ceylon was the largest exporter of desiccated coconut to the United States. The idea was to advance desiccated coconut manufacturing in the Philippines by increasing the cost of importing the British Ceylon product to the United States. The tariff was only 1.5 cents per pound, but that represented a high percentage of the 6.5 cents per pound that desiccated coconut brought on world markets. The margin was high enough to get the interest of Philippine entrepreneurs who realized they could make a profit. P.H., who had been watching for such a moment, smelled opportunity; he had capital, and he invested heavily, taking over a manufacturing plant south of Manila in Pagsanjan at a fire sale price. His business plan was to manufacture desiccated coconut until world demand for glycerin returned.

§

It was in this financially super-charged, overextended business climate that P.H. wrote to his sons in 1924, explaining the financial difficulties he was having with his hemp machine and how he had invested much of his capital taking back Zamboanga Autobus, starting his electric utilities, and purchasing the desiccated coconut plant in Pagsanjan. However, he had another reason in recalling his sons. In 1922 he had shared with Cody his thoughts about prospects for his sons' continuing their educations after completing San Antonio Academy, "I'll not ship any package off to the university without knowing its contents," he wrote. Now was the time to make manifest his words and the plant at Pagsanjan would be the test. [4]

Chapter 16

"I'll not ship any package off to the university unless I know its contents."

Patrick Henry Frank, 1922

P.H. opened his Pagsanjan Manufacturing Company in 1923. The company manufactured Blue Star Desiccated Coconut, but few people in the Philippines had any experience with producing desiccated coconut. The output of the plant was a low, yellow-grade material that quickly went rancid. He knew that workers in Ceylon were producing the finest white desiccated coconut on world markets. He sought advice from J. Blake Hedges, an Englishman and superintendent of the Trade school in Zamboanga. Hedges advised P.H. that the British produced white desiccated coconut in Ceylon (now Sri Lanka), was a closely guarded secret. Undeterred, P.H. hired Hedges, disguised him as a British tourist, and sent him to Ceylon where he developed some connections and gained entry to several plants where he took pictures. By the time he returned to the Philippines, Hedges had arranged a bogus port for the transshipment of the entire Ceylonese manufacturing machinery. P.H. and Hedges replaced the poor equipment at Pagsanjan and began producing desiccated coconut whiter than the best on world markets. Some industrial espionage and the timely American tariff on Ceylonese desiccated coconut had P.H. up and going again. And all the while, he was suing the Japanese for patent infringement in the Philippine Supreme Court.

§

Sam had graduated valedictorian of his class at San Antonio Academy in 1923 and was completing his first year of studying law at Texas University from which he immediately departed and returned to the Philippines in August 1924 aboard the *Grover Cleveland.* Pat had another year until graduation at the Academy. P.H. was well pleased with the first "package" Cody and Charles sent back to the Philippines. He took Sam to Baguio for vacationing, caught up on his life, and introduced him to business associates and Old Timers, Spanish-American War veterans who had known him only as a child. In Manila, Sam observed the details of his father's hemp-stripping machine manufacture. He then traveled with his father to Jolo, Zamboanga, Cotabato, and Davao where his father introduced him to his recapitalized Zamboanga Auto Bus and his new utility franchises.

Following the tour, P.H. sent Sam to Pagsanjan where he worked under Hedges to get the desiccated coconut machinery set up, hire labor, and start the manufacturing process. Everything was going well except for buying coconuts from the plantations around Pagsanjan. Hedges just did not have what it took to work with the Filipino growers.

When Pat returned to the Philippines following his graduation in 1925 as Best Scholar Athlete, P.H. was as taken with Cody's second "package" as he had been with the first. P.H. took Pat on the same tour of his businesses as he had with Sam and then sent Pat directly down to Pagsanjan where he was made the coconut buyer. Pat developed a simple way of buying the product. He would ride the railroad with a suitcase full of money which he would distribute to farmers at every station only on their promise to deliver coconuts. He required no receipts. The farmers were as good as their word, and coconuts arrived at the banks of the Pagsanjan River. There Pat oversaw bundling the coconuts into spectacular fifty-foot rafts piled ten feet deep in coconuts which he floated down to the plant with the help of Filipino raftsmen. One could see this seventeen year old boy, whom P.H. had been ready to consign to a reformatory a few years earlier for his failures at Mt. Tamalpai, coming around a bend in the river with a big smile, hopping around on the rafts and waving to his brother and proud father.

Sam was good at engineering and plant management; Pat excelled as the buyer. Both spoke the local dialects fluently, and the Filipinos trusted them. P.H. recognized the importance of his *mestizo* sons in advancing his businesses and America's interests in the Philippines.

For Pat and Sam, living and working in Pagsanjan was a pleasant time in their lives. They lived the Life of Riley; they had a company home, houseboy, cook, and *lavandera*. The plant was eight miles down river from the famous Pagsanjan Falls, a tourist resort. Pat swam every day, jumping in and swimming against the current to the wonder of the employees. It would take him forty-five minutes and the cheers of the natives to beat the current 200 yards from one end of the plant to the other. It was the real start to what would become his serious swimming career and run for the 1932 Olympics.

By the middle of 1926, both boys had had enough of coconuts and limited their intake of coconut the remainder of their lives. They remembered the employees' sweating so profusely over the coconuts that their wet perspiration flowed steadily onto the meat before it made it to the boxes of Blue Star Brand. In Manila, Sam and Pat joined their "Private Frank" for the August 13, 1926, "beer and beans" celebration of the American occupation of Manila in 1898. P.H. had a father's pride in a vision of their becoming inheritors of his place in the Philippines.

The plant now profitable, P.H. said to his sons, "You can stay here and make a fortune in coconuts when the price for oil turns, or you can finish your education." The boys chose an education, and, to finance that education, their father sold the plant to John McCord. McCord became a millionaire as the price of coconut oil turned steeply higher when Japan invaded China in 1932, and demand for glycerin skyrocketed.[1]

In late August 1926, Sam and Pat were aboard the *SS Korea Maru* steaming back to the United States, and that fall they enrolled together at Texas University in Austin. Before leaving the Philippines, the boys had a pow-wow with their father who left it clear they would have a future in the islands—Sam in his father's electric utilities and Pat in his transportation business.

116

CHAPTER 17

"I'm a little scared—new land, new people"

Frances Russell Frank, November, 1931

The University of Texas in 1926 seemed to the boys to be composed of dull buildings and classrooms in World War I training barracks. Other poor facilities in those years and a lackluster engineering department created the conditions for them to want to transfer to Washington University in St. Louis. George Perkins an academy friend, who attended Washington, had recommended the school. Sam went up for the 1927-28 academic year. "The university was ideal," Sam said, "just what a university should look like, stone buildings, ivy growing on the walls, and a fine engineering school. It was what you dream of."[1]

Washington University also had a fine swimming team: a good coach, opportunities such as swimming against Yale, Navy and other great teams of those years, and a reputation for winning. The athletic department used its recruiting prowess, and Pat joined his brother for the 1928-29 academic year. During his sophomore year he made Lock and Chain, an honor society. The organization required initiation, and it was at that event that a pretty coed named Genevieve Quinlan saw Pat wearing pajamas, chasing girls on roller skates across the quadrangle, and enlisting kisses.

Genevieve, Gen as she was called, was living in South St. Louis on Shaw Avenue, between Reservoir Park and Shaw's Park, today the Missouri Botanical Gardens. Her parents were Irish immigrants. The

Quinlans were frugal, simple people who neither drank nor smoked, and, though neither was educated, they had a respect for education that one often finds in the immigrants of that era. They sent all three of their daughters to college, an amazing feat during the Depression. Gen, however, was the only one to graduate. Pat always spoke of the Quinlans as an exceptionally close, gentle and loving family. They had a great ritual of Sunday dinner, and Pat was often invited, fussed over, and royally fed.[2]

Sam took the Camp Master position at Camp Menahga, a girl's camp in Wisconsin, the summer of 1929. There he met Frances Russell, called Fran by her family, who was teaching tennis to the young campers while he kept the weeds pulled from the court.

Fran lived with her four brothers and sisters in St. Louis, not far from Washington University, and she and Sam began dating after their return from camp. At University City High School, Fran had been on the first full-court girls' basketball team, was the school's only girl cheerleader at a time of male dominance in the activity, and played tennis. After graduation, she entered the Wilson Kindergarten-Primary Institute, completed the two-year certificate program in teacher training, and continued at the institute as a teacher for two years. Sam was welcomed into the Russell home just as Pat was with the Quinlins. Weekend dinners together became a pattern followed by singing all the favorites around the piano.

The acceptance of the boys into the Quinlin and Russell homes gave both boys a feeling for family and everything that goes with it that their home life in the Philippines had not provided. They both felt that their father just did not have a real understanding of family life, and Sam and Pat saw in those households the kind of family élan they wished they had had. The story of the two couples became one love enterprise with jobs waiting in the American colony.

In 1931, Sam graduated from Washington University with honors in electrical engineering and left for Beloit, Wisconsin. There he spent the summer at the Fairbanks-Morris Company familiarizing himself with diesel engines and the modern generators his father's utility franchises were now using in the Philippines. Wedding plans went forward despite the death of Fran's father in an automobile accident that summer. The couple married on August 29 and left for the Philippines.

Pat continued at Washington, finishing in 1932. Gen stretched out another academic year to earn a master's degree in English literature, an uncommon achievement for a woman of those times, while Pat coached the Washington swim team. He also swam against Buster Crabbe (Tarzan) in the 400-meter free style during trials for the 1932 Olympics. Pat lost but won a spot as an alternate.

On September 16, 1931, with ticketing provided by P.H. Frank, Fran and Sam boarded the *S.S. Taiyo Maru* of the Japanese N.Y.K Line (Nippon Yusen Kaiaha), which was the general passenger agent for the Canard Line in the Orient. There were 286 Third Class Passengers (mostly Asians returning for visits and adventurers), sixty-four Tourist Class, and forty-eight First Class that included the young Mr. and Mrs. Frank. The couple's cabin was the choice number 203 next to the Chief Steward's office and closest to the Dining Salon. Above them was the "B" deck containing the First Class Smoking Room, Bar that Fran called the "Gent's Room," First Class Ladies Lounge, a dark room for movies and a large veranda. The "A" Deck sported a swimming pool, dressing rooms, gymnasium, and a winter garden.

§

Two days into the voyage up the United States coast, Japanese troops took the Manchurian city Mukden following a four-hour battle with Chinese forces. The Japanese said the attack was in retaliation for an alleged attempt by the Chinese to destroy a nearby bridge on the Southern Manchurian Railway, owned by the Japanese. The Chinese denied the charge. Manchuria was an uneasy mix of competing interests. The Japanese had invested heavily in the area and because of the railway, controlled much of southern Manchuria. The situation posed a challenge to the 1928 Kellogg-Briand Pact, an international treaty providing for the renunciation of war as an instrument of national policy. Secretary of State Henry Stimson began work on a peace accord in Manchuria, and after weeks of sustained battle, the League of Nations began studying the situation as Japanese forces advanced. All of these events worried Fran's family back in the States

§

The *Taiyo Maru* picked up passengers in San Francisco, and the couple took the day for a visit to the Presidio and Golden Gate Park. On September 19, the *Taiyo Maru* slipped through the Golden Gates with a Honolulu destination. For Sam, the trans-Pacific trip was his fourth. He was an old hand at boat life and the savages of sea storms. For Fran the first few days were her first taste of seasickness, but she soon settled into the evening dinners of twenty-seven dishes. Following dinner were musical programs featuring fox trot, tango, and waltzes and terminating with a rendition of "Anchors Away" by the Japanese orchestra. Fran met several people she enjoyed, "but the rest are pretty sad company. I've never heard such broken English in all my life." She was referring not to the Japanese crew, but the British passengers.

From Hawaii, the *Taiyo Maru* sailed nine days to Yokohama. Sam had stayed in touch with Okio Yamagouchi for the last fourteen years. Now with Fran, he boarded the train to Nagasaki where he introduced her to Okio, who was selling trinkets at a Shinto shrine. They dined at Okio's home, where they met her extended family who was eager to meet the Americans and show their hospitality. Okio had never married upon return to Japan in 1917. A woman who had been a magazine picture bride had little such opportunity. Following dinner, the couple took the overnight train to Kobe where they met their ship and set forth for the mainland of China. If there was any premonition in October 1931 of Japan's move into China, Fran did not mention it in her letters.

Fran was crazy about Shanghai, writing, "All the queer Chinese signs and lights are just as you read about." In addition, she was anticipating her life in Manila, "They drive on the left side of the road in Manila with a 'right drive' car." She could hardly wait to get there but confessed, "I'm a little scared—new land, new people ..."[3]

"The narrative mixes the human content of the author's family in the Philippines from 1898 to 1946, the history of the period, and unscrambles and sorts out the messages of a complex world of four wars, imperialism, multiculturalism, racism, internment in Japanese prison camps, destruction, repatriation, return, emigration, a new start in America."

"…beautifully composed, thoroughly researched, captivatingly told…"

"…warm, enlightening, and deeply moving…"

"…truly a masterpiece…"

"…a wonderful balance of compelling narrative and historical context…"

"…a dramatic portrayal of history that captures the spirit of a family, their entrepreneurial flair, their love and sacrifices, and the survival of what must have seemed interminable hardship…"

John Russell Frank graduated from the University of the South, received his M.A. from Furman University as an Angier Duke Fellow, and his Ph.D. from Georgia State University. He is formerly an independent school headmaster and then a college professor. He and his wife, Peggy Ann, now live in Montreat, North Carolina.

On the Road Home
An American Story

A Memoir of Triumph and Tragedy on a Forgotten Frontier

JOHN RUSSELL FRANK, PH.D.

Sam Frank, San Antonio (Texas) Academy, 1923. *(Courtesy of Emory University MARBL, Frank Family Collection)*

Pat Frank, San Antonio (Texas) Academy), 1925. *(Courtesy of Emory University MARBL, Frank Family Collection)*

P.H. Frank and Filipino employees testing an early model of the Frank Hemp Stripping Machine, Manila, circa 1922. *(Courtesy of Emory University MARBL, Frank Family Collection)*

Sales of P.H. Frank's hemp-stripper ballooned into the thousands, Davao, circa 1925. *(Courtesy of Emory University MARBL, Frank Family Collection)*

Pat Frank repairs machinery in his father's desiccated coconut manufacturing plant, Pagsanjan, circa 1925. *(Pat Frank family photograph)*

Coconuts were rafted to P.H. Frank's plant where they were processed and sold as *copra* on world markets, Pagsanjan River, circa 1925. *(Sam Frank family photograph)*

Slow fire underneath the coconuts dries the meat, after which it is air dried, then sacked and sold as *copra*, Pagsanjan, circa 1925. *(Sam Frank family photograph)*

Part 5
The Jolo and Davao Years
1931 to 1940

"If anybody can light anything I can"

P.H. Frank, Mindanao Herald, 1908

CHAPTER 18

"Our boat got in at three o'clock and how excited I was"

Frances Russell Frank, October 20, 1931

After leaving the United States for perhaps the greatest adventure of her life, Fran turned to letter writing as a way of keeping up with her family. In the tradition of letter writing in the early twentieth century, her letters tended to be long, detailed missives, explaining as much as possible about her new surroundings and new acquaintances. The couple had been at sea for thirty-four days, and Fran's fresh enthusiasm for the newness of all she had experienced aboard ship and in the ports of call continued, "Everything is so different but just what it should be in a place like this." She was twenty-one years old, more than halfway around the world, and excited "almost as bad as the day I was married." In Manila the two moved in with P.H. and Annie at their home on the corner of Taft Avenue, a major thoroughfare, and Vito Cruz. The house, purchased only months before the newly weds arrived, was in one of Manila's most exclusive neighborhoods. The home had an air of permanence—much as the British colonial homes P.H. had observed in Hong Kong and Singapore in 1908.[1]

"Here we are in Manila, at home any time you would like to call," wrote Fran to her family. Her first letter from Manila contained cheery news, "I'm simply in love with my new parents and house and way of living. I'll start from the beginning and tell everything."[2]

And she did, from descriptions of her in-laws and their house to the lizards that sang to her. "You would love this house, big and open, a huge porch which is as big as mother's old bedroom and twice as high. There are three bedrooms, TWO BATHS, a living room, kitchen, and a small alcove off of the dining and living room, a nice big yard with all kinds of fruit trees (The flowers are not in bloom yet)." The home backed up to marshland three blocks from Manila bay. There was a garage "for two cars." The chauffeur, Pantar, lived in a room off the garage. Three servants lived on the ground floor. The main floor was seven feet above ground. "Mr. Frank's" library was in the alcove. There was a piano in the living room. The porch is "where bridge is fought out." The long curving driveway connected Taft Avenue to Vito Cruz. There were stairs to the kitchen in the rear and stairs to the front porch. The end of a "perfect day" included playing bridge until 10:30 after a dinner of "Real food!! (We were so sick of the food on the boat.)."[3]

Fran's way of life in Manila was different from what her middle-class counterparts were experiencing back in the States where the Great Depression had a near death-grip on the country's economy. The Frank family businesses thrived, and Fran lived in a lovely, modern home, with an eye-catching garden and an array of servants. She was not worrying about her husband's job and dwindling paychecks.

She spent most of her first days in Manila with Annie, going to the "Y" for volleyball. She reported, "It was fun, but they were mostly older women." Fran went every day and "had to buy bloomers, blouse, and tennis shoes. Maybe you think I wasn't wet with perspiration." At the Frank home, she ate three two-course meals a day. "I don't turn my hand for anything!" There were five servants, "a Chinese boy for a cook, a houseboy, a girl who washes my clothes and mends them, a gardener, and a chauffeur." For a twenty-one year old from a large middle class St. Louis family, she exclaimed, "It is great fun but I'm afraid I'll get spoiled." It was also "funny to go to bed at night with a net over your head."[4]

For Fran, Manila was made up of "great big boulevards, trees, grass and flowers. Dewey Boulevard runs along the sea and along the park or Luneta, they have all colors of flowers. We drive there about sunset every day and it is too beautiful to look out across the bay and see the sun setting behind a huge mountain on an island. Really the mountain rises out of the sea." She was describing the island fortress of Corregidor, a place of telling future events. But she missed St. Louis, "I am anxious to hear from you, I feel lost sometimes with no news from my friends."[5]

As evident by her letters, Fran fell in love with the Philippines. "Thru rice fields, sugar fields, coconut groves, and millions of native villages," the newly weds drove the countryside around Manila. "The villages are so quaint and beautiful. There is an old church in every town that the Spanish built and you can't imagine how old they are and yet how beautiful. Old fashioned bells in the belfry and moss and vines growing all over the walls." Of her father-in-law she wrote, "He sure is a fine man and reminds me of our Daddy all the time."[6]

Fran had an endless stream of social invitations and stayed busy swimming, playing bridge, and dining and dancing at the Elk's Club, Manila Hotel, and the University Club. She also spent time at Lake Tall, which was ninety kilometers from Manila, and the Army and Navy Club. Visiting the boats in the harbor and the Opera House for plays "which begin at 9:00 after dinner," were all part of her busy activity. She wrote home, "Save your money and come see me. You would love it. It is a free and easy life with people to wait on you and plenty of time to read, write, and sew."[7]

Fran was well educated, which meant she was particularly attuned to the events, both national and international, surrounding her. Writing about the Japanese invasion of Manchuria in November, "I don't want you to worry about us because of the war in China. We are so far away from it and couldn't possibly be touched...and besides we have almost the whole American fleet camped in the bay—submarines, destroyers, and seaplanes..."[8]

§

Starting in 1901 at the behest of Governor General William Taft, City planner Daniel Burnham carved out a valley for the Manila colonials in the upland Cordillera region of northern Luzon. Baguio quickly became a favored destination, one of the cleanest and greenest towns in the Philippines, and, at over 5,000 feet in elevation, one of the coolest for summer getaways from torrid Manila two hundred miles south. After a steep climb from the tropical jungles, travelers donned tweedy attire for sitting in front of large fireplaces with crackling logs. If the British had their cool retreats at Simla or Darjeeling in India, then the Americans reinvented a Berkshires resort in the Philippines. Wealthy families constructed summer homes, and businesses built compounds of small cottages.

"We came up to Baguio on the train touring third class and also by bus," Fran wrote. "It was great fun traveling with the natives. We saw and experienced some of their inside life. After we got on the bus we picked up natives in every barrio we went thru and by the time we got to Baguio the car was packed. Chickens, roosters, kitties, and every kind of bundle and oh I must not forget the babies. One woman forgot some instructions and had the bus driver stop the bus while we took five minutes to perform her household duties." [9]

Baguio was a wonderful place, mountains with huge pine trees and marvelous weather. Fran and her new Manila friends stayed at the Pacific Commercial Company (P.C.C.) Cottage. She explained that there was "No charge for staying here. We pay for our food and have a houseboy and cook furnished. Some fine way to spend a week! We eat most of the time, sew, and sit by the fire or one of us reads to the rest. We are reading *The Good Companions* by Priestly." [10]

§

The women went to the nearby Bontoc region to see the postcard-beautiful Banaue Rice Terraces inscribed in the World Heritage list as the Eighth Wonder of the World. It was an engineering marvel built over 2,000 years earlier by the Ifugao people, using their bare hands and primitive tools.

What Fran saw were paddy fields growing in terrace after terrace, rising above each other seemingly up into the clouds. Fitting into the contours of the mountainsides, the terrace walls were overgrown with green rice plants. Little cascades carried the water down from terrace to terrace like great hanging gardens. The native Igorots worked naked, with their clothes balanced on their heads to keep them dry as the laborers stooped at work amongst the rice stalks. Showers and cloud effects added to the beauty of the panorama that Fran passed.

Back at the compound in Baguio she wrote, "Right now I'm looking out on wonderful mountains, pine trees and clouds circling in and out of valleys. Don't you love my descriptions?" Later that night the women sat around the fire until midnight talking, popping corn, and eating apples, "It is much fun…and I feel wonderful and have grand color in my cheeks. I eat like a horse and that is no joke."[11]

But there was another side to her new life. As much as she loved her new surroundings, Fran battled homesickness and boredom. She admitted, "I feel so useless and lazy." Manila was nothing like St. Louis. Now her days spent socializing, shopping, and sewing did not compare favorably to the purposeful busyness of her former teacher's life and the lively interactions amongst her family members and close friends. Forging friendships with other American women, or even European women, was a kind of comfort-survival strategy for American women in the islands, and although she adored her mother-in-law, she longed for friends her own age. Shortly she even came to miss the daily chores of life, "I haven't cleaned house or cooked, or washed dishes in so long that I'm afraid I would be clumsy awhile. I'm really spoiled. No beds to make, no clothes to wash, nothing to do but read, sew, and play. It has been hard to get used to it…If any body had told me I would miss housework, I would have laughed at them. I can understand now how it is."[12]

Toward the end of November 1931, hopes were high that Henry Stimson's efforts to secure peace in Manchuria through the League of Nations were paying off. Peaceful elements in the Tokyo government appeared to be gaining ascendancy. Yet those hopes seemed inconsistent with reports that the Emperor had approved the complete occupation of Manchuria. There were also reports that Japan would drop out of the League of Nations if the League ordered any withdrawal of Japanese troops.

§

A business trip for P.H. Frank often involved a month's time, which included twelve days going and coming on the inter-island boats and business stops in Zamboanga, Jolo, Cotabato, and Davao. Sam was being brought up to speed on the family businesses and left for the Mindanao business circuit with his father before Thanksgiving, returning on Christmas Eve. Fran's Christmas present was ten shares of Davao light and Power Company from her father-in-law. She giddily wrote, "What that means is 1,000 pesos, $500 gold invested for us! Isn't that just too good to be true?"[13]

Fran's life was being shaped by American colonialism in the Philippines. She reported, "We are leaving for Jolo in about a month. We will live with the manager and his wife. She speaks Spanish only. Poor me. Oh, for a little knowledge of Spanish—but I'll manage, never fear, I'll be speaking pig Spanish in a couple of days. But look at it from the sunny side—me in Jolo—about five Americans there if that many, living with Spanish people and trying to be friendly when you can't understand what they are talking about! Oh how I love to talk too—now that is what I call adventure!! I am tickled to death about leaving for Jolo—it will be such fun seeing the Moros."[14]

P.H. and Annie Frank's home and gardens fronted Taft Avenue, Manila, circa 1931. *(family photograph)*

Sukiyaki dinner and musical entertainment at P.H. and Annie's Taft Avenue home, Manila, circa 1930s. *(Courtesy of Emory University MARBL, Frank Family Collection)*

P.H. Frank in the garden of his home, Manila, circa 1930s. *(family photograph)*

Sam and Fran Frank en-route to Los Angeles where they will sail to the orient, Dallas, 1931. *(family photograph)*

Sam *(left)* goes to work for his father *(right)*. His first assignment was Jolo in the Sulu Archipelago where he became manager of Jolo Light & Power Company, Manila, 1931. *(family photograph)*

CHAPTER 19

"I'm in a daze—absolutely—totally gone"

Frances Russell Frank, February 5, 1932

It was late January and summer in the Southern Hemisphere. A crowd of fourteen friends feted Fran and Sam to dinner and *despedida*, a festive cheerio for a Manila couple headed to the most distant sub-provinces of the Philippines. Annie and P.H. served champagne, and Fran got her first look at the chugging inter-island boat that would take her and her husband to Jolo in the far off Sulu chain, further south than any other islands in the Philippines. She described the paint chipped vessel as having a "two by four cabin, and such a little boat." The vessel was not even typical of the small inter-island steamers, but P.H. was eager to get Sam on the job and had made a charter arrangement, an idea Fran pictured as romantic. But reality sank in fast after the boat's casting away from the waving friends. This voyage would be nothing like that on the newer boats which the British Dollar Line expected to have up and going within the next three months. The cabin was too hot for sleeping and smelled of diesel fuel and oil. So from the hold below, two Chinese cabin boys, their braided queues bobbing, popped out with little cots which they placed together on the deck. "It was fun cause the moon was full and—well—Sam and I felt like we were on another honeymoon—until—oh until—the next morning I woke up and was I sea-sick! Oh, if only you knew." Sam ate every meal on the trip, "but not me," she lamented.[1]

The route of their boat took them through the Verde Islands passage between Mindoro and Batangas, skirting the Sibuyan Sea. At the island of Samar, Sam pointed out Catbalogan, far away and forgotten to most people, but scene of a massacre of a unit of the 9th Infantry by natives at the village of Balangiga during the Philippine Insurrection in 1902. It was one of the many sites and histories Sam tried recounting to his seasick wife. The second night, moving through the Visayan Sea was no better for Fran, but she woke up the next morning feeling better as their boat pulled into the picturesque harbor of Cebu. To the east, she beheld the blue ranges of mountains on Bohol Island and a lone fisherman standing on a rock and throwing his net into the sunset. The boat was coasting through the same waters in which Fernando Magellan had observed a village of bamboo huts on stilts when he went ashore claiming the islands for Spain on April 21, 1521.

A day later, Fran and Sam disembarked at the Zamboanga wharf to a world vastly different than Manila. The brilliant tropical orange of an ending day was reflecting purple off roiling clouds north to south. It was the cooling time from a late equatorial afternoon. Twenty-one year old Fran, having grown up in progressive University City in St. Louis, stepped onto the pier in the place where her husband was born. She was young, vibrantly alive, pretty, and determined to adjust and find joy in the unexpected pleasures and adventures of life in the Philippines. Fran and Sam, holding hands adoringly, moved through the crowds of various Moro groups—the Tao Sugs, Yakan, Sangil and Badjao, who for the most part were indistinguishable from the mostly Catholic Christian Filipino groups—Cebuanos, Visayans, and Tagalogs. There were thirteen different language groups among them, but Cebuano, Spanish, and broken English were the *lingua franca* on the wharf. Fran's white skin and western features drew attention from equally attractive mixed Malay, Indonesian, Polynesian, Chinese, and Spanish featured natives. Her husband enjoyed the handsome mixed racial features of all the groups.

The couple walked down streets lined with ancient houses whose second stories arcaded the sidewalks. Zamboanga had the look of a new and prosperous place, owing in part to building materials of exotic decay-resistant hardwoods. The couple stayed in Zamboanga with old friends of P.H.. They visited with the parents of Sam's childhood friends and spent an evening with the Hacketts whose daughter Betsy had recently returned to Zamboanga to join her father at the *Mindanao Herald*. The next day, Sam led Fran to the cool and quiet Episcopal Church where he had severed as an acolyte. They climbed the ramparts of Ft. Pillar where he had played war. They visited the old parade grounds of Pettit Barracks and the spots in the jungle where he and Pat had hunted monkeys. As cool shadows began to close over the Santa Maria road, they walked slowly together to the Old Catholic Cemetery where Sam's grandfather, mother, and sister lay buried.

§

At dusk the following day, Fran and Sam boarded the *Rizal* for the couple's last leg to Jolo. Pulling out of the Zamboanga harbor, they cruised toward the island of Basilan thirty miles in the distance, its rugged mountains and palisade coast backlit by the emerging moon. In the low-lying foreground, the old Spanish fort behind them looked mysterious in the afterglow, and the skies were alight with oranges and purples. The waters of the Moro Sea were awash in phosphorescent greens, and small flying fish thudded onto the deck.

Early the next morning, the *Rizal* passed the small islands leading to Jolo Island. Beneath the crystal clear water could be seen a strange world of feathery, lacelike vegetation, and depressions in the coral. There, tiny fishes played and water creatures established a little world for themselves, living in its narrow confines unconscious of what was going on in the surrounding vastness.

Sam raised his hand and waved to a man and woman waiting on the cement and rock pier of Jolo Town. There stood Francisco Suche who managed P.H.'s Jolo Light and Power Company. Don Paco, as he was known on Jolo, had served as chief engineer on an inter-island steamship before P.H. hired him to run the power company. Don Paco also ran the ice plant and water pumping system for the town of Jolo, all P.H. Frank businesses.

Fran watched on both sides of the long wharf as the boatmen in conical straw hats perched at the ends of their hollowed out log *bancas*, paddled rapidly through the water, or floated idly by, smoking their cigarettes. The boats were loaded to the gunwales with green grasses covered by canopies of matted straw. Launches, too, came chugging past, their poop decks covered with straw-screened *cascos*, small storage areas, which contained case goods, cartons, and cordage unloaded from the inter-island steamers.

As Sam carried on an incoherent conversation with the Suches in Spanish mixed with the local dialects, Fran stood bewildered and quickly realized that Mrs. Suche spoke very little English. Fran could see that Jolo was a mix of up-to-date-Spanish and American buildings, native *nipa* shacks, and old Spanish churches. Beyond the tidal flats and away from the more thickly settled parts of the town, she saw thatched *nipa* houses on stilts. On that arrival morning, as in all mornings in Jolo, Fran heard for the first time a *muezzin* calling the Muslim faithful to prayer while the bell at the Catholic Church clanged for mass.

Getting her land legs back as she walked up the wharf, Fran drank in the picturesque gray walls of the old Spanish fort. Its sentinel houses at the corners where Private Frank had relieved the last Spanish sentry in 1899 were all moss grown, and pink flowers were breaking out of the crevices of the rocks. Picturesque Moros, men wearing their traditional fezzes, baggy silk trousers and tight shirts, crowded the streets and pathways. Wide belts made of brilliant hand-woven material held partially hidden *barongs*, thick-backed thin-edged knives. Deep red stains from chewing betel nuts colored the gums and lips of the Moros, whose teeth were ground down from constant chewing. The women wore colorful silk pants, long-sleeved, ornate, silk blouses in blues, reds, and yellows. They wore silver and gold bracelets and were barefoot for comfort. A Moro *datu's* daughter accompanied by harem surfs holding green umbrellas over her head passed with two pet monkeys on her shoulders. Long, silver, false fingernails, badges of her status as part of the idle rich class of Moroland, completed Fran's first Jolo Town street scene.

That night Fran went to bed early. Her husband stayed up with Suche inspecting the electric power units, ice plant, and water pumping station. She drifted off, occasionally hearing a whisper from the street, often giggles, sometimes loud talking but unidentifiable and at other times something tinkling—all conversations in unfamiliar languages.

Jolo was only about 200 miles from the equator, and the heat was great not withstanding the electric overhead fan Fran awoke to the next morning. Sliding screens that formed the side of the room in which

Fran and Sam lived above the Suches offered cross ventilation and pleasant breezes. The shutters were like Japanese *shoji*, made of small panes of opalescent shell to soften the intensity of tropic sunlight; there were also green slit bamboo shades pulled halfway down. She began writing her first letter home from Jolo. She sat on the rattan bed under the mosquito netting where she could look out to the red hibiscus border of the garden that stretched along the narrow road to the wharf as she wrote, "I'm in a daze—absolutely—totally gone." [2]

§

Cholera was a dread disease in the southern Philippines, and the couple was in Jolo for just two days when Fran became frightened, "...I got diarrhea. I had a pretty bad case of it and suffered so with pains in my tummy that we finally called in the doctor but couldn't find him—he was out hunting." Fran refused an injection, "They scare me—and we had to find the pharmacy girl and about nine I got my medicine!! I was tearing hair out by then...I was suffering." She took three doses, was better, and got up to wash her face, "and for the first time in my life fainted. It was a terrible feeling and thank goodness Sam was there to bring me to. I was just weak and it took me another two days to feel good again. I'm fine now and have forgotten all about that piece of bad luck." A Moro woman living next door to the Frank's home brought Fran an *anting-anting*, a silver embroidered leather amulet to ward off further disease and shield her from her enemies. Of the Japanese advances in China, she wrote, "Don't worry about the Japanese trouble. We are well protected and even if we do feel a little close to it, we are a long ways from the fighting." [3]

As the cholera and typhoid epidemic ran unabated, Fran, none too reluctantly, overcame her fear of needles. She was in line when the Red Cross relief boat arrived from Cebu with vaccines arranged by Sam who had been appointed Vice-Chairman of the Jolo Red Cross by Jamalul Kiram, Sultan of Sulu. Kiram's son had attended grammar school with Sam in Zamboanga, and Kiram's niece was attending the University of Illinois—all of this while George Ade's comic opera *The Sultan of Sulu* was being sung on Broadway, and thus strengthened American stereotypes of Philippine Muslims.

§

Life for Fran in Jolo was isolating, "We don't get mail often here...we will only be here three months and then will go to Davao. Oh, what I would give to see you all. I simply have to tolerate this for the time being until we are definitely settled." After a month there had been no mail sent down from Manila, "so you can imagine how anxious I am. It is hard to know when you will get your mail because there are no shipping policies in Jolo. I simply send one letter a week and I figure it will hit at least one of the boats leaving for Manila the following week." Typically, from Jolo in 1932, a turn around of letters with her family in St. Louis took two months, and circumstances would extend her life in Jolo longer than she expected. She was already feeling the isolation. Homesick and culture shocked, she confided in her mother, "I wish for a nice talk sometimes about little matters that sometimes bother me."[4]

As the weeks turned to three months with no word from P.H. about the move to Davao, Fran's life settled into routine boredom. "We get up about 7:30 and have breakfast on the front porch at 8:30. At 12:30 we have dinner and at 4:30 we have tea. Then at 8:30 we have supper. When I'm not eating I'm sewing buttons on shirts, darning socks, working on my quilt, reading or writing letters. I usually sleep about two hours every afternoon. This is not the kind of life I would want to lead forever." There was the dilapidated South Sea Club—such as it was—and she and Sam would sometimes rent a *vinta* and sail to nearby islands. [5]

Fran welcomed a respite from predictability one weekend when Sam engaged a small packet to take them to Tawi-Tawi. The island was at the end of the Sulu chain, only thirty miles from Borneo where they spent the night on the beach. For outings, the two attended Moro dances featuring music with brass gongs and nose flutes which she enjoyed. Less appealing were the bloody cockfights and the horrific goring of *carabao*, water buffalo, duels accompanied by frenzied bloodlust betting by the Filipinos and Moros. She began a stamp collection, played dominos until almost midnight, and "would straighten and do odds and ends," but always rushed back from wherever she was for the radio news dispatches at 6:30 every evening. She embraced news from a world beyond Jolo. The BBC from Hong Kong or Singapore, depending on atmospherics, provided war reports from China, and the familiar voice of reporter Don Bell in Manila brought news from America and the social chatter of doings in the Philippine capitol. Hearing English was her comfort, and she cleaved to the voices, news, music, and sounds.

§

There was always the gnawing uneasiness that accompanied Moro country, and fear was a part of Fran's everyday life. Even with Constabulary guards at the gates of Jolo, she confessed, "I don't like to go out after dark alone…Sam is often too busy to go with me." When they did go out at night, Sam wore a .38-caliber pistol.

One day their cook slammed through the door yelling that a Moro native was going *juramentado*. The cook, exhausted from running, was terrified and shaking. The attack was happening just up the road, yet crowds from the native barrio where they lived ran to see the excitement. For Sam and Fran, it was no incident to see first hand, and they crouched indoors, Sam with pistol in hand and Fran sitting close by. Both watched through the bamboo awning slits for any movements, their pump shotgun leaning against the wall. Finally, the crowds of Moros, chattering and laughing, returned. Fran recounted the tale that a Constabulary officer called up an explanation to Sam that "a young Moro girl was 'being excused' behind a coconut tree and a Moro gentleman came along and 'peeked'." Fran shared the event comically, profoundly understating the tensions, adding, "Whereupon the lady lets out a yell and all her boyfriends came to the rescue and ran the man out. Not one killed, hurt or injured."[6]

Weeks later a more serious incident occurred. Fran explained, "The Moros out in the mountains have been fighting the Constabulary, a week Sunday. One officer killed and around seventeen soldiers; no telling how many Moros dead—no way of checking up but they will fight to the last man. One house was full of women and children and the soldiers fired on the house not knowing it and killed about fifty. It was quite terrible, but those Moros are hard to handle—they have guns and will not surrender on any terms so the Constabulary has to fight until they get their guns." The Moro uprisings provided a kind of spectator sport. "This is all going on about thirty kilometers from Jolo. Sam and I drove out Sunday, when the fighting first started, to within three kilometers of the fighting—we could hear the shooting quite distinctly but were in no danger. We heard on the radio of an announcement in Washington. Hope if you heard about it you would not be alarmed as we are in no danger whatever. No one seems to know the cause of the uprising—many rumors but nothing definite." [7]

§

There was a palpable tension in the Philippines, a result of Japanese military advances in China. In early February 1932, Japan was pounding Shanghai and had taken Manchuria. Efforts by the League of Nations had failed miserably, and President Hoover sent the 31st Infantry to Shanghai as a military reinforcement to protect American interests. He additionally ordered the Asiatic Fleet to proceed from Manila to Shanghai and join fleets sent by Great Britain, France and Italy. Fran was nonchalant. "We are not bothered about things there as far as safety is concerned because we have a fleet here, soldiers, and lots of protection." Sam was strategic, "If Japan came to attack the Philippines, she would leave her cities defenseless, and open to an aerial and naval attack from the Pacific Fleet which stays on our coast. The Asiatic Fleet, which ain't no plaything, stays in Chinese, Japanese, and Philippine waters. Japan knows this, also the fact that there are many islands here for her navy and army to attack and each one of any size has a nice garrison, and would give any landing force a stiff fight. We sure aren't worried cause we know of 367 other islands they would rather land on than Jolo. Papers play things up, but America is wise to stay out as long as it can." [8]

§

By March 1932, it was becoming clear that the couple would be in Jolo a great deal longer than originally expected. A boycott of electricity by Chinese merchants seeking lower rates was hurting Jolo Light & Power's profitability. The merchant class in Jolo, as in most of the southern Philippines, was Chinese or Chinese-Philippine *mestizo*. The Public Service Commission in Manila, modeled after a similar government agency in the United States, set rates, but civil war in China between the Nationalists and Communists was emboldening young Chinese merchants throughout Asia who were willing to try out the collectivist lessons of Mao Tse-tung and thus organize.

143

P.H came down to Zamboanga on the *Mayon*, the new Dollar Line inter-island boat "which is a miniature ocean liner," Fran reported, remembering her recent "yacht" ride. Sam and Fran met him in Zamboanga and stayed at the Plaza Hotel. Fran was thrilled to hear English again in the markets and among friends. The three discussed the Chinese boycott and other business for two days with Fran happy to be included and her opinions valued. P.H. needed Sam in Davao to take over Davao Light and Power Company, bring it fully on line, and take complete command of what P.H. saw as his family's future flagship enterprise. Nevertheless, P.H. was not happy with Suche's management in Jolo and needed his son to stay on to keep an eye on things. Fran expressed her disappointment in the decision saying, "It is hard to go on back to Jolo, now that I know how lonesome it is there."[9]

Fran was determined to adjust and find joy in the unexpected pleasures of life in Jolo, "It feels so queer to find your self in a place where conveniences are not!!…but Daddy used to tell us how disappointed he would be if we could not adjust ourselves to the situation we find ourselves in!!…Well, he would not be disappointed." There was an unexpected visit from the famed British explorer Richard Halliburton because his airplane ran out of gas and coasted into Jolo. For the next several days, he awaited a petrol supply from Cebu and spent the time as a guest of the Franks before continuing his around the world flight.[10]

The delights of the exotic side of the islands continued to thrill Fran as she exclaimed, "Oh, what a sight I just saw. A Moro wedding procession!! It is the first I have seen and I will tell you about it. The bridegroom was on his way to the bride's home with money for the father of the bride (The more money it takes to get a bride the more valuable she is.) He was preceded by a group of well-dressed Moros and by two boys beating on tom-toms. The bridegroom mounted his horse, his face painted a ghastly white and dressed in a white embroidered shirt with a colored turban on his head; following him is his page on the shoulder of a man, dressed in bright colors, also a man carrying a trunk with money and gifts for the bride. I didn't see the bride but maybe I'll see her some other time. The people were shouting and yelling and having a glorious time."[11]

Still, she missed her family and wrote them saying, "I laugh and cry over your letters. Mostly, I cry."[12]

§

A typhoon in the orient is a gargantuan hurricane, a *baguio*—hulking, stupendous. "I never want to be in another…rain and wind…Jolo is down to the ground, including trees, wires, and telephone and electric light poles," Fran wrote. There were no meteorological warnings, only darkening sky, rising tides, and pounding surf. There was no place to go, so Sam and Fran held tight in their house. To be outside meant to be swept away in the advancing ocean's backwash. The couple's home was the strongest in Jolo, but their tin roof peeled back, the porch and its roof blew away, and Fran bemoaned, "Oh, how this house did shake," for eight hours. There was a short calm as the eye crossed over Jolo, and then the fury continued. For three days, the rain came in torrents, "all clothes, bed clothes, shirts, pillows—everything is drenched." Boats were dashed against the pier and sunk, freighters were washed ashore, "There is hardly a tree standing—also houses."[13]

When Sam and Fran walked out at dawn of the third day, Jolo was a terrible sight. Wires, poles, trees hundreds of year's old, houses—everything was demolished. The mountains were swept clean of their foliage, hemp, coconut trees, and banana trees. "Oh, it is impossible to tell you the damage," Fran wrote, "Sam is doing his best to get lights in as Moros are stealing and people are afraid of them going *amok* and killing people." Sam helped refuel relief ships and got the electrical system operating so that the town could pump water. He worked long hours keeping the ice plant running. The roads became impassable because of dead animals, "Terrible isn't it to think about," Fran described, "but oh if you could smell it."[14]

Five days later, the town was still dealing with the aftermath of the storm. The Manila and Zamboanga newspapers were reporting thousands killed. Sam opened the electric plant to survivors, and Fran opened the remains of their home to the Moros. Sam's office below their quarters as well as what remained of their upstairs living quarters filled up with native women, children, and men. Fran, Sam, and the Moros together hung clothes all over the house, "and still it rains. This has been a terrible catastrophe." [15]

The mildew settled on surfaces wet or dry; it did not matter. But if the surface was wet, the growth and odors became terrible. For a week Fran had three *lavanderas*. They washed and used heavy, charcoal-burning irons to dry the clothes in order to stay ahead of the mildew. Then they helped their neighbors do the same. Fran observed thankfully, "We are lucky 'tho. We have electric lights, our clothes are dry, and we are sleeping in our bed now. Natives have no lights and are without roofs over their heads." Red Cross boats and five airplanes brought food and medicines in a continuous stream. "I guess this typhoon will keep us in Jolo even longer," Fran predicted and P.H. confirmed in a radiogram from Manila, telling them that until repairs to the plant and transmission lines could be made, the couple would be in Jolo indefinitely.[16]

It was getting Fran down. "I really don't mind—I like it here—but oh for the companionship of young people...Poor Sam feels so badly when I get blue and I can't let him feel that way; I don't want to be selfish. I must be a good wife now as well as a daughter...the flies are about to drive me crazy...since the storm we have had terrible flies, mosquito and bugs of all kinds and description. So many things have happened to me."[17]

§

In late July, P.H. and Sam planned an inspection trip to Davao where the power company was installing the new Fairbanks-Morris generators with which Sam had familiarized himself in Beloit, Wisconsin. It would be a good time for Fran to take a month in Manila, and this time she rode in luxury on the new Dollar Line inter-island steamer. She also had an important appointment to keep.

On August 3, 1932, Fran wrote to her mother from Manila, "Some great news. You are soon to become a grandmother!!!...I'm so happy I want the whole world to know. Another thing—we will keep our house in Jolo, just us two, and Mr. Suche might be let go." As lonesome as she was in Jolo and as engulfed in culture shock as she might have been, Fran shortened her stay in Manila from a month to just eight days, "I had been so lonesome for Sam. It seems like now that the baby is coming I need him more than ever." She began reading the *Women's Home Companion* she found in Manila; her letters reflected the glow of motherhood, and she had found a grand new purpose. By the second week of September, P.H. had asked for Suche's resignation, and Fran proudly shared with her family that, "Dad turned the plant over to Sam. Business has been very bad here and it had to be done." [18]

§

The U.S. Congress passed the Hare-Hayes-Cutting Act in 1932, which set a date for Philippine independence. The act was a fulfillment of the vague pledge of in the Jones Act of 1916 of future independence; it was also responsive to the demands of a series of "independence missions" sent to Washington by the Philippine legislature. But this unprecedented transfer of sovereignty by a colonial power was decided upon in the dark days of the Great Depression and with the help of some incongruous allies. The Depression had caused American farm interests to look desperately for relief, and those who suffered real or imaginary hurt from the competition of Philippine products sought to exclude those commodities. The farm lobbies had already failed in a direct attempt to establish tariffs on Philippine products but found that advocating for independence of the islands increased the effectiveness of their efforts. Tied to independence was the end of free entry into American markets of Philippine sugar, coconut oil, rope, and other less important items. That these agricultural interests were able to accomplish what they did is partly explained by their political influence which was greater than that of the small group of American traders and investors in the Philippines. The bill passed the Senate in December 1932 but was vetoed by President Hoover. To Hoover's surprise, Congress promptly overrode his veto, and the bill became law on January 13, 1933. The act, however, required approval by the Philippine Senate, and this was not forthcoming. Manuel Quezon was leading a campaign against the bill because of provisions in it that allowed the indefinite retention of U.S. military bases on the islands.

The juxtaposition of U.S. democracy and imperial rule over a subject people was jarring to most Americans. From the beginning of American presence in the Philippines, the training of the Filipinos for self-government and ultimate independence was an essential rationalization for U.S. hegemony in the islands. Differences between Democratic and Republican politics focused on the speed with which self-government would occur and the date on which independence should be granted.

During the debates in the Philippine Senate, Sam reflected the feelings of his father, whose views mirrored an evolved, weighed, and pragmatic viewpoint—a moderate Republican view of slow emancipation, as he wrote, "Now that the Philippine Independence Bills are so near passing in Washington, the people are getting worried. The Philippine Legislature is in session, and they are holding debates on the Hawes-Cutting Bill. It seems that many would prefer going on under the Jones Bill, on which the government is based, with nothing definite ahead, than to look forward to the complete separation as is being proposed by the leaders. As long as they don't do anything too hurriedly it doesn't make any difference to us."[19]

Manuel Quezon, President of the Philippine Senate, denounced the act as "shameful and unfriendly" and "not an independence bill at all," describing it rather as a tariff and immigration bill aimed at Philippine products and labor with "the elements of independence being merely a sugar coating."[20]

§

Sam took over the Jolo Light and Power Company from Suche, and the Spanish community feted the popular couple to several merry *despedidas*. A final party was held at the club, and Fran described the scene, "When it was time for the boat to leave didn't the brass band start down the street and the whole town walked after it and weren't there some fond farewells. It was quite touching but every time I think of that brass band…" But business changed the direction of Sam's and Fran's lives again.[21]

Suche went directly to Manila where he talked with P.H. about finding an investor to buy the power plant in Jolo. The idea was not a bad one because P.H. needed Sam in Davao. The population was growing, hemp was a major export, and he needed to secure Davao Light & Power's fifty-year franchise. P.H. did not think Jolo would ever be a big money maker. The Chinese boycott continued to hurt earnings; his daughter-in-law was unhappy with life in the Sulu archipelago; his expected grandchild would be safer in the healthy clime of Davao. And the sale of the Jolo companies would be highly profitable with the resulting capital useful for expansion in Davao.

Suche had many friends in the Philippines, so he arranged the sale of Jolo Power Company to a wealthy Spanish *illustrado* named Ramón Aboitiz from Cebu. Aboitiz would put up the capital and Suche would operate the power plant. That was the beginning of the Frank family's thirty-year relationship with Aboitiz who became the majority stockholder of the Jolo Power Company and afterward began expanding his holdings to include other provincial utilities. By February 1933, the sale was completed; Francesco Suche was back as the superintendent, and Fran and Sam were in Manila where their son Sam, Jr. was born on March 7, 1933. A week earlier the German Reichstag burned in Berlin and Nazi authorities opened their first concentration camp in Dachau, ten miles outside of Munich.

P.H. and Annie, with handsome profits from the Jolo sale in hand, departed for a voyage around the world. A month earlier, Adolf Hitler, the recently named German Chancellor, had assured Ambassador William Dodd that Nazi attacks on American nationals would cease, but just in case the Frank's bypassed Germany on their tour.

Before departing, P.H. assigned Sam the job of looking after the Manila office and turned the Taft Avenue home over to him and Fran. That same month, Franklin Roosevelt was inaugurated which ushered in a post Woodrow Wilson era of closer relationships between Filipino and American interests that could possibly move toward Philippine independence at some time in the future. Japan announced it would quit the League of Nations, and Albert Einstein, a self-exile, arrived in the United States to settle in Princeton, New Jersey.

Fran and Sam stayed in Manila for seven months. There on November 1, 1933, they left for Davao where Sam assumed responsibilities for his father's Davao Light and Power Company and Mindanao Sales and Services. For Fran it was once again preparation for a move. "You would think I was going out of civilization for years and would never see a drugstore or dress shop again!!" But Fran was ready to get to Davao; her earlier Sulu island home to the south had its shortcomings, but the social bustle of Manila contrasted too sharply with the simplicity of Jolo, which she came to remember and value more than the hardships, loneliness, and dangers. She wrote her mother, "I'm glad this is my last day in Manila!!"[22]

CHAPTER 20

"You know what a big 'fraidy-cat' I usually am"

Genevieve Quinlin Frank, November, 1933

On the same day that Fran and Sam left for Davao, younger brother Pat and his wife Gen pulled out of Long Beach, California, heading for the Philippines on the *Penrith Castle*. Gen had completed her master's degree and Pat his coaching at Washington University. Like Fran and Sam, Gen and Pat had left for the islands immediately following their marriage, and now they were leaving depression times in America and looking upon Pat's return to the land of his birth as a great adventure. Pat would have a position with the Manila Trading Company, known as Mantrade, the sole agency for Ford automobiles in the Philippines. P.H. Frank had slated his son to take over his Mindanao Sales and Services in Davao, but Pat first had a great deal to learn about Ford automobiles and the transportation business.

P.H. and Julius Reese, who owned Mantrade, devised the deal. The two men were friends and business collaborators from the earliest days of P.H.'s transportation companies. When Reese was looking for someone to handle the sale of Ford automobiles on Mindanao, he approached P.H., and their agreement was made. P.H. expanded his Mindanao Sales and Service Company in Davao, which was also handling his Universal Hemp-stripper, and began the exclusive sale of Fords on the island as well as all of the parts and service they required. On November 20, 1933, the boat threaded its way through the San

Bernardino Straits and docked three days later in Manila. P.H., Annie, and Julius Reese met the couple. Pat and Sam were now both on their native soil and were among the first generation of American *mestizos* who had reached their maturity in the United States and returned to the Philippines. A week into Gen and Pat's voyage, Hitler had joined Japan in withdrawing from the League of Nations, and the *Penrith Castle* bypassed Japan and China on its Pacific voyage.

§

Family business interests prevented the sisters-in-law from spending much time together. As Fran settled into Davao, Gen settled into Manila. Gen taught kindergarten for several months at the American School in Manila, giving it up when she was pregnant and because her husband asked her to. She and Fran would not live together in Davao until 1936.

For Gen as it was for Fran, Manila was a beautiful cosmopolitan place, "a tropical Paris." On almost any day of the year, American and European children played along Dewey Boulevard under the close supervision of their Chinese and Filipino *amahs*. Cars, mostly made in America, drove leisurely down the boulevards. Young and old enjoyed the sunsets, the gentle sea breezes, and the sight of the American fleet silhouetted against the sky. The fleet was larger now and included aircraft carriers. Roosevelt was showing the flag as Japan advanced in China, and Pat and Gen were regular invitees to shipboard cocktail parties.[1]

At one end of the famous boulevard, American officers played tennis, swam, and enjoyed cool drinks at the Army-Navy Club. Next door at Legaspi Gardens, the famous hangout of American soldiers, the jukebox played all day and into the night. And tenders came and went bringing new sailors in to enjoy their hours of shore leave and taking others out to their ships—the mariners sometimes a little worse for wear. At the Yacht Club, "front porch sailors" rocked. In the distance was the Polo Club with the greenest imaginable playing fields. Hooves of the polo ponies kicked up the turf at a bare rumble that from that distance echoed two beats behind their flashing legs.[2]

Gen recounted her impressions of her father-in-law, whom she described as a strong man of strong character, "a natural leader, and highly respected and trusted by the men who had served with him in the army—the Old Timers. There were any numbers of these men who chose the easy life of the tropics. They would turn to P.H. to manage their affairs when, in poor health, they feared for their children's futures... while he had little formal schooling, he was an educated man. When Pat and I first arrived in Manila, we lived with Dad and Annie. During that time, I was happily reveling in the fine books Dad had acquired over the years, a gem of a small collection. Dad had read all the Harvard Classics and could discuss them as well as the great lectures. Here I was fresh out of college with a M.A. in English Literature and Dad could remember events and names of characters better than I could. It was not easy to send away for books and to wait such a long time for them to arrive."[3]

At Mantrade, Reece started Pat on the right foot but at the bottom-rung. He had Pat memorize every Ford part, nut, bolt and screw by name, number, and model. In the service department, Pat learned how to take a Ford apart and put it back together. Moreover, in marketing he learned about strategic planning, advertising, and sales. For three years, he and Gen lived in Manila, a time which she described as a "beautiful, happy, and carefree life." Their first son Dennis was born there on October 26, 1934.

In 1935, P.H. lost his hemp-stripping patent case to what he considered a Japanese-influenced Philippine Supreme Court. The Court had ruled for him in 1933, but yet another Japanese company attacked his patent, and in 1935, the Court overturned its own precedent and found in favor of the Japanese. P.H. had the option of appealing to the United States Supreme Court. His Manila attorney J.W. Ferrier advised him of the several years and thousands of dollars it would take to engage American attorneys and make the appeal. P.H. considered his options for a year, finally deciding that the Japanese would continue to infringe on his patent, so he said "To hell with it."[4]

CHAPTER 21

"So many things have happened to me"
Frances Russell Frank, October 14, 1932

In Davao, Sam was taking over management of his father's Davao Light and Power Company, an American corporation operating on a Five-Year Legislative Franchise and regulated by the Philippine Public Service Commission. Mindanao Sales and Services was also an American corporation, which sold P.H.'s Universal Hemp-stripper and all the parts and lubricants needed for their maintenance. Billy Gohn had been managing the two enterprises for P.H. and held 5% of the stock in the power company. But he had no training in electrical engineering or business management. He was sixty years old and his energy level as well as his expertise could not match P.H.'s vision of a modern, expanding electric power company and a fully integrated Ford franchise.

During the 1920's, P.H. observed the growing population of Davao and how it supported the abaca plantations and infrastructure for the production and export of hemp. There were also huge coconut plantations, and Del Monte was establishing a pineapple plantation larger than any the company had in Hawaii. At that time, Davao was also the largest consumer of P.H.'s newly patented hemp-stripping machine which was revolutionizing hemp production and contributing to the surge of population growth in Davao City and the surrounding district. In 1929 the means of generating electricity had been crude; the machinery was made up of leftover parts from old U.S. Army portable generators that had seen little maintenance and could no longer support the increasing demand for electricity. P.H. had applied for and received a five-year municipal franchise from the government. Under the franchise, he would have five years in which to build a power plant and meet all the specifications of the Philippine Public Service Commission. If he could accomplish that, he would then receive a fifty-year legislative franchise, a powerful incentive. Sam began the immediate installation of the four powerful Fairbanks-Morris diesel generators he had studied in Beloit. He also formulated new systems of electrical distribution that would carry Davao's explosive growth well into the future. Sam got the job done in two years by adding synchronized diesel-electric units at its central unit in the city, which supplied customers with 220 volt, 60 cycle single and three-phase current from 2,300 volt distribution lines and a 13,800 volt transmission system. His father's fifty-year franchise was won.

The Japanese population continued to grow around Davao. "Little Japan" was a name sometimes given to Davao because the Japanese were so instrumental in the growth of the town and district. They had quickly seen the possibilities there and acted promptly, entering into hemp production on a large scale. Powerful Japanese interests sent trained executives and managers to manage the plantations and dispatched thousands of Japanese laborers to work the plantations. Japanese women were also brought over, and soon large families of Japanese children were growing up around Davao. Japan's largest corporations had a presence in Davao, and Japanese banks in Tokyo, Osaka, Yokohama, and Kobe were silent partners. A peaceful colonization had gradually taken place. In the Philippines, Davao had the largest immigrant population of Japanese. They had their own schools, hospital, restaurants, and club. A Japanese enclave, so large and important, also required the maintenance of a fully staffed diplomatic consulate. The Imperial Japanese Consulate General at Davao was the most sumptuous edifice on Mindanao. The Japanese executives and diplomatic officials would often entertain the top American business families and Philippine government officials. The banquets and *sukiyaki* parties were elaborate, and Fran and Sam attended often. Japanese party manners were catching; Fran observed,

"Soon the Americans would find themselves bowing and noisily sucking in air before making a remark."[1]

Davao was home to Fran and Sam for the next eight years. While living there, they had two additional sons, P.H. II born on September 30, 1937, in Manila, and on July 4, 1940, I joined the family after my mother requested a jostling rickshaw drive over Davao's roughest roads to promote my birth on America's birthday.

Pat and Gen moved to Davao in 1936, when Pat took over the operations of Mindanao Sales and Services from Billy Gohn. That couple also added two more children—Mike on September 9, 1938 in Davao, and Pat Jr., born in Baguio on August 4, 1940, the last of the six grandsons of P.H. Frank and Eugenia Garcia, all born in the Philippines. Gen and Fran organized a small school for the several American and European expatriate children and used the Calvert School curriculum adopted by many missionaries.

By the late 1930's the population of Davao City was between 40 and 60 thousand. The Japanese population was 20,000 and the American community less than 100. The main street in Davao was crowded with Japanese bazaars of all kinds and descriptions which sold cheap imitations of American clothing, cosmetics, toys, and household goods. Even the boxes and jars were imitations of well-known American manufacturers. The common Japanese people wore western clothes "which were not becoming to them," Gen observed, adding, "The women with their bowed legs, ill-fitting shoes and stockings and dresses which hung without any fit or style certainly did not have the charm of the women in Japan who have clung to their own fashions." Of the men, Gen observed that Japanese commoners "were robbed of all natural grace and looked like they had donned Sunday clothes in which they were not at ease." In contrast, the Japanese executives and diplomats dressed in well-fitted tropical whites as did the Americans.[2]

§

By the time the Frank brothers and their wives reunited in Davao, Japanese corporations were some of the largest there. In the city proper, there were only about fifty American and European residents. Another twenty Americans resided on the outlying plantations. Many of the Americans and Europeans, besides the Franks, were representatives of companies which were built around the hemp industry and did business in Davao, that by the 1930's was thriving—International Harvester, Standard Oil, Shell Petroleum, Luzon Stevedoring, Standard Vacuum, Saleeby Fiber, Ker and Company, Singer Sewing Machine, Manila Rope, as well as small contractors, mechanics, and others. In addition, there were American government officials who administered the school and health bureaus. The Davao Gold Mine employed American master mechanics, engineers, geologists, metallurgists, executives, and managers. Walter Tong, a United Church of Christ missionary serving under the American Board of Commissioners for Foreign Missions, administered the Davao Mission Hospital.

Additionally, there were twenty or so remaining American pioneers, the "Old Timers," who lived on the outlying plantations. These men came into Davao only at rare intervals to purchase supplies and to celebrate the Fourth of July, Thanksgiving, Christmas, New Years Eve, and other special occasions. They were long, lanky, lean men, fearless, and undaunted by the buffetings of nature and dangers of Moros and Pagan aborigines that had been present in years past. Most had married Filipino women. The center of activities for all these Americans and Europeans was the Davao Club, built by the early settlers.

The roster of the Davao Club included Americans, Canadians, British, German, Swiss, and White Russians. Social mixing with non-Americans and Europeans at the club was limited to business occasions. Sam and Pat, now American citizens, were members. Sam was secretary-treasurer of the club which allowed women, but not in the bar; women and couples had drinks in a pleasant seating area in another part of the club. Sam was also president of the international Rotary Club, which excluded women but included the men of the racial and culturally diverse business community. Japanese Consulate socials included a limited number of the top business and political leaders of Davao and their spouses, and the Franks were always included.

The Japanese formed the Davao Golf and Country Club in 1939 and opened its membership to Americans and Europeans. Seven of the directors were Japanese; three were American—Pat Frank, Dick Bownass, and Sam Fraser. The club desired a more heterogeneous membership, and Pat Frank considered himself the first "token."

Davao was a frequent stop for naval vessels. Gen and Pat were invited out to dine with the fleet as guest of some officers they met socially at the Davao Club. The affair was quite elaborate—lots of braid, starched whites, and all spoken in very solemn French. Before they sat down, the captain read something from a book—in French of course—while all the officers stood behind their chairs. It was a regulation of the French navy that the captain read the section of the Articles of War about mutiny to his officers before the midday meal. Gen, however, thought he was saying grace, bowed her head, and made the sign of the cross when he had finished to the great amusement of the officers. The captain raised his glass to her and said something like, "You are right, Madame; the Navy is also a religion."[3]

§

Gen and Fran described life in Davao as "carefree." For the Americans it was like living in a small town in the United States. Social life revolved around what people planned for themselves. In the homes they occupied in Davao, the two families lived a gracious life. Fran and Sam were first in their rental on Escario Street for a year, and then they moved to a larger home on Magallanes. Finally, they moved into their dream house on the North Road. A Japanese architect designed the home which overlooked the Davao Gulf. Gen and Pat moved from Manila directly into their home which had been designed by an Egyptian architect. Both residences were typical of successful business class Spanish and American homes in the Philippines.

Most people, when they went abroad to live, enjoyed socializing with others like themselves. The Americans visited back and forth, dropping in on each other for a drink before dinner, sipping tea in little groups, and heading to the beach for picnics, swims and rare, eye-appealing shells. There was a library at the Davao Club to which both Old Timers and newer residents contributed. After 1937 the club added a bowling alley on the lower floor and tennis courts. It became customary for the men to go straight from the office to the club. Sometimes someone would call in for chow at the Chinese Restaurant. On Sunday evenings, the American community gathered at the club for a buffet supper prepared in turn by the women. Traditions had grown up—the Fourth of July baseball game and a Thanksgiving Eve dinner party for which turkey and trimmings were ordered weeks ahead of time from Manila. There was the annual Christmas party with a tree ordered from the States, and on New Year's Eve, a masquerade party followed the next day with an eggnog party. At an earlier time in Davao, Old Timers used their pistols on the bells of the next-door church, plinking out some sort of tune that only they claimed to recognize.

Both Gen and Fran spent the 1930s focused on motherhood and planning trips back to the States. Most of Fran's letters from the mid-1930s contained plans and wishful thoughts of a visit back home. This was finally realized in 1936. She knew her lifestyle had become different. She later asked her mother, "Was I terribly clumsy about the house? I tried to overcome all my careless habits. How I wish you could be here with me and acquire the same habits I have." Fran's visit to the States coincided with continuing Japanese advances in China, Germany's entrance to the Rhineland, Italy's conquest of Ethiopia, and General Francisco Franco's leading his Fascist rebel troops against Republican Spain. Gen managed to make the trip home in 1937. Bringing her sister Catsy with her when she returned to the Philippines, she described their stop in Yokohama, Japan. "Japan is certainly a hustle and bustle these days due to the war (in China)," she observed. "Japan is for the Japanese and they intend to keep it that way. Every building has a flag flying from it and there are soldiers wherever one goes. Japan is opening all the mail, which leaves the country," she wrote. "In Japan, you just can't buy anything that is not Japanese-made. Anything American has an enormous duty on it. Japan is for the Japanese and they intend to keep it that way," but she did not speculate about what that might mean for Americans in the nearby Philippines.[4]

What Gen had witnessed was a Japan plainly intoxicated by its military victories in China. The occupation of the Shanghai and Nanking areas was complete. In early December 1937, Japanese planes sank the United States gunboat *Panay* and two Standard Oil ships in the Yangtze River twenty-five miles from Nanking. The incident killed five Americans, and Japan claimed the episode was an accident.

§

Every year the Davao Fair and Agricultural Exposition opened two days before Christmas. Sam's responsibility was lighting the entire grounds, including program areas, tents and booths. The two-week annual fair required a lot of electricity as Filipinos, Moros, and non-Christian tribes came into town from the outlying province. Another boom time for power company sales was the first day of November—Decoration Day at the cemeteries. Many families built permanent pavilions over their ancestors' tombs; others erected temporary canvas and nipa awnings over the grave plots. However, all strung thousands of strings of lights that lit the Davao night for ten days of weeding and cleaning graves, superb eating, singing, folk dancing, and recalling stories about the dead.

They were pleasant years for the Franks, as the easygoing life of the tropics rolled smoothly along under bright sunshiny days, coconut palms, dense vegetation, and brilliant, vary-colored flowers. Native men and women wore leather sandals, *shannalas*. Women dressed in garb of every description from homemade versions to styles straight from *Vogue*, to the colorful *sarongs* of the people bathing at the wayside water faucets. Nipa shacks, built from bamboo with ties of hemp and not a single iron nail or fastener, congregated into *barrio* communities from which arose a conglomeration of aromas ranging from that of dried fish and fragrant fruits to the bouquet of tropical flowers.

However, Davao also had its tropical dangers. Within months of her arrival, Fran contracted her first case of dengue fever, a serious disease of the tropics that comes in several sub-types, all maintained in a virus-mosquito-human cycle. Her symptoms included fever, with severe headache, and brutal muscle and joint pain that that gave the disease the name "break-bone fever" or "bone-crusher disease." The dengue rash, a red plague, spread to cover most of her body. Her demoralizing fever lasted seven days, the trailing end of which included an additional peak fever before abating, and weeks of recuperation from which she thought she would never recover. Both women repeatedly contracted malaria, fortunately a less virile form than was the most common around Mindanao. Moreover, Davao, like the rest of the Philippines, was subject to intensive earthquakes though it was not in the typhoon corridor.

Davao like much of Mindanao had a substantial population of Mohammedan Moros. The Muslims lived in their own nearby villages outside Davao where Gen and Fran often visited the markets. However, one day Gen, Fran, and some friends drove by car to the Lake Lanao region far from Davao and visited the Moro market. The Moros around Lanao were noted for their skills, and the women enjoyed examining the interesting hand-woven cloths of startling colors, and belts with fine metalwork. Both Gen and Fran experienced an uneasy feeling when they realized that crowds of Moros were gathering around them and staring in an unfriendly manner. "They were dark and strong-looking and had a way of staring at us with a wooden expression which was rather alarming," Gen wrote. Following that field trip, the two confined themselves to visiting the Moro *barrios* nearer Davao but remained more comfortable with the cosmopolitan and friendly mix of Visayans, Bocolanos, Tagaolgs, Zamboanganyans, Cebuances, Japanese, Americans, British, Egyptians, Italians, and Arabians in the market centers of Davao. [5]

§

As virgin jungle around Davao was cleared for new plantations and brought into cultivation, Davao Light & Power's electric service reached out. Sam's distribution plan envisioned that until the new area became fully developed and settled, small, high-speed diesel electric units would serve the embryo community. These units were easily transported and could be moved to a new territory until the larger transmission lines from the main system in Davao had reached the developing area.

Another unique innovation Sam brought to Davao was the use of reinforced concrete poles, the first in the Philippines. In Manila, chemically preserved timber poles protected against tropical funguses and wood rot. But due to high inter-island freight rates, Sam found the use of reinforced concrete poles to be more economical. He designed the poles with the idea of casting a few standard sizes to meet all the company's transmission requirements. By manufacturing locally, Sam added a small industry to Davao's largely agricultural economic base.

Diesel fuel for the plant came by Standard Oil Company from British North Borneo. Oil tankers made regular trips to Davao and discharged their cargo into large supply tanks near the shore. Sam had the fuel pumped to a company tank farm at a higher elevation, and gravity flow brought the diesel into the generators at predictable rates.

Davao was developing as a highly agricultural area with only small industries in the city. This type of development accounted for a heavy peak demand for electricity during the early evening hours when power was needed to light homes and streets. During daylight hours, with low electric demand, the extra generating capacity of the plant went toward supplying the city's ice plant. In Jolo and Cotabato, P.H. owned the ice plants, too. In Davao, however, a Japanese company owned the ice plant and purchased its electrical needs from Sam's DL&P.

It was also during this time that P.H. purchased the municipal electric franchise in Cotabato, a day's drive east of Davao. Sam had responsibility for bringing his father's new Cotabato Light & Power to a fifty-year legislative franchise, which was accomplished in two years.

Pat's Mindanao Sales and Services prospered under his management. The iron mines at Surigao were mining and sending ore to Japan at the rate of nearly 2,000,000 tons a year in pre-war times, and Pat supplied the trucks and company automobiles. He also supplied vehicles to the gold mines opening in the hills around Davao. Prosperous and politically involved Filipinos and Japanese owned most of the private automobiles. Pat, too, increased automobile sales by financing purchases while also earning interest on the notes. Typically, he carried a half-million dollars in customer financing at nine percent interest.

Pat also grew the service department, installing fine machine tools and overseeing the training of his Filipino machinists. Soon he was bringing in large repair and tooling jobs for Davao Gold Mines, heavy machinery work from the docks, and anything else that came through the doors.

Both Frank companies enjoyed the goodwill and respect of their employees and the Davao community. Pat and Sam each worked closely with the Filipino mayor, city officials, the Japanese Consul General, and Japanese plantation interests to keep in step with Davao's progress. The top Japanese executives and consulate staff were educated in some of America's finest universities and spoke fluent English, which in those years was the language of business and commerce in the Philippines. As children, the Frank brothers had also picked up from Okio the rudiments of Japanese, which helped them communicate with Japanese workers and shop keepers.

§

Davao Light and Power Company and Mindanao Sales and Service Company, while separately incorporated by P.H., jointly owned a five-acre compound in the city. In the rear of the compound were employee cottages. There was also a large house with single men living upstairs and clubrooms downstairs. In the clubrooms, natives from the same provinces who understood one another's dialects and common cultural interests could congregate and rest after a hard day.

Sam and Pat also offered training for their employees. For the power company, the Filipinos developed into excellent linemen and technical maintenance personnel. For Pat's Mindanao Sales and Services, they grew into superior automobile and truck mechanics as well as fine tool and die makers and fabricators. All the company managers were Filipinos as were the accountants, sales, and clerical personnel. Sam found that Moros could not be used on high voltage line work except where new, isolated construction was in progress. They were excellent pole climbers but had a complete indifference to death and danger, a cultural trait characteristic of their Mohammedan ancestors. They insisted on working around line equipment without protection, weaving in and around hot wires with catlike precision until it became necessary to remove them from this type of work altogether and place them in other positions.

The greatest sources of line outages around Davao were not lightning storms or wind. They were fruit bats, enormous creatures with wingspreads of up to forty inches, which at night became screeching demons. During the fruit ripening seasons, these flying mammals would dart in and out of the trees along transmission lines. Invariably the creatures would make contact with the transmission lines. Fried fruit bats and resultant short circuits were frequent. Sam finally had to solve the problem by buying up and chopping down the disturbing fruit trees. From then on electrically roasted bats were out of season.

The Frank family's Davao Light & Power Company, and Mindanao Sales and Services, Davao, circa 1939. *(family photograph)*

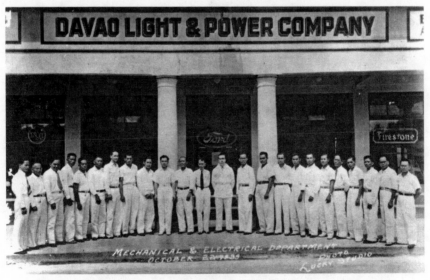

Davao Light & Power Company's Mechanical and Electrical Department, circa 1939. *(Courtesy of Emory University MARBL, Frank Family Papers)*

Sam Frank, Davao, August 1940. *(family photograph)*

Fran Frank, Davao, 1938. *(family photograph)*

Sam and Fran Frank's company home was designed by a Japanese architect, Davao, 1939. *(family photograph)*

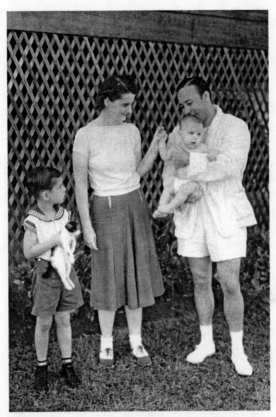

Gen and Pat Frank with children Dennis (left) and Mike (right),
Davao, 1938. *(family photograph)*

Part 6
The War Years
1941 to 1945

*"Today I don't know if you are alive or dead
and perhaps until this war is over"*

Frances Russell Frank, December 7, 1941

CHAPTER 22

"Don't worry about the Japanese trouble"

Frances Russell Frank, March 3, 1932

By 1935 there were two distinct events on the minds of the Franks. The first was Philippine independence. The Philippine Autonomy Act, also known as The Jones Act, had passed in 1916. This legislation called for the withdrawal of American sovereignty over the Philippines "as soon as a stable government can be established therein." The Jones Act was superseded by the Tydings-McDuffie Act in 1934. The law's promise of absolute independence of the islands on July 4, 1946, had P.H., his sons, and their wives talking about whether to stay in the Philippines or sell out and make their way in the United States. "You sort of set your time clocks to work something out before 1946," Sam recalled.[1]

For the next ten years, according to the Philippine Autonomy Act, the Philippines would operate as a commonwealth even as it remained a United States territory. Monetary matters would remain under the jurisdiction of the United States as would Philippine defense and foreign affairs. All other internal matters would gradually be placed in the hands of the Filipinos. "I think all Americans in the Philippines had misgivings of what was going to happen when the Philippines got its independence," said Sam. "They just didn't have confidence in the Filipinos to govern themselves and maintain a good disciplined government." There was also concern on the part of the Franks that Japanese influence was growing in the islands, especially in Davao where

Davao Light and Power Company and Mindanao Sales and Services were the flagships of P.H. Frank's businesses. The power company in particular would be subject to government regulatory changes and even nationalization under amendments to the Tydings-McDuffie Act. In addition, what Japan might not take by war, as in China, it might take by the oriental means of doing business—bribes, promise money, favors. "You could see the Japanese had developed quite a lot of influence among top Filipino politicians and government leaders," Sam remembered.[2]

The second event was a possible war with Japan. "We followed what Japan was doing in China and Manchuria," Sam recollected. "We knew Japan was very ambitious. I wouldn't say that we knew that a war was coming back two or three years before the war actually came, but we realized that it could possibly come."[3]

Sam addressed both currents of concern in a letter to Fran's mother in late October 1939. He was convinced that Japan "cannot accomplish anything in this direction." He saw an ambitious Japan with a strong navy and large army, but her army was busy in China, and her navy was occupied with keeping captured Chinese ports closed from foreign business and war supplies. In the orient, the combined forces of the United States, Britain, and France would make a notable obstacle to Japan. The American Navy was also formidable, and Sam believed that the fleet in Honolulu could join the fleet in Manila at any time. He noted that six additional submarines had just arrived from the States and that the Philippine Army had been training a force of 100,000 under supervision of the United States Army. As for the Army Air Force, he counted "fourteen of the latest type twin engine bombers which flew out from the U.S. More planes and fliers are coming out." Then there was the British Navy at Singapore and "a large army was being raised in India which can be used against the Japanese." Sam's correspondence resonated with strategic analysis. "If Japan starts any trouble here she will be bombed from the air and blockaded. She will then be unable to get fuel for her ships and planes or food for her people and if her navy ventures out in search of fuel for her ships in Borneo or the Dutch Indies she will require so many navy war ships for the venture that her own shores will be left defenseless." Summing up the analysis with a picture of Japan surrounded by American allies and "afraid to start anything," he concludes, "I have dismissed the idea of any attack on the Philippines by Japan and feel we are completely safe on that score."[4]

Then there was the business side of staying in the Philippines. Gen, Fran, and their husbands had been planning a trip home to St. Louis, departing Manila the end of October 1939 aboard the *Sorholt*. They were looking forward to Christmas in America. It would be Fran's and Gen's second trip home since their Philippine arrival and Sam's and Pat's first trip to the States during the same period. For the cold weather, Fran was making pajamas for the boys. Gen was making a red knitted snowsuit for their youngest son, Pat, Jr. "We are practically ready to sail!!" wrote Fran.[5]

The trip did not happen, "postponed for the present and I hope not for long," Sam wrote to Fran's mother. "The reason is certain laws, government policies recently started which affect our business, and which make it impossible to leave as planned. Fran doesn't want to go ahead without some assurance of when I will follow."[6] The cause for the delay was serious business. P.H. wrote Sam:

> For some time we have known that the Philippine Government has been trying to take over all public utilities. We assumed, of course, she would do it slowly and start with poorer and backward companies to build them up. This does not seem to be the case. Taking the present European war as an excuse for a 'National Emergency,' President Quezon has just been empowered to take over and operate any public utility. We are supposed to be 'compensated' but his idea of compensation will be practically the same as confiscation. They have also passed other laws, which will empower the government to take over public utilities less drastically but practically on their own terms. We do not expect any protection in this respect from the U.S. High Commissioner as that office or the U.S. has never done anything to help Americans here, except in the case of General Leonard Wood. What Sayre, the new U.S.H.C., will do we don't know. The fact remains, however, that we must get ready for any

eventuality and take the best steps possible a jump ahead of the other fellow. We may decide to sell out our entire interests before they are taken away from us at the government's own price. Alternatively, we may sell that part most likely to be taken first. At any rate, we have to all be on the job and watch every move and possibility. We will know in a few months the route the government will take, and until then our plans for a vacation will just have to stay on ice. Our plans have been to sell out more or less before independence in 1946 and go back to the States. We could all live very comfortably then. The government may force us to sell out earlier than we expected.[7]

The canceled trip to the United States also meant that Russell Frank was born ten months later at the Mission Hospital in Davao and his cousin Pat, Jr., a month after that in Baguio. Daily the Franks listened to the war news from Europe—the entry of German troops in Paris, the aerial blitz over London. And in late September, Japan joined the Axis pact forming a tripartite military alliance with Germany and Italy. Three days later the Japanese advanced into French Indochina.

§

During the 1930's, the United States government had been somewhat concerned about Japanese aggression in Asia, but that main concern centered on China. In 1939 the State Department asked American citizens living in China to relocate temporarily to the Philippines until hostilities in China ended. By the end of the following year, the State Department refused to allow Americans to land anywhere in China. The U.S. High Commissioner in the Philippines Francis Sayre assured Americans that there was no reason for anxiety or excitement, "Manila is one of the safest places in the Far East." But the Franks knew there was going to be trouble with Japan. They just didn't know when. "We're up against a tough problem of when to send Fran and the boys home," Sam wrote his mother-in-law Bessie. It was not a matter of "if" but "when," and Fran began making inquiries of her mother in late October 1940 as to the availability of her deceased grandparents' farmhouse in Tucker, Arkansas as a possible home until they could establish themselves back in the States or in the event she had to come before Sam. Fran had fond memories of vacations to the farm and staying at the Tucker home built in 1905, the "Big House" as the family called it. Bessie wrote back that the farm home could be fixed up and made available.[8]

On November 30, 1940, Fran wrote to her mother that P.H. Frank was keeping an eye on ship departures from Manila and clarified the difficulty of the trip by writing, "You can appreciate the complications (of) such a trip and can realize how I would hate to leave Sam and break up our home for such an indefinite time. Should it be the wisest thing to do, however, then I will have to think of the children and not of myself." She mentioned nothing specific about the Japanese though clearly, when she referred to thinking of the children, she was thinking of their safety, by keeping them out of a war zone. Yet in a letter to her sister in January 1941, Fran admitted she had still not made a definite decision. Available berths on ships headed to the States were "not the best and that too has held us back, as well as the seemingly quiet spell the Japanese have been enjoying. Sam and I simply hate to break up our family unless we have to, and naturally, that makes it harder to decide. So, thus far we have made no definite plans."[9]

In a follow-up letter to her mother, Fran expressed optimism that developments in the European war and the strengthening of the U.S. navy and army air force in the Philippines would forestall a Japanese attack. "But whatever happens," she wrote, "as long as our fleet is in the Pacific, Japan will do nothing to us, and that is all that concerns our immediate safety." Breaking up the family was an absolute last resort.[10]

The fence straddling of both young Frank families came to an abrupt halt when an old fraternity brother of Sam and Pat flew to Davao from Manila. His name was George Perkins who in 1927 had convinced the brothers to transfer from Texas to Washington University. After graduating from Washington, George had been an Army Air Force dentist and had also flown for the air force in the Philippines. He had mustered out to become a commercial pilot in the islands where he flew for the gold mines. The drumbeat of war with Japan took him back into the service as a major. He knew the Mindanao area well and led flights of bombers from Nicholas Field on Luzon down to Davao.

George stayed with Sam and Fran at their house, and was usually accompanied by the senior officer from the flight. It was on one such flight that Perkins had a reunion with Sam, Fran, Pat, and Gen. The group visited long into the night. Perkins told them that the Army was sending all the dependents home and that even non-combat types like him were issued a complete set of combat fatigues, helmet, and side arm. He told the two families and their guests, "When we get the signal, at a moment's notice, I have to be at a certain place at a certain time." Sam and Pat stated that splitting up their families was still a last resort. Perkins abruptly sat forward, bolt upright, his right fist coming down on the chair arm and shouted, "You better get your families out of here! Get them out of here!"[11]

CHAPTER 23

"Frances Children Leaving End March
Proceed Tucker"

Western Union Radio Telegram, February 26, 1941

That very evening, February 26, 1941, with a time sent of 11:22, a Western Union Telegram went out from Davao by Radio Telegram to Fran's mother who was visiting her daughter Jeannie in Hutchinson, Kansas, "FRANCES CHILDREN LEAVING END MARCH PROCEED WITH TUCKER LOVE TO ALL—SAM." In Manila P.H. began a daily haunting of the shipping offices to try to get the women and children on a ship.

There was no time to waste. Packing commenced; the last of a series of anti-rabies shots were administered to the children's dog, Big Boy, and a home was found for the ducks and canary. Magno, the Franks' gardener, was assigned the care of Dickie-Dickie, Sam, Jr.'s pony, bought from a circus and good only for riding in circles. All articles of value Sam did not need for living alone were stored away. Sam prepared a detailed list of his life insurance policies, bank accounts, and investments. Two weeks later Fran and Gen, accompanied by their husbands, left with their six sons for Manila. P.H. was working there to arrange transportation to the States, all the while receiving reassurances from the American High Commissioner that there was no need to leave the Philippines.

P.H.'s frequenting the shipping offices day after day finally paid off. A Norwegian freighter, the *Fern Glen*, was to arrive in Manila on March 19, and set sail again on the 23rd for another Philippine port to retrieve a cargo of sugar, then proceed directly to Los Angeles. As to arrival in Los Angeles, Sam could only advise Fran's mother in the United States that shipping agents in Los Angeles would know when the ship was due just after it left the Philippines. Unlike passenger ships, cargo vessels were often unpredictable, and the *Fern Glen* did not sail on March 23. P.H. and his sons hung around the shipping offices pushing to get a sailing date and filling their time by taking young Sam and Dennis to the Polo matches. In Manila, Sam and Fran had some friends with a boy Sam, Jr.'s age who invited him to go up to Baguio with them. Unfortunately, he could not because of the uncertainty of the *Fern Glenn's* sailing date. Sam, Jr. was eight years old and even though feeling apprehension, he said, "Going to the States was mostly just a big adventure for me." As if a premonition, he continued, "We had a really big earthquake in Manila while we were waiting. I remember us all standing in the doorway of the house on Taft Avenue and all the sparks flying from the power lines...I never really knew why we were leaving the Philippines. I was told we were going to visit Grandma Bess (Fran's mother) in the States and that Dad would be along to visit with us at a later time." The *Fern Glen* left port on April 1, 1941, after some minor adjustments to the ship to accommodate the baby crib being shared by the two young toddlers. Getting the crib through the stateroom door finally required that the crib legs be sawed off. [1]

Gen recalled the freighter's slipping its moorings, "Whenever I hear that haunting song, "The Last Time I Saw Paris," I always think of Manila, for the last time I saw Manila 'her heart was young and gay'...a beautiful cosmopolitan city, a tropical Paris, was Manila in April '41 when I had my final glimpse of her as my ship sailed slowly out of Manila Bay just as the sun set over the staunch and rocky fortress, Corregidor."[2]

That night Sam wrote Fran from his father's Taft Avenue home, "You will be on the high seas right now and I'm ready to leave for Davao. I miss you all very much and find myself worried to death over all the extra care and hardships you will run into with all the youngsters. I'm anxious to hear about your trip across in detail. The 'detail' can come regular mail, as it would cost too much by Clipper. Just let me know the high spots by air." His letter ends, "After you left

I had lunch, siesta, a nice golf game, drink with Chuck, and dinner at the University Club, games and dancing."[3]

In hindsight, it is easy to say that breaking up the families was the most logical decision. War, as Margaret Mitchell tells us in *Gone with the Wind*, is men's business, so it made a certain kind of sense that the men should be left behind to deal with the Japanese, should they attack.

§

The *Fern Glenn* was a Norwegian ship, and Norway was at war with Nazi Germany. To avoid German submarines the captain plotted a circuitous, zigzagging route across the Pacific. The ship was on the water twenty-two days, maintaining radio silence, and out-of-touch with a single port. There were twelve passengers on board with the six boys and their mothers making eight of them. There were many days of rough waters, and almost everybody got sick early on. The captain maintained blackout conditions, and all portholes were curtained. Sam, Jr. and Dennis thought the drill was like war games and lifted the curtain one night. The captain confined the boys to their cabin for three days, their mothers joining the captain and crew in reading the riot act to them. The voyage ended at San Pedro, California, where the captain and crew sought and received asylum in the United States. [4]

Even as Gen and Fran were on the Pacific, Pat wrote to Gen and shared his view that the non-aggression treaty between Russia and Japan in mid-April was a harbinger of war. Without the threat from Russia, Japan could become bolder. His guess was "that war between the United States and Japan will be either this year or next." Pat continued that the destruction of ships by German submarines was also having its effect on the Philippines "where the British have been using every ship they can spare in the Atlantic." Sam wrote Fran that even if Japan did attack, "The U.S. will simply destroy anything they can lay a bomb on."[5]

If business were to continue as usual, Pat had to count on dependable shipping to bring in the automobiles and parts for Mindanao Sales and Services. But this did not happen. Few ships were docking in Davao. Thus, Pat was getting low on merchandise, hemp was backing up from the shipping wharfs into the fields, and consumer goods were becoming scarce—all of which resulted in inflated prices. Not only Pat but also others in Davao were equally concerned with events. Peg Tong, wife of the medical missionary in charge of the Davao Mission Hospital and mother of three young children, wrote to Fran in June 1941, "We Tongs are still sitting on the edge of our chairs wondering what the next broadcast will bring. The latest report is that the *Pierce* is taken over by the government to be used as a merchantman, and the passengers who are booked for the June sailing will have to find other means of transportation." Davao families counted on the *Pierce* for their transport and connection to Manila from which there was no other way out of the Philippines. Sam wrote on July 18 that General MacArthur had been put in command of a combined force of United States and Philippine troops and "that planes, equipment, and men have been pouring into Manila steadily." As Sam saw it, the United States had "something to fight with now and Mr. Jap had better watch his step."[6]

At the same time Sam noted in his letters, "The Japanese here have been doing lots of buying and importing which is a sign that they expect normal conditions for some time to come, for which I am pleased." However, the brothers were being cautious, "I'm going to send you all the extra cash I have, so put as much away as possible. If things get bad that may be all we'll have for awhile, so be careful with it." When Davao Light and Power declared a ten-percent dividend from accrued profits, he had his father immediately wire his and Fran's earnings plus a bonus directly from Manila to Crocker National Bank in San Francisco, payable to Fran. This was done even before she had landed in the States. Ten days later Sam wrote, "I got a little jittery last week and that I'd better get money across to you before any control is placed limiting amounts that can be sent at any one time," and dispatched other cash by Postal Money Order to Tucker. In addition, he worried about his family, "...let me know how this 'evacuation' is working out." Pat was doing the same, "I am economizing in every way possible that I know how, and sending you all the money I can to buy Postal Savings Bonds with. I want you to do the best you can, Sug...because there may come a time real soon we shall need every cent we can get our hands on." In mid-June Sam wrote, "Just remember that world conditions are greatly upset and our source of income is in the Philippines, not the U.S.A.. We might be in this war ourselves almost anytime, and anything could happen to me and to our business out here."[7]

Fran and Gen arrived in Los Angeles April 27, 1941, the day the Greek army capitulated to Germany. Halfway through Fran and Gen's voyage, Moscow had signed a non-aggression treaty with Tokyo, allowing Russia to transfer its troops from Siberia to guard against the Reich. U.S. military chiefs began meetings with Dutch and British counterparts, making plans for the transfer of Japanese troops from the Russian border, which threatened Cambodia and Thailand.

§

The two mothers were tired and frazzled after their twenty-six days on the Pacific Ocean with their six young sons. Gen struggled on to St. Louis with her three boys and took a duplex apartment up the street from her parents. When Sam sent his family to the States it looked like Tucker, Arkansas, would be the right place. Fran's grandfather John Tucker, a Confederate soldier with Nathan Bedford Forest's cavalry, had gone west following the Civil War and had carved out his own cotton plantation in the rich, fertile Arkansas River delta. He grew cotton and erected a cotton gin; when the Cotton States Railroad came through, it named the station "Tucker" after John himself. Tucker grew into a tiny settlement of tenant farmers, and included John Tucker's store. Fran's mother Bessie, who was born at Tucker, met her daughter and grandsons at the station and helped settle them into the "Big House."

The evacuation of the mothers and their children was not meant to be permanent, but rather was a rushed response to what was felt to be a developing crisis. Meanwhile, in the Philippines matters were moving rapidly. Gen and Fran would soon face going from some of the best years of their lives to some of the worst. On June 30, Germany launched a massive attack on Russia.

§

Aboard the *Don Isidos*, P.H. arrived in Davao to discuss the sale of Cotabato Light and Power Company (C.L.P.) with his sons. He was to meet with Don Paco Suche and Don Ramon Aboitiz about sale of the power company and ice plant. In the company car, a Lincoln Zephyr, Sam drove his father to Cotabato and checked into the New Midway Hotel ("midway" between Davao and Zamboanga). A week later, Sam was writing Fran, "Flash! I have just received a telegram from Dad to proceed to Manila by *Don Isidos* with papers, so they may have reached some agreement" on the sale of Cotabato Light and Power Company.[8]

On July 1, 1941, Sam wrote dramatically, "You can draw a big 'X' across the C.L.P page. Dad went up to Baguio to rest after the deal, and I haven't received any further particulars on it." Sam telegraphed $3,000 to Fran, proceeds from the sale of his personal C.L.P. shares, saying, "Please be good to it. It's capital." Pat wrote Gen that Aboitiz was also interested in purchasing Davao Light and Power Company, "but (P.H.) decided to hold on and take a chance on what will happen out here." On July 26, President Roosevelt nationalized the Filipino army under command of General Douglas MacArthur.[9]

On July 28, Sam wrote, "the war situation is very odd. When Germany invaded Russia, and especially when she started to bog down, there was a clear expression of joy from the Japanese here. They were sure relations between Japan and the U.S. would improve...but the new cabinet is stepping on Uncle Sam's toes by moving into Indo China. Japanese and Chinese assets have been frozen in the Philippines, and until regulations are out to explain how they can do business, they can't draw money out of the banks to pay their electric bills. We are only accepting payments from them in cash." Continuing his assessment, "It was announced over the radio this morning that General McArthur has been put in command of the combined U.S. Army, Philippine Scouts, Constabulary, and Philippine Army, a combined force of 80,000 men to start with. Planes, equipment, and men have been pouring into Manila steadily. And we have something to fight with now, and Mr. Jap had better watch his step...I feel that the U.S. means business now and another incident will start the fireworks... just cross your fingers and sit tight and hope for the best." Assuredly he tells Fran that he does not see himself in the line of fire. "I'll be busy here keeping the town lit up, refrigerators and radios running, and motors turning, and won't have much time to worry."[10]

There were large Japanese businesses in Davao and twenty-thousand Japanese civilians. "I would say that 95% of the Japanese here do not want to see trouble with the U.S.A.," Sam stated. However, he recognized that the attitudes of Japanese businessmen in Davao might not reflect Japanese political reality, "They not only have too much to lose, but they are off where they can get a good perspective of Japanese policy and the opinions of other nations and people." As for relations with the top Japanese in Davao, his opinion was, "We get along fine with them and have done a lot of kidding back and forth during the present crisis, especially at the golf course, where we see a lot of the leading Japs." As to the possibility of the Philippine government using the emergency as an excuse to nationalize utilities, Sam wrote, "They (the Philippine government) have so many other things to do that they will be only too glad to leave well enough alone, and I don't expect any interference as long as we keep the plant running, and will certainly do that."[11]

§

Nevertheless, in Manila P.H. was worried about the Philippine government issuing emergency decrees, freezing bank deposits, and the possibility of war. After selling Cotabato Light and Power, he deposited $60,000 with the Crocker National Bank in San Francisco, and $100,000 at the Mellon Bank in New York, "...just for precaution. It has made him feel much easier," Sam wrote. P.H. also approached Aboitiz about also selling his Davao Light and Power Company, "This of course all 'Q.T.' altho the rumor is well circulated."[12]

On August 23, 1941, Aboitiz, Suche, and P.H. met in Davao to discuss a possible sale of Davao Light and Power. P.H. was undecided as to what to do. He believed there was a tremendous business opportunity in Davao—a large growing city, and the possibility of business several times its present volume. He had developed a company that had a foothold in one of the most important economic regions of the Philippines. Still he saw uncertainty in the political situation and the possibility of war to the degree that he was transferring assets to the United States, as were his sons.

Sam's feeling was that there was no better opportunity than in Davao. He could not see twenty years into the future with certainty, but he dreamed "of our children carrying on our business and investments." There was uncertainty after Philippine independence, and war was looming yet he wrote, "This uncertainty has always been the rule out here, and large profits are the rewards for those who have been willing to gamble on the future, and it has turned out to be safe for over 40 years so far." Sam saw his father as vacillating, "He cannot seem to decide what he would do after selling out. He can't remain idle...Dad has always been a solitary figure. There are so few people he considers friends, and I believe our children and we have been his greatest thrill in years and the first outlet for love that he certainly has plenty of."

Another big part of the equation was Annie who was unsure of where she fit in the plans being made with her husband's sons. Sam shared that P.H. and Annie had been having bitter quarrels, "Dad has said things he found himself surprised to have said what he did...What will come of it I don't know, but Dad likes to go thru with things he has started, and he will stand a lot for the sake of harmony."[13]

P.H. and his sons also talked about what Sam and Pat would do in case of a decision to sell out. He anticipated that the boys would have to stay on for six months to a year until they could train the men who would replace them. If they wished, they could probably keep their jobs with the new owners as long as they wanted, as such positions were not easy to fill.

P.H. anticipated that the sale would probably bring two for one for all Frank shares, as they had the controlling stock. Sam would receive about $14,000 for his shares. P.H. would get $300,000 for his interests. He was indefinite about the division of his own share with his sons, indicating that if each of the boys went his own way and returned to the United States, he would let Pat and Sam have $50,000 each. P.H. would keep $200,000. Thinking toward his estate, P.H. anticipated Annie receiving $100,000, to which she would be entitled under Philippine law, and Sam and Pat would each receive an additional $50,000.

Sam shared all this and more with Fran, "I would be interested in locating in a town of 20 to 30,000 with good schools and probably a college or university, buy a small suburban farm which could be developed for investment and on which we could eventually build and live." The dream he shared with her was going into business in the town, "I could go into real estate, automobile dealership, merchandising electrical supplies and appliances, or even a drug store. In the mean time, our money would have to be invested safely for some returns." He asked Fran, "Now what do you think of all this? Am I planning right, or do you want to return to the Philippines indefinitely? If you do, you'd better let me know pretty quick so I can ask Dad to hold on." The day after Sam sent his letter by Clipper, Secretary of State Cordell Hull warned Japan to leave the Pacific open to United States shipping. In retrospect, with all that was going on in the world, "hold on" did not seem a reasonable prospect.[14]

While all these business and family decisions were being discussed, air raid and black out practices were beginning in Davao. Sam wrote, "The people have taken a keen interest in all this and believe me the blackouts have really been black, including the small shacks back from the roads. And if any lights have been left on, the Wardens come right in and put them out." The American aircraft carrier *Langley* put in at Malalog Bay, and "Davao was full of Navy. Of course you must know what sailors have on their minds soon as they get ashore from a long cruise—well these boys were no exception." [15]

Sam wrote to Fran on October 21, "This is one of those beautiful mornings we get on the hill when it is almost crisp. Everything is green from recent rains, and the sun is just refreshingly warm...I've been writing Dad regarding his deal with Aboitiz and believe me an awful feeling was running thru me to urge him to hold on. This sort of morning makes you want to live here all the time. I didn't let it get me down, and have been urging him to sell out. As it stands now, he has made his proposition in writing, the deal to take place between December 15 and January 1, and both parties can change their minds and back out. There is nothing binding so far." [16]

Sam's pessimism about war was growing, yet he continued to express optimism about island defenses, "The situation out here doesn't look good and may lead to war...Philippine mobilization is not yet complete, but it is being done properly from the ground up and will be a strong capable force. They are building a camp at Malaybalay, near Dansalan, centrally located for Mindanao for 20,000 men. We all feel quite safe out here now with our navy and air force especially."

In Tokyo on November 3, 1941, warning of a possible secret attack on U.S. positions, U.S. Ambassador Joseph Crew cabled Washington. On November 17, Japanese Ambassador Nomura began talks with the State Department and Sam wrote the same day, "We're supposed to know this week whether Japan backs down or we go to war. I'm not the least bit worried. We're well prepared with plenty of Flying Fortresses, large new submarines, and a good number of troops. If Japan wants to commit suicide, we may have to help her do it. The islands are well patrolled daily from the air and sea, and there can be no surprise attacks." [17]

On November 19, Fran began a letter that never made it to the Philippines, "The Far Eastern situation is graver every moment. How will you and Dad feel when bombs begin exploding—and there is the point I get to a thousand times a day, and there is where I begin to shudder." Her reply to Sam's earlier question about whether she wanted to stay in the Philippines, "Yes darling—let's do live in the P.I. It is much cheaper and seemingly healthier!!"[18]

Gen was equally worried, "I am all for the plans if Dad can carry them through in face of this war which it looks now will start any minute." Responding with equal enthusiasm to Pat's suggestion of staying in the Philippines she wrote, "Disregarding the war—by that I mean if the war were out of the question—I think the plan to stay in Davao is really fine... From a practical view point I can see that Dad's offer is truly wonderful...Between the two lives (U.S. or the Philippines) I prefer the life we live in the Philippines...Personally I think to have the children in the Islands would be beneficial rather than harmful...Mike, Denny, and Paddy could have a really grand time there."[19]

The drumbeat of war was getting louder. P.H. reported to his sons that fifty tanks landed at the pier in Manila "which went clattering down Dewey Boulevard to their stations." On November 25, Sam posted an airmail letter by Pan American Clipper reporting that the army had taken over the three inter-island steamers serving Davao—the *Mayan, Don Esteban* and the *Don Isidos.* "Army airbases are under construction in Zamboanga, Malabang, Delmonte and other places in Mindanao, larger than any in Manila...we have had 5 or 6 air raid black out practices in Davao." No further letters arrived in Tucker from the Philippines. The next day a Japanese carrier force left its base in the home islands—moving east. Another smaller Japanese carrier force moved south toward Palau off the coast of Davao.[20]

§

Premier Hideki Tojo rejected a U.S. proposal for a Pacific settlement as "fantastic" and "unrealistic," the same day Fran wrote from Tucker, "I am terribly worried about you and Dad and all, with the situation growing more and more tense each hour. Try to take every precaution for yourself should anything happen out there. I am afraid I will not be so brave and noble!! Don't worry about the children. I am trying to take good care of them. Darling—come to us when you can and as soon as you can. Life is not the same without you." On December 6, 1941, President Roosevelt issued a personal appeal to Emperor Hirohito to use his influence to avoid war.[21]

Pat Frank tuning 12 o'clock news from Treasure Island, Davao, circa 1941. *(family photograph)*

Fran (left) and Gen (Right) Frank with sons (left to right) Russell, Pat, Sam Jr., Mike, Dennis, Pat Jr. before evacuation to the United States seven months before Pearl Harbor. *(family photograph)*

Ramon Aboitz and P.H. Frank in Davao November 1941 where they
concluded terms for the sale of Davao Light & Power Company to
Aboitz. Sale to take place January 1, 1942, which could not take place
as war with Japan started December 7, 1941. *(family photograph)*

CHAPTER 24

"Those were Japanese planes bombing our airfield."

Samuel Boone Frank, Remembrances, 1990

The Japanese task force lay off Palau eighty miles directly east of Davao in an ocean covering the Mindanao Trench. The trench, regarded at that time as the deepest point of the earth, was the result of a collision of tectonic plates where the Philippine Sea Plate shifted itself under the Eurasian Plate and melted the hot mantle of earth, a part of the Pacific Rim of Fire.

Below the Emperor's ships, the ocean floor reached 34,440 feet. At 0400 and 0445, two hours after the initial Japanese bombing runs on Pearl Harbor, December 7, 1941, the Japanese aircraft carrier *Ryujo* launched thirteen dive-bombers with nine fighters as escorts. Destroyers *Hayashio, Kuroshio, Natsushin, and Oyashio* broke from the formation to make a high speed run toward Davao to attack any American vessels escaping the *Pyujo's* planes.

§

It was Sunday in Davao, and west of the International Date Line the calendar announced December 8, 1941. Lying in his bed, listening to the news broadcast from the immense radio tower above Treasure Island off the coast of San Francisco, Sam heard loud explosions. The time was 0600. The sounds were Japanese bombs, the first to fall on the Philippines. The airfield at Baguio was hit at 0930 and Manila at 1135.

Then the radio broke out with the news that Pearl Harbor was under attack by Japanese planes.

For about a week before the war started, there had been a general uneasiness around Davao. Pat and Sam's Japanese friends had expressed their concern. There were also rumors about someone seeing submarine signal fires on the hilltops above the gulf. Much of this information was speculation and rumor; but people, including Japanese golfing friends at the Japanese chartered Davao Golf & Country Club, were expressing their nervousness,.

Davao held important strategic objectives for the Japanese high command. First, the occupation of Davao was designed to secure airbases which would impede a possible southward withdrawal of American forces in the Philippines. Second, the Japanese needed Davao as a staging point for the invasion of the South West Pacific—Java, New Guinea and Australia. Third, acquisition of the vital resources of the Southern Philippines like hemp, gold, and iron would not only cut off the flow of materials to the United States but also place Japan in a favorable economic position for prosecution of an extended war. Fourth, Japan wished to extend protection to her corporations and twenty thousand civilians around Davao. Finally, the Japanese also knew that quinine plants on Mindanao supplied America with its drugs for fighting off yellow fever and malaria.

Among Philippine exports essential to war was Manila hemp or abaca. No other fiber in the world could match the qualities of hemp in the manufacturing of long lasting, high quality rope. The U.S. Navy and Merchant Marine required thousands of tons of rope. But the Army, especially in the time of war, used more rope on a tonnage basis than the Navy. Millions of feet of tent rope were required. Additionally, engineers required millions of feet of steel cable, and nearly all the steel cable had a core of Manila hemp. The Davao plantations produced sixty percent of the total Manila hemp production in the Philippines. Approximately ninety percent of the Davao hemp was exported and accounted for eighty percent of the total exports from the Philippines. After July 1941, when the U.S. Export Control Act limiting critical war material shipments to Japan went into effect in the Philippines, shipment of hemp to Japan was no longer allowed. The stock of hemp in Davao, together with protection of the Japanese hemp plantations, became critical for Japan's war aims. Thus, the small city of Davao with its outlying hemp plantations, port on the Mindanao Gulf, and shipping facilities became a target for early Japanese landings in the Philippines.

Listening to the news about Pearl Harbor, Sam picked up the phone and called his good friend Louis Rodaeche a successful Spanish businessman and civic leader, whose children were the ages of Sam and Fran's children. Yes, he was also listening to the news, and moments later, there were loud explosions. Running outside, Sam could see the Japanese sun emblazoned on the wings and sides of the cream-colored planes as they flew over his hillside home to drop their bombs on the Sasa Airfield. He called his brother Pat, and the two headed for the power plant and transportation companies.

The bombing damaged Sasa's main runway, the hangar, one airplane owned by the Elizalde Company, and killed a Filipino mechanic. In the harbor, the *U.S.S William B. Preston*, a seaplane tender, escaped serious damage and sailed south. Two of her PBY's, aircraft designed for takeoff and landing on water, were destroyed on the water—a third was on patrol. One Filipino was seriously injured. Elva Burchfield, a friend of the Franks, counted seventeen planes but was never sure how many there actually were. She recalled in her memoirs many years later, "They did their evil deed and climbed into the blue so fast it gave no one an opportunity to sense what had happened, to say nothing of counting them." About noon, four Japanese planes returned and machine-gunned the Standard Oil Company petroleum installations near the airfield and the power company fuel oil tanks near Sam's home. Rumors flew back and forth all day—about Japanese landings all along the coast guided by signal fires lit by Japanese nationals, and about uprising of armed Japanese civilians. Radio news brought reports of Japanese attacks on Clark Field in Manila. Filipinos were all about town, briskly moving from place to place and stopping for excited conversations. Japanese disappeared from sight. Radios were turned up in Chinese market stalls. Anger, fear, and apprehension were thick in the air; for some, nerves were shattered and there were the beginnings of panic. Others reacted with retribution to the bombings and rumors that Japanese civilians were assisting the landing. Some Filipinos sought revenge on the large Japanese civilian community in Davao, often with manic ferocity.

§

In Manila, P.H. learned by Radio Telegram from his sons that Japanese bombs had fallen on Davao. Later in the morning, he and Annie heard planes swooping over Manila and the thuds of bombs falling on the U.S. naval station at Cavite, leaving smoke, dust, and flame in the clear sky. Starting at a quarter past noon, from their manicured lawn, the two witnessed black smoke billowing over Clark Field far in the distance across the bay. Waves of bombers and fighters made by the Mitsubishi Corporation obliterated thirty-six American P-40 fighters and seventeen B-17 Flying Fortress bombers, all parked wing tip to wing tip. At Iba Field, sixteen more fighters exploded in fire and oily smoke. The dawn raid at Davao and later morning raid at Baguio had given notice that the Japanese did not intend to bypass the Philippines, yet the American bombers and fighters at Clark and Iba Fields were not moved. Even today, the failure remains an unresolved question.

Over the next two days, P.H. watched as Japanese war planes darkened the sky over Manila, repeatedly attacking Cavite and Nicholas Field. Historians have called Pearl Harbor the greatest military disaster in American history; the same is equally applicable to the Philippines.

§

For security and for protection from marauding bands of Filipinos and Chinese, Major Firriol, a Filipino who commanded the Constabulary in Davao, began an immediate internment of the large Japanese population in and around Davao. By the next day, 12,000 Japanese children, women, and men entered internment in school and government buildings; by December 20, 16,000 were interned. Others left the city seeking shelter and safety at the outlying Japanese plantations. The top Japanese nationals were taken to Davao Penal Colony, twenty-five miles from the city. The job of guarding and feeding so many people was a momentous task, but the Japanese nationals needed protection against lawless, revenging Filipinos and Chinese. More and more infuriated, many Filipinos and Chinese took to the streets with bolos and clubs, beating and chopping to death Japanese civilians. Hysteria had taken root. There were reports of Constabulary guards going berserk and shooting civilian internees.

Americans kept in touch with each other and passed along information, true or not. The good news especially made the rounds. Likewise, the Filipinos knew what was going on because they had Westinghouse radios sold by Pat and powered by Sam's electricity.

§

In Tucker, Arkansas, Bessie Tucker Russell, Fran's mother, was up early on December 7. Fran was asleep. Later in the day, the Arkansas sky would be clear and blue, but at six o'clock, the dawn was still gray, the early December sun not yet showing tendrils of orange. The local gleaners were already working the fields, gathering for their personal sale the last sprinkling of cotton left from the fall picking season. There had not been a hard freeze yet that would turn the stubble to mush, but it was cold enough for a frost that crunched under her black shoes.

Bess stopped at the chicken coop, twisted the double hung latch, let herself in, twisted the inside latch back, and watched the hens display their eggs for gathering. She filled her basket and left. The hens made a ruckus. The rooster strutted and pecked in the side yard, for it was not yet light enough for him to wake up the world.

Sunday lunch was always fried chicken, biscuits and white gravy, iced tea supersaturated with sugar, turnip greens, and mashed potatoes. Bess stopped at the house garden to pick the tender turnip greens and dig for the smallest white turnip bulbs, which she would dice and boil with the smothered greens and chunks of bacon side.

The day before, Bess had caught two chickens, quick-handedly snapped their necks, and finished the job with a hatchet over a dark stained piece of upright chestnut log. After quickly dunking the carcasses in boiling water, she and Fran plucked, fire-singed, and removed any remaining feathers. This morning they would cut up the pieces, dust them in paper bags filled with flour and a sprinkling of salt, and fry them crisp in bacon fat.

Cleaning up in the kitchen after lunch, the two women were listening to the radio and heard the news at the same time. President Roosevelt was speaking from the White House. Together with young Sam, Jr., they listened to the announcement that Japan had attacked the

United States at Pearl Harbor on the island of Oahu in Hawaii. Sam, Jr. remembers asking, "How is Daddy?" There were no answers, only assurances that his Daddy would be fine. Sam, Jr. does not remember how many phone calls were received or made that day, but he does remember that his mother talked to every member of the family.[1]

On Monday, Fran listened to the radio all day and long into the evening. It was 10 o'clock at night. Her mother moved around upstairs. Her sons, except for Sammy, slept; he was writing his father. The radio crackled and faded in and out as was often the case in those days, especially in remote places like Tucker, Arkansas. Fran listened intently for news from the Philippines. The Sunday that had begun just cold enough for frost under a blue sky had turned bitter. Then she heard barely distinguishable place names: Manila, Baguio and Davao. Whatever the announcer said disappeared in the impaired radio waves.

On Tuesday, an ice storm moved across Arkansas. After still another day of sitting close to the radio and reading the *St. Louis Post Dispatch* delivered daily by the Cotton Belt Railroad, Fran watched out the second story window of her bedroom. The cotton stubble in the fields accepted layer upon layer of ice, freezing the dead cells that would be mush at thaw, and finally flatten in the fields. She took pen and wrote her husband.

December 9, 1941
Tucker, Arkansas

Dearest Sam,

> *Today I don't know if you are alive or dead and perhaps until this war is over, I will be constantly feeling this way. But, I shall keep my chin up and always hope for your safety. I shall try to keep a sanity about me and look forward to the day when we will be reunited.*
> *Sam dear, I don't know what I am writing!! Please forgive me. I am so jittery and upset that I hardly know what I am thinking.*
> *We got the news of Japan's attack as soon as the White House released it. I was completely stunned although I realized it was inevitable that this would be the final outcome. We listened to the radio all afternoon and last*

night got the news that Davao and Baguio had been attacked. Later last night we got a direct report from Manila and the announcer said that Davao had been temporarily taken over by the Japanese population. We have not had a confirmation on that, and undoubtedly it was a false report. You can imagine my feelings.

Everyone is concerned about your safety. Jeannie called as soon as she got the word and Uncle Sid also called. All the relatives have been in to see us and all wish you the best.

I have just heard an account from Manila of their first bombing. It was horrible to hear and my thoughts are all confused and muddled up. Don Bell was broadcasting and he was uncertain as to what was hit—he named Nichols Field and Fort McKinley. I am instantly aware of Jim (Brokenshire) *and George* (Perkins).

Oh, darling—what will be the outcome—I pray for faith to keep me going and I pray for your courage and safety as well as our friends and our Dad and Annie. It is all too horrible to realize and to believe. Can you stand it for long, yes—you can and will and we will win out in the end. Our lives will be changed, but I am confident for the best and so at least we can look back and have no regrets.

My dearest love,

Frances[2]

RETURNED TO SENDER
SERVICE SUSPENDED

In St. Louis, Gen wrote her own undeliverable letter.

John Russell Frank, Ph.D.

December 9, 1941
St. Louis, Missouri

Dearest Pat—

How are you darling? I am so terribly worried about and your safety and the safety of Dad and Annie and Sam and all of our friends. It is horrible and I wonder just how very bad things are with you.

I love you, dear Pat. I feel like I never really made you understand how very, very dear you are to me and how much I love you. If only we can come out of this bad dream whole and well, I shall not ask any more.

The news broke on Sunday at 1:30 P.M. and I have done nothing but stick by the radio ever since. Sunday evening at 10 P.M., I heard Davao and Baguio had been bombed. My heart leaped into my throat and I don't believe I have ever felt so thoroughly terrified. I sent you a cable immediately but knew it was doubtful you'd ever get it. Last nite I sent one to Dad in Manila but he also will probably not get it. This is to be a long war they say—surely there will be some way of hearing from you. The clipper is out, so I shall take a chance and send this by boat.

I carry Denny's little radio with me from one room to another. Bert Siler and Dan Bell come in on the N.B.C every once in a while. But they don't seem to know anything about Davao. I suppose Davao can't connect with Manila.

I am so worried because they say the Japs in Davao are armed and will cause an uprising. Perhaps they have done so already. Darling Pat, in case theirs trouble remember to keep out of the way. Please, please be careful. What's the good of anything if you get hurt? The japs are really treacherous and it gives me chills to think of them uprising and causing trouble in Davao where you are so few in number and so far from help.

I can't express in words dear Pat how terribly anxious for your safety and well being I feel. Whatever the

194

circumstances are I'd rather be with you than here. The lonesomeness of waiting for news is truly heart breaking. Of course, I'm glad we saved our 3 boys this experience and got them out in time.

All I can do is wait and pray for the best. Denny is so concerned about all this and his eyes fill with tears when we speak of you. We all love you, dear, and I dread to think of the years that may elapse before we will be together again.

I am worried for fear Dad was in Davao also and Annie alone in Manila which would have been horrible for her.

President Roosevelt will make a speech at 9 o'clock to-nite and Catsy is here to listen with me. All our friends have called to express their sympathy for my anxiety and to express their hopes for your welfare.

Darling tell Rose, Madelyn, Helen, Evelyn, Enos, Elissa and all our other good friends that I have thought of them and hope they are all well and safe.

All my love dearest Pat. If only you could be with me, and if only I could do something to help you. All I can do is tell you I shall look out for the children and wait patiently and bravely until I can have some news.

Your loving wife,
Sug (Gen)[3]

RETURNED TO SENDER
SERVICE SUSPENDED

CHAPTER 25

"SITUATION NORMAL
ALL WELL
LOVE SAM"

Samuel Boone Frank
Western Union Radio Cablegram
December 12, 1941

In Davao the population made a mad run on the stores, which were practically emptied of food and clothing. After that, all business in town just shut down. It was too late to escape by boat. To Sam and Pat, heading for the jungles offered no sane alternative. Instead, the first thing the brothers did on Monday morning was to go to the Davao branch of Philippine National Bank and transfer money to Fran and Gen. The men also withdrew money from their accounts. Pat cashed a check for his entire balance. Sam had a balance of 1,158 pesos from which he withdrew 100 pesos. The bank president called them that afternoon reporting all transfers stopped. He explained the banks would not cable funds because they could not stand behind the money if the Japanese took over. On December 10, Sam returned to cash a 40 peso check. By the fifteenth, the bank was limiting withdrawals; Sam took out the maximum he could draw, 200 pesos. "I should have followed my brother's advice to get it all when I could. I didn't and it was a mistake."[1]

§

Commanded by Americans Lt. Sharp and Corporal M.E. May, Philippine army troops arrived in Davao the day after Pearl Harbor. The following day, in Army trucks, Col. Roger B. Hilsman arrived with three more Filipino army companies, all from Malaybalay. On December 12, another battalion of Filipino army troops, under Maj. A.T. Wilson, arrived from Bohol. There were an additional couple of hundred trainees, boys in their teens, bringing Col. Hilsman's strength to 1,200 men. Hilsman, Sharp, and Wilson moved in with Pat where Pat briefed the three of them on the situation. Hilsman held the rank but was new to Mindanao and had never been to Davao.

Hilsman called a meeting of the Americans at the Davao Club. During the past two years, the number of Americans in the District of Davao had shrunk to fewer than forty, and most of those were on the plantations. There were fewer than twenty Americans in Davao City. At the Davao Club, Hilsman gave orders. The roundup of twenty thousand Japanese civilians and the organization of their internment were huge undertakings. These men, women and children needed protection from angry, roaming Filipinos and needed guarding as well. Hilsman had to collect food and get it into central locations. He also had to commandeer the gas and oil in town and establish a defense. He told the dozen Americans at the Davao Club that he would need their help; then he appointed the men as his aids.

Sam's responsibility was maintaining electrical power and keeping the telephone and wireless communications going. Hilsman was going to put in telephone lines to his defense sectors. Pat opened his service shops at Mindanao Sales and Services where his machinists worked on the firing pins of old WW I single-shot Springfield rifles issued to the Constabulary. The heaviest gunnery included two WWI water-cooled, .30 caliber machine guns.

Hilsman asked Clayton Jones, the local Standard Oil Company man, to be in charge of keeping track of all the gasoline there was in Davao. Dave Burchfield was to be in charge of transportation. Hilsman put others in charge of accumulating canned goods and rice and storing them in a safe place. He put several in charge of working with the town's established civilian authority to help intern the Japanese civilians. Col. Hilsman also appointed Pat and Bob Zack his *aide de camps*. Both had a military bearing, Pat having graduated from San Antonio Academy and Zack from West Texas Military Academy where he was student commanding officer of the ROTC. They stayed close to the Colonel and played a key role advising him on who was who among the civil government and vetting his visitors. Pat explained, "Everyone wanted to see Hilsman, from the mayor to the police chief. Zack and I screened people at the headquarters. I could explain who people were. I also knew the politics; by being present in the room, I kept them from pulling the wool over Hilsman's eyes." Chuckling, Sam recalled the scene, "We all drove around in cars with American flags on the fenders. We were all playing soldier." Blackouts occurred nightly.[2]

Bob Crytser, branch manager of Luzon Stevedoring Company, called together all two hundred of his Filipino dockworkers and told them they would be responsible for law and order at the water front piers and *bodegas* until the army arrived in sufficient numbers to take responsibility. Also under the direction of Col. Hilsman, Bob took over the nearby port of Santa Anna. Crytser and his stevedores immediately seized all Japanese launches, lighters, and other floating equipment in the Gulf of Davao. These vessels were then used to transport men and materials from the outlying plantations and to help build up a stock of food in the port. A boat patrol system was set up, and Crytser named his conscripted unit the "Davao Marine Coast Guard." It was to send advance warning of any Japanese vessels rounding St. Augustine Point and entering Davao Gulf. However, since none of the "Coast Guard" vessels was equipped with radios that idea failed.[3]

Walter Tong and Frank Cary kept the Davao Mission Hospital operating, busily worked to convert a nearby hotel into an emergency hospital, and tried to alleviate the suffering of Japanese civilians now going into the hastily arranged concentration camps. He and the Mission Hospital staff began making rounds of the camps with medicines and bandages, and arranged for keeping the Japanese hospital open with its doctors and nurses on duty. Walter, from New Haven, Connecticut, was thirty-six years old. His wife Peg and three children, Eloise, Curt and Annarae were in Baguio when war broke out. Walter had no way of knowing if his wife and children were alive or dead.

By order of Hilsman, everyone was to observe the strictest blackout. A member of the Constabulary stood under every streetlight. "We could not even strike a match that a whistle was not blown at us," recalled Sam, "The only light allowed in houses was a flashlight with a piece of blue paper or cloth tied over it." Ships ceased to come into the harbor and no one considered doing business. Sam recalled that with a show of money, a little *baksheesh*, Chinese groceries could be entered through the back door, but their stocks were low. You merely took what remained. "Butchers finally gave up trying to procure and sell meat. Hundreds of wild stories were woven out of people's imaginations. There was promiscuous shooting and uncertainty as to the Japanese next move. After a few days, the Filipino army began rationing food. It began to look as if we were deserted and left on our own." Many Filipino families left for the hills, and a dog wagon went around picking up abandoned pets and putting them out of their misery. [4]

In Davao things steadily grew worse, and the men still with families felt they were no longer safe in Davao because of the danger from more and more desperate Filipinos. Also, for years, the Americans had closely followed the news of Japanese atrocities in China and the Rape of Nanking. Therefore, the men, concerned about the safety of their wives and children, organized a caravan led by Gary Lane to evacuate them to a safer place. Most felt they should motor to Malaybalay, thirty-nine miles west of Davao where the headquarters of American and Filipino troops on Mindanao was located. There it was felt the women and children would be the safest. Those in agreement formed their caravan and departed Davao.

One man, Dave Burchfield, disagreed. He felt that the caravan would be driving right into the hands of the Japanese who would obviously attack Malaybalay. As a result, Enos Emory, manager of a large American owned plantation thirty-four miles north of Davao, offered his guest quarters to the remaining women and children. Included were Evelyn Burchfield and her son Jimmy (13), Glenda Crytser and son Steve (4 months), Helen Lane and son Johnny (4), and Alberta Stumbo and daughter Helen Louise (8). Enos also wanted to protect Italian friends George and Tamara Vigliada and Al Menigini—citizens of an Axis country and subject to internment by Hilsman—who also joined his caravan to Madaum overlooking the Davao Gulf. Many Filipino families moved out of Davao to homesteads in the interior.[5]

An American planter down the coast, John McGhee, was a veteran Major of artillery in WW I. Because of a wound in WW I, he had a silver plate in his head and easily became disoriented. Occasionally he would wander into Davao and get lost. He had memory problems and often required assistance to get him where he was rooming. He heard about the war, came into town, and reported to Col. Hilsman who said, "Get a decent shirt on and you can be my major."[6]

For the next twelve days, Hilsman, with the help of the American and European civilians and Davao civil authorities, interned increasing numbers of Japanese nationals, placing them under guard in public buildings and schools. The top Japanese managers, Consulate staff, and plantation and business owners were taken to the Davao Penal Colony about twenty-five miles from town where they had barracks and food which included fresh vegetables grown at the colony.

Sam worked with the telephone company and used their linemen, plus linemen from Davao Light and Power Company, to get telephone lines out to areas Hilsman had designated as defense perimeters, where he thought the Japanese would be landing. More and more food accumulated in strategic, guarded locations. Intermittent Japanese bombing of the airfield and waterfront continued.

Hilsman gave Sam orders coming directly from MacArthur's headquarters in Manila to prepare to blow up the electric plant. Davao Light & Power was his father's flagship enterprise, the key to the family's future. Sam was being ordered to destroy the generators; if he hesitated, it was only momentarily. He called Davao Gold Mines and spoke to Ludvig Sundeen, a forty-year old Minnesotan who had been in Davao for a year and a half. Sundeen immediately sent down his dynamite crew to drill the necessary holes and plant the explosives. Sam saw to it that the crew properly prepared for the destruction of the power plant's large generating engines. Others were responsible for placing dynamite at the ice plant and water works insuring their destruction when Hilsman was ready to give the order.

Sam and Pat were also able to send off radio cables, the last direct word Fran and Gen would have from their husbands for three and a half years. Sam's words were: "SITUATION NORMAL STOP ALL WELL STOP LOVE SAM STOP."[7]

§   §   §

December 13, 1941
Tucker, Arkansas

Dearest Sam,

   Just about an hour ago I got your cable. Maybe you think I wasn't happy to hear! Yesterday Gen called me after receiving a cable from Dad saying all was well.
   The boys and I danced a regular jig in the hall when I read them your cable. We have been very hopeful all along but I did get so upset at first. Now I am so certain that we will come out all right in the end, in Davao, Manila, and here. So thumbs up from now on. Perhaps that now the job has been started, it will be finished just that much sooner and joy on joy—we can be together again.

Lots of love,

Frances

RETURNED TO SENDER
SERVICE SUSPENDED

CHAPTER 26

"How helpless and forsaken we felt."
Evelyn Burchfield, unpublished manuscript, December 8, 1941

In the still, dark hours before the dawn of December 20, 1941, the Davao harbor filled with the Japanese invasion force of a cruiser, six destroyers, and fourteen troop transports holding a landing force made up of the Japanese 16th Army under the command of Major General Shizuo Sakaguchi. The fleet of twenty-one ships had staged off Palau Island, taken by Japan from Germany in 1914. The fleet had departed Palau for Davao on December 17, arriving there three days later. The command included Sakaguchi's own detachment made up of the 146th Infantry Regiment, 1st Battalion 56th Artillery Regiment, the 1st Company of the 56th Engineering Regiment; the Miura Detachment, which included the 1st Battalion, 33rd Infantry Regiment; two platoons of the 2nd Special Landing Force of the Kure Detachment; and the Japanese Navy's 2nd Airfield Construction Unit. The landing at Davao was parallel to the landing of Japanese forces on Luzon. The overall Japanese invasion plan called for the seizure of the small American-Filipino forces at Davao, including the airfield at Sasa, followed by landings at Cotabato, Zamboanga, and Jolo.

The thudding explosions of heavy shelling awakened Pat. It was still dark. Pat recalled, "Colonel Hilsman and I jumped in the car and drove to the waterfront. Shells were hitting the *bodegas* and starting fires in the warehouses." Through the smoke and flame, silhouetted by

202

moonlight, Pat could see the Japanese armada in the Gulf—a sinister, apocalyptic projection. The two men turned the automobile around and went back to a building in town that Hilsman was using as his headquarters. The population of Davao was racing to every kind of conveyance imaginable and leaving town. The roads were full of men, women, and children with their belongings piled high on cars that had not been requisitioned by Hilsman, bicycles, or overstuffed carts pulled by people, small ponies, and lumbering water buffalo. Horns blared, people shouted, children cried, and hundreds of dogs barked. To their barking was added the squealing of trussed pigs and the clucking chatter of crated chickens and ducks. Japanese planes soared overhead spitting fire, and a white cloud of macadam dust rose from the roads to mix with the oily smoke from the burning warehouses and wharfs. "A whole population was on the move," Pat said, "It was some sight. Suddenly it was 50,000 to 60,000 people leaving at once."[1]

The main Japanese attack included landings north and south of Davao City and spearheads toward the center of town. Sam awoke to the same detonations as Pat did and took off for the power plant where he waited for the miners to show up and set off the dynamite they had planted around the generators. While there, he decided to take the company's spare fuse link and hide it in case the demolition plan failed to work. Driving back to the house, he opened the septic tank, tossed the link in, and headed back to the plant. Japanese planes were strafing the roads, and he could hear thunderous, earth-quaking explosions north and south of Davao.

Facing the onslaught of the Japanese landing at Davao was Col. Hilsman who was commanding the Filipino Army's 2nd Battalion, 101st Infantry, and other local Filipino troops. The battalion, lacking unity and poorly trained, had arrived in Davao eleven days earlier and there had been insufficient time to correct these conditions before December 20. Hilsman had Bob Crytser and the forty men of Crytser's newly formed Davao Marine Coastguard deployed in shallow trenches on the beach next to the pier. Corporal Milton May mounted the battalion's second machine gun on the bed of a truck and positioned himself and his Filipino Army gun crew on the wharf.

Returning to the power company on the North Road, Sam diverted to the pier where he joined May and his Filipino Army crew. On the beach, Crytser and his men allowed the Japanese landing crafts to get within 200 yards of the wharf then opened fire with rifles and their machine gun. May opened up with his machine gun. Those Japanese soldiers not killed in the landing crafts turned around and headed back to their ships. The resistance brought on salvos of fire from the Japanese cruiser and destroyers. On the pier, the truck holding the machine gun exploded under the naval barrage killing every man except May. Sam watched as May, wounded and bloody, limped away from the carnage and disappeared toward the town. A more intense shelling of the waterfront by the Japanese followed. Within minutes, the entire port area was in flames, and the staccato fire of small arms fire reverberated on both sides of Davao. Crytser ordered his men to retreat to the hills to connect with Col. Hilsman. According to Major John McGhee in his memoir, *Rice and Salt*, "The battalion disintegrated against the Japanese," who rapidly secured the area around Davao.[2]

Sam and Corporal May fled the area. Sam went to Davao Power Company where Pat joined him. The dynamiters had assembled to blow up the engines and generators. Clayton Jones, the Standard Oil man in Davao, arrived to detonate the company oil tanks. Col. Hilsman's plan called for the men to wait there for final orders to blow up the machinery and oil tanks.

The dynamiters from the gold mine were anxious to get away. Nobody wanted to be in Davao when the Japanese came in. Sam finally called Hilsman's headquarters to find out when to ignite the dynamite. Walter Tong, the United Church of Christ medical missionary, answered the phone. When Sam asked about blowing up the plant, Walter told him the Colonel and his troops had retreated from Davao in autos, trucks and busses. There was nobody at the headquarters, and Walter was on the way to the Davao Mission Hospital to join in aid to the wounded. Tong said that orders had come from General MacArthur's headquarters remanding the order to destroy the utilities in Davao. Walter Tong also knew that destroying the utility would leave the Filipinos in a terrible situation with no electricity, drinking water, or ice. Sam immediately dismissed the dynamiters who fled in their truck.

In the frightful, confusing moments of indecision as to where to go, Sam, Pat, and Clayton moved into Pat's Mindanao Sales &

Services building next door to the power plant and in the corner of the downstairs display room pulled together large truck tires to form a barricade. Pat had a 1917 Enfield rifle, Sam a .45 caliber pistol and shotgun, and Jones a 1903 Springfield rifle.

About that time, a young Spanish boy who had been serving Hilsman as a messenger and dispatcher came by on his motor scooter. He confirmed that Hilsman and his forces had left town, that the Japanese were very close, and that the Americans were at the Davao Club. Sam, Pat, and Clayton hopped into a car and hightailed toward the club.

As the three men were making their way through the town, they witnessed the horror of Filipinos murdering Japanese nationals, hacking them to death with knives, hatchets, and bolos and beating others to death with baseball bats. A Constabulary guard went berserk opening up with a machine gun on Japanese civilians interned in a schoolyard. In the streets, other Filipinos in their frantic attempt to escape continued to clog the roads.

North of Davao City, in the hills overlooking the beach, the American wives and their children, sent from Davao days earlier, watched as the Japanese ships slipped through the water. Some with field glasses could see the Japanese landing craft invading Davao. "We could see smoke, and shelling went on unceasingly; all day long it continued," Evelyn Burchfield wrote. "Where were our men folk, were they lying dead somewhere? How helpless and forsaken we felt."[3]

---------------------------------- CHAPTER 27 ----------------------------------

"We surrendered at the club."

Samuel Boone Frank, Remembrances, 1990

The Americans and Europeans fled to the Davao Club and the Davao Mission Hospital. Thirteen men made it to the club—Bob Bennet, Alex Brown, Otto Bruderman, Dave Burchfield, Crame (a Filipino), Bob Crytser, Sam and Pat Frank, Clayton Jones, William Park, John Stumbo, Paul Trub, and Henry Umstad. The men knew they had to find a way to surrender. As they began thrashing out what to do, Alex Brown, the honorary British Consul in Davao, proposed a letter to the Japanese Consul General. Sam was the club secretary and wrote the surrender letter, the only such known document in existence, surrendering American civilians to a foreign power. Bob Crytser went out to the street, found the young son of a Japanese friend, and the boy took off on his motor scooter for the Japanese Consulate as the men opened the Club bar in the library.[1]

Philippines
December 20, 1941

The Honorable Consul of Japan
Davao

My dear Sir:

Please permit me to advise you that a number of American and European civilians have quietly gathered at the Davao Club. We hereby place ourselves subject to your orders and assure you of our peaceful intentions.

Yours faithfully,
Sam B. Frank
Secretary, Davao Club

The Americans squinted through the bamboo curtains as Japanese tanks and infantry pushed down the road, firing fusillades of bullets and cannon to their front and sides. Japanese were also walking in through the woods paralleling the road, shooting down everyone in front of them. Right behind these shock troops, Japanese in marching formation moved down the road into the town. The fighting was over and thousands of troops were now making their entry. Sam had left his shotgun at the Davao Power Company but still carried his revolver which he threw as far as he could into the undergrowth. Sam also opened the club safe, and removed the Edward C. Bolton pistol which he also hoisted toward the sky. Bolton had been a popular governor of the Davao District in the early days and was murdered by Tagacaolo natives. The club members had preserved his pistol at the clubhouse, the early planters taking it out for target practice.

After the first company of troops had filed by, a staff car approached on the road with an imperious looking Japanese officer standing in the rear seat. It was getting dark. The men had eaten most of the ham that was in the bar, and some of the fellows had drunk just about all the highballs they could handle. There was not time to wait for a response from Consul Mori.

The men debated about how to get the Japanese officer's attention. Undeterred by the lack of unanimity, Otto Bruderman, a Swiss national, grabbed a pool cue, took a white tablecloth, tied it to the end of the cue stick, stuck it out a window and waved. The officer immediately stopped, signaled to his troops, and forty Japanese soldiers surrounded the clubhouse. The officer entered the club library and, speaking clear English, expressed displeasure over his soldiers' finding Pat's Enfield rifle on the bowling alley floor. After a few tense moments the officer satisfied himself that the men were only civilians and confined all thirteen to the library. The officer posted guards, assigned an interpreter, left the club, and got back in his command car. The line of soldiers, some mechanized, some on horseback, kept moving. Sam and Pat were prisoners of war.

At Madaum, Enos Emery, manager of the International Harvester Plantation, loaded the wives and children into the plantation station wagon, drove down the road, and entered the jungles of the Agusan Valley, hoping that the husbands would find a way to join them. Undoubtedly, Fran, Gen and their six sons would have accompanied this group of their best friends had they not evacuated to the United States six months earlier.

§

Japanese civilians, previously interned by the Filipinos, flooded the streets welcoming their country's soldiers as they came into Davao. For some it was now their turn for revenge against the Filipinos. It was the Japanese civilians who now had bats, golf clubs, bolos, or anything they could grab. They were seeking revenge for the deaths of their children, wives, and husbands at the hands of Filipinos. Some came to the club where the Japanese army guards turned them back. Then the Japanese army officially sanctioned the slaughter by executing any Filipino pointed out by their nationals—a time for settling old slights or disagreements as well as revenge for murder.

It was dark now, and outside the club, Japanese soldiers were executing Filipinos accused of attacking or killing Japanese civilians as their Nipponese army came into Davao—all on the basis of fingers pointed by the mob. There were other executions—Filipino civil leaders, teachers, and business people. The American prisoners, three of whom took turns carefully squinting through the bamboo slits of the window curtains so as not to be seen, witnessed all these massacres. "The executions went on all night long," Sam recorded. "We could hear the shouting and knew they were bayoneting them. The whole atmosphere was killing, killing." For Sam that was the only time during his period of internment that he thought he might not make it, "We could hear the Japanese bayoneting Filipinos that they had captured and had reason to think had treated Japanese nationals badly. We could tell what it was and the Japanese interpreter explained it to us. They would get a little distance and run toward the Filipino, and shout aloud when he bayoneted the man. We could hear that all night long. It was touch-and-go that night. We didn't know if we would survive." Sam estimated that hundreds died outside the Davao Club.[2]

§ § §

In St. Louis, Gen listened to the radio, "I don't believe I have ever felt so thoroughly terrified before in all my life." P.H. Frank cabled from Manila that he and Annie were safe—then nothing. In Tucker, Fran wrote[3]

> *December 20, 1941*
> *Tucker, Arkansas*
>
> *Dearest Sam,*
>
> *Today at noon we got the report that Davao was being attacked and invaded by Japanese forces in great number. My only thought is of your welfare. My anxiety it too great to express and it is heartbreaking to sit and wait and wait. However my heartbreak is nothing compared to your hardships, trials, and horrors. I had so hoped and prayed you would be spared any real trouble. But this whole world is to suffer, each individual, and I know now that we can each expect the worst. None are to be spared. So we must take it on the chin. I know you will do that. I know that you will do the right thing always and I know that you will some day come to us, and we will be waiting. We will be better people, our boys will be better boys, for we will have all shared and suffered together and hardships make us stronger ...*
>
> *Good night, sweet dreams, and love.*
>
> *Frances*
>
> *RETURNED TO SENDER - SERVICE SUSPENDED*

CHAPTER 28

"We volunteered to go beyond the Japanese lines"

Samuel Boone Frank, Davao Internment Camp Diary

The men in the club slept little that night. There were two guards at the door to the library, and there was no electricity. The power plant had stopped, the engine men having fled the Japanese as they moved into Davao. There was a flickering candle burning on the bar. The noises of bloodlust lingered in the hot air trapped in the room. The two guards kept out the curious crowds and soldiers, but as the night wore on it became increasingly difficult for the guards to maintain the prisoners security. One Japanese soldier managed to push by the guards, walked in, looked around at the Americans, and headed for Dave Burchfield, who was sitting at the bar with his shirt open, chest and stomach exposed. There was a bayonet, sharpened to a razor edge, on the soldier's gun. Sam described the tense scene, "There was blood on the Jap's rifle and clothes. Outside you could hear the yelling and screams of the Filipinos as they were executed. He stood there in front of Dave with his bayonet pointed right at Dave's stomach—Dave didn't flinch. The soldier, after two or three minutes, finally pulled his gun away and walked out. I don't know why or what he had in mind, but that is what happened there." The guards relaxed their own fears and resumed their positions at the door.[1]

One American who figured Japanese property fair booty after war broke out had blown a safe at one of the Japanese hemp plantations.

He was captured and that night paraded onto the club tennis courts in view of the American prisoners, who, peeping through the slit of a bamboo blind covering the window, watched in horror as he was forced to kneel and was then run through with bayonets. The stench of perspiration and fear permeated the room.

Another incident occurred the night of December 20. Fran and Sam had frequented a Japanese bazaar for several years and had made friends with the owner and his two sons. One of the boys had grown up over the years knowing the Franks and other Americans in Davao. Sam said, "He came to the door of the library that night. The Japanese boy told the guards who we were, and I think that helped a lot to give those guards a reason for not letting the Jap soldiers who were on the loose that night, to get in." The young man slept the rest of the night on the floor, protecting them as best he might.[2]

Forty-eight hours later Japanese guards awaked Pat in the night, took him to a nearby house, and threw him into a room. Shortly thereafter, another soldier came in and, at the point of a bayonet, directed Pat into an adjoining room. "The room was dark except for a light that was shinning on me," Pat said. A Japanese officer began questioning if Pat was a military soldier. Over and over Pat responded that he was not. "Oh, oh, is that so, is that so?" the officer kept repeating, leaning forward on the table, inches from Pat's face. Finally, the officer placed a picture of Pat in front of him—a picture of him as a thirteen-year-old student at Mt. Tamalpais Military Academy in San Rafael, California. The officer also produced a pile of military gear found with the picture in Pat's home. The military gear was that of Colonel Hilsman and Major White whom Pat had billeted at his home before the Japanese arrival in Davao. As Hilsman and White retreated, they had left their equipment behind.[3]

The arrival of another Japanese officer, a former Stanford University student and familiar with Mt. Tamalpai, explained about American military academies, and Pat was allowed to return to the club. Sam was relieved, believing that his brother might have been executed; the brothers embraced as Pat walked in.

The men slept on the hard floor of the club library for the next twelve days. The guards strolled through from time to time, counted the men, looked around, and departed. The prisoners had received no food for two days when the guards brought in cans of sardines, squid, and bread. Finally, the Japanese made available canned goods, oatmeal, and rice, which before the invasion had been stored on the concrete slab beneath the club by one of Col. Hilsman's committees. At the request of the prisoners, the Japanese authorities allowed the club cook, Salvador, to come in to prepare meals.

The Japanese permitted the prisoners only thirty minutes outside the library in the morning and afternoon for toileting, exercise, and washing. One of the men whom the Japanese captured at the Davao Mission Hospital was Frank Cary, a missionary gifted in Japanese language and culture. The Japanese brought Cary to the club, and he became indispensable translating for the Japanese and Americans, thus easing communication burdens.

§

Before the Japanese invasion on December 20, Colonel Hilsman and the Filipino civil authorities had interned two hundred of the most important Japanese nationals at the Davao Penal Colony twenty-four miles north of Davao. By December 23, the Japanese Army's perimeter around Davao extended only twelve miles outside Davao. The Penal Colony was another twelve miles beyond the Japanese lines, and the Japanese command was concerned about the safety and welfare of these high-value citizens. Major General Shizuo Sakaguchi, the commanding officer of the Japanese forces in Davao, came to the club with Consul Mori, both concerned that if their army marched straight to the Penal Colony some of the Japanese civilians might be hurt or killed by the Filipino Constabulary guarding the internees. Mori wanted help figuring out how to release the Japanese and get them to safety. The phone lines were down in several places, having been cut by Hilsman's troops as they retreated from Davao. Mori explained to the assembled prisoners that there would be dire consequences to the American and European civilians at the club if anything happened to the top civilian Japanese at the Penal Colony.

Mori and the American prisoners huddled in the Club library. They knew the superintendent of the Penal Colony well, but his top employees and the guards were Filipinos. None in the group could be sure of the outcome—release or massacre of the Japanese civilians.

Mori left no doubt that the lives of the Americans depended on the outcome. In response to earlier Japanese atrocities and promiscuous cruelty as their army entered Davao, Filipinos were arming themselves, forming guerrilla bands under Hilsman's leadership, and resisting Japanese advances. The Americans finally came up with a plan. Their lives depended on its working.

The men concluded that if they could get to the place on the North Road where the telephone line was intact, they would be able to talk with Superintendent Rubin of the Penal Colony and arrange the provision for safety and release of the Japanese. Sam told Consul Mori they could get a telephone field set from the phone company, hook onto the end of the last cut in the line to the Penal Colony, and make contact with Rubin.

Under guard, Sam accompanied Mori to the telephone company and told the manager what he needed. The Filipino hesitated. Sam insisted that he knew the field set was there. Knowing that his life and the lives of his friends, both American and Japanese, depended on the plan working, Sam ordered the man to produce the set right then and there. "We have got to get those Japanese civilians out of there." Sam shouted, "I know you have a field set," and slamming his hand on the desk continued, "so bring it out!"[4]

Sam, Clayton Jones, John Stumbo, two Japanese officers, a Japanese interpreter, and two men from the telephone company climbed into two cars and drove toward the Penal Colony. After reaching the Japanese perimeter, one of the officers ordered the cars to stop. The Filipino linemen spliced the field telephone to the wire. Sam dialed the number; Superintendent Rubin came on the line. The two talked, all the while the Japanese interpreter translating Sam's end of the conversation. Sam asked Rubin to get Masumoto, the top Japanese civilian, on the line. Sam could not hear Masumoto's end of the conversation, but he listened attentively as the interpreter translated the Japanese officer's end of the conversation. The officer stopped his conversation with Masumoto several times to confer with Sam through the translator.

The arrangement worked out was for Sam and Clayton to drive toward the Penal Colony, meet the Japanese civilians, and bring them back to the perimeter. The Japanese officer kept a pistol on John Stumbo, the Superintendent of Schools in Davao, and told Sam and

Clayton through the interpreter that if they tried to escape Stumbo would be shot.

Carrying a large Japanese flag, Sam stood on the running board of the automobile while Clayton Jones drove. Both sides of the road were thick with banana and coconut trees. The men passed barrio after barrio with no Filipinos in sight. The roadside was littered with the debris of the hurried evacuation of Davao. Stray pigs rooted in the detritus beneath the nipa houses. Chickens scattered off the road. "Any good Filipino farmer who didn't like the Japanese could have taken a shot at somebody waving a Japanese flag and very understandably so." Sam leaned in the window and told Clayton to step on it.[5]

A station wagon driven by Superintendent Rubin with the three highest-ranking Japanese civilians inside—Matsumoto, Sugimoto, and Kumagai—met Sam and Clayton as they approached the Penal Colony. Sam and Clayton stopped just long enough to tell the superintendent to follow them and both cars sped back to the Japanese lines. This time Sam furled the Japanese flag and rode inside with Clayton at the wheel.

Back at the point where Stumbo was being held at gunpoint, the Japanese officer conferred with the leading Japanese civilians. The Japanese officer returned his pistol to its holster as he spoke to Sam, Clayton and Rubin, the interpreter translating, "Now, your lives will be spared."[6]

The next day was Christmas Eve, December 24, 1941. Consul Mori and the Japanese commander sent Christmas gifts to the internees at the club—six chickens, tobacco, and two bottles of whiskey.

Sam's diary entry on Christmas day, 1941, recorded, "No service or carols."[7]

CHAPTER 29

"Somehow I have made myself believe you are still alive"

Francis Russell Frank, December 28, 1941

Pockets of Japanese civilians guarded by Philippine Constabulary troops found themselves encircled and cut off as the Japanese perimeter around Davao enlarged. Just as at the Davao Penal Colony, the military and civil authorities needed someone to negotiate release of their nationals. On December 26, the Japanese sent Pat Frank, Billy Gohn, and Edward Christensen beyond the front lines on the Tigatto Road to secure more releases. The next day, Clayton Jones was ordered to drive once again to the Penal Colony and then to the Bincongan Ferry. In every case, the Americans were successful in securing releases, but it was dangerous, nerve-racking work.

A day or two later the new Japanese-appointed manager of Davao Light & Power and a Japanese military engineer took Sam to the power plant. The turbines were not operating. Sam knew exactly what the problem was. The main generator fuse had blown, and he had hidden the spare in his septic tank. Sam explained this to the new Japanese manager, the owner of the Davao Ice Plant, with whom Sam and Pat had enjoyed a solid business and personal relationship for many years.

Accompanied by two guards, the men drove to the house and opened the septic tank. Sam was ready to descend into the offal when the Japanese engineering officer stopped him and gave a command. One of the guards stripped and eased himself into the tank, fished out the fuse link, and set out across the manicured lawn and gardens to the water faucet. Sam quipped, "That soldier never flinched. I could have done it, expected to, but I was glad it wasn't me, and surprised I'll tell you."[1]

§

In Manila, P.H. and Annie felt little but anxiety during the Christmas season. Air raid sirens wailed day and night, low flying Japanese warplanes dominated the skies, and P.H. and Annie took shelter in his large concrete safe built into a cement slab on the ground floor. An unofficial American coordinating committee did what it could to maintain communication and provide support. On December 26, MacArthur declared Manila an open city and lifted the blackouts; American and Filipino troops began final withdrawal to Bataan and Corregidor, and the civilian coordinating committee now advised everyone to stay in their homes. Within three days, the city was deserted of a military presence except for demolition detachments destroying remaining military installations, stores of supplies, and gasoline and oil dumps to keep them from falling into enemy hands. The report of thousands of storage drums exploding, oil tanks blowing, and heavy detonations at the bridges thudded and reverberated as illumination from the conflagration danced its shadows across the Frank's gardens and home in a surreal dance of light, sound, and memory.

P.H. and Annie, leaving their lights on as warning against the looters who were now carrying off whatever they could in the port areas, made their way to a district meeting held by the civilian coordinating committee. Francis Sayer, Governor General of the Philippines, fled to Corregidor. P.H. along with thousands of American children, women, and men felt abandoned in a silent and foreboding Manila.

§ § §

Snow fell heavily outside the "Big House" in Tucker, Arkansas as Fran wrote:[2]

December 27, 1941
Tucker, Arkansas

Dearest

No word yet, continued bombing of Manila and not a word from Davao for two or three days. It seems like years. Gen called Tuesday and said she has no news from Davao. Economize. I know if Dad has not heard by now that he must also be as frantic as we are. All that we are concerned about is your safety. Darling, are you all right? Is Pat all right – God – if we could only get some word!!

All my love,

Frances

RETURNED TO SENDER - SERVICE SUSPENDED

Tucker, Arkansas
December 28, 1941

Sam dear,

Still no word. I wish I could hear some news—but now with Manila under severe bombardment, Dad's messages might be delayed. I don't even know how to mail this letter. I doubt very much if you will ever receive it; but still, there is a chance, so I will mail it.

Somehow I have made myself believe that you, Pat and Dad are still alive; I do not think any further than that; I dare not.

To read and listen to the news is heartbreaking. We read and listened to London, but only feared it might happen to the Philippines. Now, it is happening. Perhaps by this time next year the United States will be experiencing it. The outlook is dark and grave, but we can always hope for the best, and still do. There are times when I'm not so cheerful, and the thought of living without you for so long is almost unbearable. Just so it will not be forever, just so you are alive; then I can carry on.

I'm keeping clippings from the paper. You will be interested in reading them someday. Davao splashed all over the headlines!! And no one knew how to pronounce it!!

All my love,

Frances

RETURNED TO SENDER - SERVICE SUSPENDED

Tucker, Arkansas
December 28, 1941

Dearest Dad and Annie,

We are all more concerned over your safety than over the business. I realized what this means to you, but Dad, let's be grateful for all we have enjoyed these last ten years and look forward to a certain recovery of everything in a few years. I get courage thinking of you. Undoubtedly, you are one of the finest men I have known and I am proud to be your daughter-in-law. I firmly believe that Sam and Pat are well, and will continue to be so. They are strong and brave and are like their father.

I hope you and Annie will take all necessary precautions and that you will be spared. We all love you and pray for you.

Dearest love to you all.

Lovingly,

Frances

RETURN TO SENDER - SERVICE SUSPENDED

§   §   §

On January 3 Japanese forces entered a dark and chilly Manila and drove down Taft Avenue. P.H. could see soldiers dropped off in front of his house where they set up a machine gun and stationed three men. The sun, merely an orange orb, filtered through the haze and smoke. The next day P.H. had little recourse but to go with the Japanese soldiers who had come politely to his door, helped him onto a truck, and transported him to Vallamor Hall in the Conservatory of Music at the University of the Philippines on Taft Avenue, several blocks from his home. Annie, a Portuguese citizen, escaped internment. They had celebrated twenty-five years of marriage the same year that the war now separated them.

The sovereignty of the United States had disappeared. The Japanese flag flew over Malacanan Palace, home of former Spanish and American governor-generals and more recently the president of the Philippines, and other government buildings. The red sun on a white field also flew over the Intramuros, and other places so familiar to the Frank family—Elks Club, Army and Navy Club, and the Manila Hotel where Fran and Sam had dined and danced.

The next four days, imprisoned with over a thousand other Americans, P.H. slept on a tile floor with inadequate toilet facilities. There was no food except for that brought in by the prisoners. Slowly, guardedly, Annie and Filipino friends began to bring in food and other necessities, a loyalty demonstrated repeatedly throughout the war. On January 6 the Japanese transferred P.H. and the other Americans to Santo Tomas University, founded in 1611 by Spanish Dominican priests, where the Japanese military congregated the thousands of civilians captured around the city. The university which had once had a student body of six thousand students and employed three hundred teachers, sat on sixty acres surrounded by a twelve-foot high concrete and stone wall, interrupted by a run of iron fence. In the middle of the run were two enormous iron gates opening from Espana Boulevard onto the spacious grounds. Three prisoners ventured an early escape, were beaten to death with rolls of barbed wire, and their mangled bodies left as testimony.

§

In Davao, on January 3, 1942, the Japanese transferred the internees to the Rodaeche house on Tomas Claudio Street, which had been taken over by the army. The guards did not permit the prisoners to take the remaining stores of food at the club nor the club cook, Salvador, and this caused considerable grief among men used to housefuls of servants.

The men first turned their attention to cleaning and sanitizing the home. Japanese soldiers billeted in the house, one of the larger, finer Davao homes, had defecated in all the rooms, kitchen, and stairways. The infantrymen did not relish giving up their posh quarters and left their scent. There were piles of human excrement everywhere. The officer gave the Americans mops and disinfectant to kill the odor. "You clean, you clean," shouted the officer, demonstrating his mastery over the Americans in front of the Rodaeche's Filipino servants. For several weeks, the men slept on those floors.[3]

§

The organization of the internees had been simple at the beginning. Initially there had been thirteen at the Club, but within three days, the number was up to seventeen. The internees knew they had to do more about letting the Japanese leadership know about the seriousness of their plight and the fact that they had no food. It was clear that the Japanese had no plan for dealing with civilian prisoners, their housing, food, and health care. The men were accustomed to the organization of Davao Club of which Clayton Jones was president, Walter Tong vice-president, and Sam secretary. For the time being, the Japanese were keeping Walter at the Mission Hospital. To reorganize, the men held an election and Jones, Bob Crytser, and Sam formed the executive committee. The executive committee then met with Ogata, Consul Mori's secretary; the committee and Ogata became the contact with the Japanese military. Sam had been the club secretary so he continued to keep the minutes. Soon after, the Japanese authorities ordered him to keep a diary for reading and approval by Lt. Hosaka, who stamped his signet *chop* next to the daily entry.

During this initial period of internment, the prisoners were the responsibility of the *Shinsei*, or Military Government. The Japanese Imperial Consulate was permitted to provide provisions to the men.

Consul Mori, his wife, and several Japanese civilians provided food and essentials, and Mr. Ogata visited daily. At first, the supplies were limited. On January 6 Ogata brought six papayas, ten small towels, six cakes of soap, and one brush and comb. In the days that followed, Mrs. Mori brought mosquito nets, and Ogata delivered vegetables— Pechay, Camotes, and potatoes—and 21 assorted glasses, 2 steins, one strop razor without strop, 5 toothbrushes and 5 toothpastes, 3 dozen assorted dishes, 8 bars laundry soap, and some clothing for Bob Zach and Eugene Stevens recovered from their own homes. On January 9 Ogata delivered further supplies including 5 packages of tea, 3 small bags of table salt, 48 tins of sardines, 5 lbs. Purico lard, 10 pounds brown sugar, and the promise of beef and bananas the next day. Ogata also suggested that the men try to purchase food and supplies directly in the markets but could offer no guarantee that military authorities would permit this. Desperate to secure a steady source of nourishment, the men raised from among themselves 5 pesos for a trial purchase of vegetables, to which the military thankfully agreed. Filipino friends made the purchases in the markets and brought the food to the Rodaeche house.

That system worked for a few days until Ogata informed the internees that they were now under a new military group, the *Gunseibu*, Department of Military Administration, and conditions formally agreed upon verbally were suspended "pending further negotiations." However, Japanese civilians continued to the aid the internees. Ohmori, Hirata, and Takakus brought cigars, chewing gum, and biscuits and promised newspapers, cigarettes, and slippers. Supplies were brought by a Japanese civilian, Iwasa with International Harvester Company, a colleague and friend of Henry Umstad, one of the internees. On January 16, Iwasa brought 2 dozen bananas, 6 oranges, 2 pomelos, 2 large cans of fruit, and a box of cigars. On January 24, Ogata delivered old newspapers for toilet paper.[4]

Then suddenly the *Gunseibu* said that supplies would no longer be allowed from outside individuals. Nor would the internees be permitted to purchase food from the markets. However, the new directives carried little weight with the Filipino families and friends of the prisoners who continued to make deliveries. The Jerry Roscom family's gift of supplies was an example. The sixty-one year-old

Roscom, a planter in the islands for forty-two years and originally from Mexico, Missouri, was married to a Filipino who was free and living at home. Another Filipino family, unrelated to the prisoners, delivered eggs, sugar, corn, peanuts, squash, tobacco, chickens, and three sacks each of rice, flour, salt, and a welcome gift of 12 cans of Carnation milk. The prisoners' Japanese friends likewise paid little attention to the army's directives.

For twenty-eight days, the Japanese never searched the internees. Neither Japanese soldiers nor authorities took watches, rings or money from the internees at the club. The first search undertaken by the Japanese military was when soldiers searched the entire Rodaeche house and removed an electric lighter, a broken radio, valet razor, and encyclopedias of the Philippine Islands. The soldiers searched not a single prisoner.

The internees received little benefit in the way of food and supplies from the new Japanese group now taking responsibility for the internees. Lt. Hosaka, still in charge, advised the executive committee that a shortage of supplies was imminent and left them with one-half a sack of dried corn used to feed field animals. Over the next several months, thirteen of the top Japanese civilian business and civic leaders made regular visits to the internees bringing food and personal effects. These Japanese friends—Yamaka, Kumagai, Matsumoto, Ogata, Mori, Sugimoto, Katsuyama, Ohmori, Hidatsa, Takakua, Iwasa, and Idoh—interned at the Davao Penal Colony before December 20 owed their lives to Sam, Pat, and the other Americans who rescued them.

§

The Japanese guards set up an office in a building across the street from the Rodaeche home. Filipino employees, friends, and family came with baskets and cartons of food. Guards first made an inspection after which the internees made pickups. The number of internees increased each day as the Japanese Army rapidly expanded its control outward from Davao. By February 1 there were thirty-eight internees confined to the Rodaeche home.

Some of the internees were able to have clothing brought to them by family and friends. The homes of Sam and Pat had been thoroughly looted during the days following December 20, 1941. There were no clothes left in their homes, and purchasing clothes was out of the question because any cash was needed for food. Both brothers went into internment with only the clothes on their backs. Each wore short duck pants, cotton shirt, underwear, socks and a pair of shoes. They would wash, mend, and keep up those clothes for the next two years.

CHAPTER 30

"Lt. Hosaka advised that the internees would be used for labor."

Samuel Boone Frank, Interment Camp Diary, February 1, 1942

Eventually the Japanese captured the American wives and children who had fled to Malaybalay, returned them to Davao, and interned the women and children separately from the men. The group who fled with Enos Emory survived two years in the jungle until rescued by Filipino guerrillas and escaped aboard an American submarine bound for Australia. Enos left the group to join remnants of the American Army fighting with the guerrillas and was never heard from again. The Filipino wives of several of the internees remained outside the camp at home with their children.

On February 1, Lt. Hosaka advised the internees that they would be used for labor around Davao. He then requested lists of those able and unable to do heavy work. At this time there were thirty-eight men interned by the Japanese at the Rodaeche house. The internees supplied a list of seventeen men able to do heavy work and twenty-one unable to do heavy work. Eighty percent of the men unable to work were over age sixty. Three were over age seventy.

The next day, due to the inauguration of the new civil government in Davao and the appointment by the Japanese of Alfonso Oboza as City Mayor, there was no work. But on February 3, the labor gang began with sixteen men digging, hauling, and spreading road material from Tibuncogco to the new bridge at Banquerohan. The following day the Japanese inspected the twenty-one men previously listed as unable to do heavy work and selected seven to add to the work gang. On February 5, the Japanese officer in charge of roadwork asked for five more men but, after inspection, decided none was fit for hard labor. Day in and day out this work continued; fourteen men, including Pat and Sam, were assigned to "special work" all day at the docks in Santa Anna on May 14. All wore numbered armbands; Sam's was number four.[1]

At Santa Anna, the Japanese were expanding dock and warehouse facilities on the Davao Gulf. The work was hard, and at times the Japanese guards could be cruel. The work crews were marched to a busy lumberyard and made to move heavy construction timbers. Some of the pieces were six by twelve by thirty feet long. It was a job for six men, but only four were put to the task. The guard was a little man and mean in character. When men buckled under the weight, he kicked and pushed them until they fell exhausted. Sam and Pat staggered into the Rodaeche house that night ashen, fatigued, and physically spent. The next day aboard a heavily laden cargo ship in the Davao harbor, unsympathetic guards leered as the internees drenched in sweat and gasping for breath, struggled in the suffocating heat and humidity, to carry heavy material from the ship's deep holds.

Other Japanese officers and enlisted men were kind. This kindness was evident when a large cargo vessel tied up at one of the new piers for the prisoners to unload a cargo of sugar. The Japanese officer in charge was young, no more than eighteen or nineteen. He was a happy fellow who joked and played around with the prisoners. Next to the pier was a recreation room with a pool table. Late in the day, the young officer, playing pool with other guards, waved the men over, gave out cues, and invited the whole gang to join in the fun. Afterward the guards took the internees back to the ship where they were allowed to load their pockets with the sugar. So tight did the men pack in the sugar that granules oozed out the pores in the cloth. The sugar lasted for a year in camp. On yet another occasion, the internees were hauling large rock. The Japanese guards were happy, cheerful, clean-cut, nice young soldiers. This group of guards scheduled plenty of breaks and allowed the prisoners to fashion fulcrums, working two men to a rock. For special occasions, the Japanese declared holidays from work. The camp diary records on April 29, 1942, that, "Today being the birthday of His Imperial Japanese Majesty, The Emperor, a holiday was observed and no gardening and work undertaken." Another break came on May 18; the fall of Corregidor and surrender of American and Filipino forces in the Philippines ten days earlier brought a day of Japanese celebration devoted to a parade and speeches. Flanked by soldiers, Pat and a gang of other prisoners were marched through Davao as a Japanese show of Asian superiority. But the Americans did not wholly cooperate. The men marched square shouldered in tight formation. Pat, who had recently shaved his head and grown a mustache, swung his arms in high cadence. Believing their charade a success, Japanese officials smiled as Filipinos broke out in spontaneous applause, but the Americans knew their Filipino friends were admiring their pluck and courage. The next day, Lt. Hosaka advised the internees that there would be an additional day of no work. For the internees, their rest was no consolation for news of the fall of the Philippines. Filipino and American troops defending Bataan and the island fortress of Corregidor had capitulated to the Japanese Army, and General Wainwright surrendered all remaining American and Filipino forces in the islands. For Sam, "It was accurate news, but we wouldn't believe it. We just wouldn't believe it." [2]

§ § §

Fran watched sprouts of cotton barely emerging from the turned black soil of spring plowing. Robins, picking through the rows for worms, on a clear blue day, flitted and bobbed in the fields. High in the tupelo-edged coppice beyond the railroad track, a Red-Shouldered Hawk perched high in an oak. Lifting, the hawk presented a translucent crescent patch of rust showing at the base of her primaries. Fran stepped outside, the spring of the screen door snapping it shut behind her.

A breath of late frost melted on the grass blades as Fran hurried down the path to the Tucker Store. Mail awaited, maybe a letter from Sam, but though she had almost given up on replies, she had not given up on his eventual return. Without slowing its thundering forward motion, toward England, Arkansas, the next small town down the track, the Cotton States Railroad mail car attendant had deposited the strong leather mail sack on the snag pole at the small depot. The Postmaster had emerged from the store on his morning fetch.

Unfolding the newspaper across the store counter Fran scanned the stories in the *St. Louis Post Dispatch* headlining, "Corregidor Gives in after 300 Air Attacks." The date was May 6, 1942. She had begun to dread the coming of this day. She knew the fall was going to happen following the surrender on April 9 of 36,000 badly outnumbered, sick and famished, Filipino and American troops after four months of ferocious fighting on the Bataan Peninsula. Still she was staggered at the reports already circulating of the savagery of Japanese atrocities in the Philippines. Where were Sam, Pat, and P.H. Frank? Were they alive or dead?

She returned to the big house, entering quietly so as not to awaken her children. She joined her mother in the kitchen, began to sob, and then make plans.

Davao Internment Camp, early 1942. This is "Gift Day" and prisoners are carrying across the street to their camp, food left by Filipino friends at the guardhouse. *(Left to right)* Henry Peabody, Sam Frank, Ludvig "Sunny" Sundeen, Bob Crytser. *(Courtesy of Emory University MARBL, Frank Family Collection)*

Prisoners of War, Davao Internment Camp, early 1942. *(left to right standing)* George Thompson, Leslie Daniel Thompson, David Jacobson, Sam Frank, Harry Hughes, Leslie "Cap" Stevens, Ludvig "Sunny" Sundeen, Eric Oscar Erickson. *(left to right kneeling)* Robert Bennet, Bob Crytser, Billy Patstone. *(Courtesy of Emory University, MARBL, Frank Family Collection)*

CHAPTER 31

"They shot him in the back of the head…"

Patrick James Frank, Charlottesville Daily Progress,
February 27, 1994

On January 7, 1942, eighteen days following capture at the Davao Club and four days after internment at the Rodaeche home, Lt. Hosaka advised the internees that the Japanese Army Hospital would handle emergency medical cases and surgeries. The prisoners were to be provided with limited supplies: milk of magnesia, Epson salts, aspirin, Bromo quinine, bandages, Mercurochrome, and antiseptics if available. Three days later, three Japanese medical officers came to treat three internee cases. The officers then returned on January 22 and February 4 to see to the internees' further medical needs. At those times, the only promised medical supplies delivered were a small quantity of aspirin, quinine, and Epson Salts. For the next seven months the internees were seen by Japanese doctors for a total of only four times—twice in March when the doctors made additional promises of care, once in April, and once in June. No additional medical supplies were ever provided.

When the Japanese entered Davao on December 20, 1941, Walter Tong was captured at the Mission Hospital. The Japanese authorities allowed him to remain on duty as the administrator along with Doctora Esteban Sexon, a Filipina surgeon, and Doctora Natividad, a Filipino dentist. During the next several months the Japanese authorities allowed Tong to attend as best he could to the care and treatment of the

Filipino population. In addition to Tong and the other two doctors, there were Filipino nurses staffing the hospital. With the supplies Tong was able to receive came from the Japanese authorities, the Mission Hospital took responsibility for the internees' health care needs. By May 15, Drs. Natividad and Sexon were making regular weekly sick calls in addition to handling emergencies and treatments that required hospitalization.

The internees received little food from the Japanese military authorities. What they did receive consisted primarily of small sacks of dirty rice, ground field corn usually fed to the chickens and pigs, occasional tins of sardines, and squid. Rarely a tin of evaporated milk would appear. For the most part, it was Japanese civilian friends, Filipino friends and the Filipino wives of some of the internees who brought what little food the men received. In addition, former Filipino employees were generous. For example, on February 18, Pat received supplies of Purico, onions, tomatoes, fish, pork, garlic, and eggs.

On February 10, Mr. Yamaka came to the camp and advised the prisoners that they could expect no further supplies from the Japanese army other than corn and rice flour until Mr. Matsumoto at the Japanese consulate returned from Manila. At that point, clarification of the policy of handling and feeding was expected. On March 7, Mr. Idoh informed the internees that they should elect officers in order to facilitate and simplify regulations of the camp by Japanese authorities. In addition, Idoh ordered a daily diary kept and submitted at 8:00 every morning to the authorities. Clayton Jones was elected president, Walter Tong, vice-president, and Sam Frank, secretary. Tong was later elected President, a position in which he served throughout the Davao internment.

As the length of imprisonment stretched into the third month, the internees increasingly began to suffer from sanitation and diet-related conditions. The first cases of skin sores began in early March with six to ten men out of a roster of thirty-seven, requiring daily bandage changes. The first case of anemia was reported in the camp diary of March 20, and by March 27, cases of chronic intestinal worms required treatment. Treatment for intestinal parasites often required hospitalization at Mission Hospital. Sam awoke one night in severe pain and was taken by Lt. Hosaka to Mission Hospital where he stayed for two days. Pat was treated for intestinal parasites and had a narrow escape with appendicitis. On April 7, there was a case of typhoid fever, and on April 20, two cases of dengue fever were diagnosed. Skin conditions including sores, abscesses, and boils, on legs, underarms, and ears became common with seven to twelve internees being treated at any one time. Tooth infections, abscesses, and extractions by Dr. Sexon became commonplace. In June there were two cases of malaria, and on July 7, the first case of beriberi was diagnosed. The medical statistics bore witness to the condition of the internees during the summer. On July 20, twenty-three men received treatment for other serious illnesses and disease, with three requiring hospitalization. In a three-day period starting July 25, one internee was treated for dysentery, another was coughing up blood, and eight were treated for tropical ulcers, and foot infections. Additionally, treatment was provided for six skin infections and two nephritis cases. And there were only forty-seven internees at that time.

In March the Japanese allowed the men to establish their own vegetable garden, but the garden never produced enough vegetables to meet basic nutritional needs. Additionally the men shared their produce with the women internees who were held separately. The American prisoners also shared the vegetables produced in the garden with the Filipino war prisoners who were living next door in squalid, desperate conditions.

The vegetable garden, such as it was, also provided a psychological benefit to the internees. They could organize around a common task, engage in teamwork, and feel some sense of control over their destiny. Everyone was expected to work according to his physical ability. The men received professional guidance in their gardening from Mr. Yamaguchi, Ludvig Sundeen's Japanese gardener—another example of how Japanese civilians in Davao tried to assist the American and European prisoners.

As the growing season progressed, the improved diet showed immediate results: on March 25, sixteen men showed up for work; twenty appeared the second day; and by March 31, thirty-three reported in the morning and twenty-six in the afternoon. But the garden was small and could not sustain the men. The number of gardeners leveled off and then began to diminish as disease, illness, and forced labor outside the camp began to take their toll throughout the summer. On June 17, sixteen men reported for gardening, twelve on June 19, and eight on July 21. By late summer, fully eighty-three percent of the internees could not report for gardening, an activity that could mean living or dying.

Despite these privations, the men had their moments of good humor reflected in meetings during which they discussed camp business. At one such meeting in June, Sam's minutes recorded that Edward Christensen, born in New York and a Davao planter for twenty-nine years, read the proposed "Toilet Rules" for both "squatters and sitters." Pat Frank objected to the height of the urinal for short men. Christensen, who had installed the urinal, replied that he used Eugene Stevens and Henry Umstad as measuring sticks, to which vice-president Sundeen suggested, "There may have been a typographical error in the computations." [1]

§

Early in 1933 just before Sam, Jr. was born, Fran and Sam had been living in Manila and had purchased a Lloyd Baby Carriage from an army couple who were returning to the States following a tour of duty in the Islands. The "Lloyd" was a Cadillac among baby buggies—there were none available in the Manila stores at the time that were quite as good. The buggy had good lines, the top could be raised and lowered. The well-contoured handle, ball bearing wheels, and well-balanced springs made for pleasant strolling. In addition to its use with their three sons, the Frank baby buggy became the popular, much desired, pre-walking conveyance of many babies born to their friends in Davao between 1933 and 1941.

From the window of the building where he was being held, Sam saw strolling down the street toward him a Japanese mother proudly pushing her baby in his and Fran's old Lloyd baby buggy, which had obviously been looted from their home.

Both the Japanese mother and carriage showed the marks of war, but the woman walked proudly by, her head tilted back. To Sam the buggy seemed to be proud, too, that it could still provide a useful service. Sam did not see or hear of the Lloyd again. The incongruity of the scene with the melancholia of missing his family stayed with him the rest of his life.

§

In August the Japanese permitted Sam and several of the internees to attend the funeral of an old friend, Guleahtah, an Italian marine engineer. Italy was an Axis power, so Guleahtah had been immune from internment. He had worked for the International Harvester Company, and his war sympathies were with his old Davao friends. Several guards accompanied the internees to the funeral which was held at the Catholic Church. A small crowd of Filipinos mingled together, dressed nicely in starched white pants, shirts, and coats with ties. Without decent clothes, Sam and the other internees looked bedraggled and stayed far back in the crowd. Sam knew the Filipinos attending the funeral, but also knew the dangers if the guards saw them talking to each other. So the two groups remained apart, acknowledging one another with the briefest, obtuse nods of comfort. A Catholic nun gave Sam almost imperceptible motions to come stand by her. She handed him a plate of cookies. Sam marveled, "My God, eating cookies during a funeral and trying to keep it hidden from the Japanese guards."[2]

During the period of internment in Davao from December 20, 1941, to December 24, 1943, when the internees were moved to Santo Tomas Internment Camp in Manila, six men died. "I watched some people grow weak, give up and die," Pat recalled, "I also grew weak, but I didn't give up." There was one death at Davao Internment Camp that was neither starvation nor disease related. It was an execution. For British captive Robert Bennet of Glasgow, Scotland, captivity was too great a burden. Bennet was twenty-eight years old, single and had lived in Davao less than three years as assistant manager of Kerr and Company, a British trading company. He wanted Pat to escape with him. Escape was easy enough with few guards and many opportunities, but where to go was the problem. Pat told him that having grown up in the Philippines, hunting and fishing throughout the islands, he knew what it was like in the jungle. One could not drink the water. There were mosquitoes everywhere carrying malaria and dengue, and leeches were in the water. "I told him camp wasn't good, but we were a hell of a lot better off there than out in the jungle. But he wouldn't listen and took off. A few days later, the Japanese brought him back."[3]

Japanese guards and an officer drove Pat and two other men down the South Road, an area of flat agricultural land, about two miles from the camp. There the Japanese officer ordered Pat, Harry McKenzie from Boston, master mechanic at Davao Gold Mines, and Thomas Garley from Northampton, England, foreman of the mines, to dig a grave for the young man. When the men finished, the Japanese soldiers made the young Scott stand at the edge of his grave. His face and arms bore the deep cuts and scratches of cogon grass and the welts of jungle insects. The dirt was of rich, dark-gray, volcanic soil laid down over the millennia by Mt. Apo, off in the distance. "They shot him in the back of the head," Pat said. "We buried him and walked back to the camp."[4]

§ § §

Tucker was not the ideal place for Fran and the three boys to live until the war was over. The home lacked many necessary conveniences. Distances to market and medical care were great, and the savings in rent were more than offset by the higher cost of living. Since there was a war on, the local draft board gave agricultural deferments in numbers sufficient to keep farming alive, but there was no extra help for heavy work, repairs, and garden planting. Plus the winter cold penetrated the big house. With three children to wash, cook and care for, it was just too much for Fran. The school system offered a teaching position in Tucker, but the salary was negligible. Additionally, she was unsuccessful finding work in Little Rock and had to stop looking after gasoline rationing went into effect.

Fran had friends from St. Louis working in Washington, D.C., her brother was stationed at an army base outside the capital, and she had the promise of a clerk position at the War Department. She moved to D.C. in June 1942, where she arranged for a small apartment. Sammy went to live with Fran's sister in Hutchinson, Kansas; Pat and Russell stayed with their grandmother in Tucker.

In Washington, Fran reread a letter she had just received from Alexander Abercrombie (Ack) Brown in October 1942. It was written aboard the *SS El Nin* when he was returning to England following his repatriation from internment in Davao. Ack Brown was a British subject, a Scott from Glasgow, forty-one years old, single, and an honorary British Consul in Davao while employed as manager of Kerr & Company, prominent importers and exporters. His consular duties primarily involved getting drunken British sailors out of the city jail and back safely to their ships and representing the king at parties held at the well-staffed Japanese Consulate. As honorary as his responsibilities were, they entitled him to diplomatic exchange. On June 9, the Japanese had flown Brown to Manila, and to Santo Tomas Internment Camp, and then by ship to England, all arranged by the International Red Cross.

The letter Fran was reading was the first news she had received that Sam and Pat were alive—or had been alive when Ack last saw them four months earlier than the dated letter. For the first time she was able to get a sketch of conditions in Davao after Pearl Harbor—the surrender at the club, and short personal notes about the men, including Sam and Pat. "Sam is the camp secretary-treasurer. He is always around where work is to be done, and he certainly did more than his fair share to make our living conditions as well as they could be under the circumstances, and is in good health." Of Pat he wrote, "Pat was threatened with appendicitis, and we managed to get him to the mission hospital for observation. It proved to be a false alarm, however, and he was back with us after a week as well as ever. At one period, he shaved his hair and grew a beard, and was known as Ivan the Terrible." Brown shared his concern for the internees. "I feel sure that the food given them by the Japanese will be entirely inadequate to maintain reasonably good health, and it is of utmost importance that some means be found of supplying them with food or the money to buy it." Gen received the identical letter and both women began immediate correspondences with the International Red Cross to let that organization know the location of the prisoners and their plight.[5]

CHAPTER 32

"Fourteen men were driven to the former Happy Life Blues Cabaret"

Samuel Boone Frank, Internment Camp Diary,
August , 1942

On August 14, 1942, eight months following their capture, the Davao internees learned from Lt. Hosaka that there would be a new internment camp for Anglo-Americans and the prisoners were to build it. Civilian men, women, and children captured in the southern Philippines and interned in small groups throughout the southern islands were being consolidated. The Japanese were moving the prisoners to Davao, now an extensive headquarters and supply depot of the Japanese army holding the southwest Pacific Islands. Some groups had already arrived and were temporarily housed in various compounds around the city, the men separated from single women and mothers with children.

Shortly thereafter, Japanese guards drove fourteen men of the Davao group, including Sam and Pat, by truck to the former Happy Life Blues Cabaret. The cabaret had been a carefree Filipino nightspot known for good jazz but also for partying and fighting. The knife wheeling-brawls there earned the cabaret the nickname "Bucket of Blood." This new camp was located two and a half miles from town center on the Davao South Road near Matina Reservoir. Upon arrival, the internees were ordered to drive fence posts deep into the ground and string three strands of barbed wire around the area. The prisoners completed the fencing by noon the second day. That afternoon, the prisoners cut grass and weeds between the fence and jungle. Then at five o'clock, the internees returned by bus to their compound in Davao. The following day the internees returned to build a gate and adjoining guardhouse.

On Friday, August 21, several high-ranking Japanese officers came to inspect the premises, followed in the afternoon by Major-General Monimoto, the new chief of the *Gunseibu*, the military authority responsible for civil affairs. Accompanying Monimoto were Tanaka and Hirata, top Japanese civilians in the *Gunseibu*. A few speeches dragged on about the new facilities, but everyone knew that the camp had many problems including lack of facilities for cooking, bathing, washing, toileting, and partitions for privacy in the large cabaret.

At four-thirty on the afternoon of August 24, a senior officer of the Japanese military assembled the internees for inspection in the street in front of the camp. He advised the prisoners that transfer to the cabaret was postponed because some pigeon eggs were in the process of incubation and could not be moved.

Meanwhile at the Davao wharfs, the prisoners continued hard labor unloading freighters and working in the deepest parts of the steaming ships. Medical sick calls reached a peak. The Mission Hospital saw forty-nine cases, mostly of tropical ulcers and sores, diagnosed by Dr. Lamora as being due to a lack of vitamin B. Shortly thereafter, the Japanese informed internees that the Mission Hospital was now closed to them and that no longer would a doctor be sent to the camp to treat tropical ulcers and change bandages. Lt. Hosaka provided no further explanation, yet paradoxically Japanese doctors arranged for vitamin B shots to be administered to the internees, which saved many from further suffering. Twice more during internment, Japanese physicians provided lifesaving injections.

The internees followed the war news smuggled in by Filipino wives and friends at great danger. The Japanese had confiscated radios from the Filipinos, but there were a few clandestine sets kept tuned to the American broadcasts from Treasure Island. In this way, the prisoners learned in early June that Admiral Chester Nimitz forced a badly beaten Japanese naval force to withdraw near Midway Island. The prisoners also had access to the local newspaper taken over by the Japanese authorities. Reading the newspaper stories, the men would learn that the Japanese had repulsed attempts by American forces to land on

Tulagi in the Solomon Islands, Port Moresby on New Guinea, and Guadalcanal. However, a week later, the newspaper would report heavy damage to American positions on the same islands. Reading between the lines, the men knew that American soldiers had actually made successful landings and were island hopping toward the Philippines. The worst cases of internee mistreatment came concurrently with bad war news for the Japanese.

§

By September 22, 1942, the pigeons had hatched their eggs, and Sam and Pat began the second phase of their internment. All the men were transferred to the new camp to be interned with thirty-nine additional prisoners who had come from Zamboanga as well as 112 men, women and children who had been interned at Impaluato. A month after the men entered Happy Life Blues Cabaret, the women prisoners and children were brought from Davao, and that added twenty-six to the number. On Christmas Day, a group of fifteen men and their families from Surigao further increased the number.

§   §   §

A bitterly cold winter arrived early in Tucker. The calendar read November 22, 1942. Bessie managed as best she could for Pat and Russell. She awakened before the freezing sunrise to prime the oil furnace that squatted in the downstairs hall near the steps, doing its best to put out heat that would rise to the bedrooms. In the small hearth room off the kitchen, she cleaned out the clinkers and added small pieces of coal to the tiny fireplace.

The insulation in the walls consisted of cotton sweepings from the gin floor packed between the wall studs. Over the thirty-seven years since the house was built, the dirty cotton had settled in the walls, and whatever protection it once might have provided was gone. Bessie had enjoyed stays in the home during periods of warm weather, but the winter of 1942 and what was already proving to be a forthcoming icy 1943 were more than her sixty-year-old body wished to endure. She packed Pat and Russell into her 1936 Packard, and by Thanksgiving was in Hutchinson, Kansas, with her daughter and her grandson Sam, Jr. Fran came by train from Washington to join them for Christmas.

Santa Claus left Sammy a chemistry set, Pat a Lionel train set, and Russell a red rocking chair. Fran returned to Washington after Christmas, and Pat and Russell returned to Tucker in March with Bessie, just as the sharecroppers made ready their plows for turning.

§   §   §

Forty-two more civilians from Cotabato were brought in on December 31. Then on February 28, 1943, thirty-seven more civilians from Zamboanga were added, most of them Protestant missionaries and their wives and families. Next came thirty-seven from Malaval. Most of the prisoners were American, but many were British, British-Australian, British-Canadian, Egyptian, and Norwegian. There were also a number of Catholic priests, but the Japanese authorities had no consistent policy on priests remaining in their parishes so their numbers in the camp at any given time were variable.

The eventual internee population at the camp was 279, which included all of the men, women, children, and the Catholic priests. For the next fifteen months, the 279 lived together on that postage stamp of land—less than two acres—surrounded by barbed wire. There was a large sign over the door of the old cabaret building that read "Happy Life Blues;" no one ever disturbed the ironic shingle.

The barbed wire fence surrounding the internment camp formed a square approximately 295 feet to a side. The enclosure ran north and south. The gate was at the northwest corner. In the center of the compound was the cabaret. The open-sided building was tin roofed and had a stage at one end with steps. The internees built a shelter for Protestant church services at the northeast corner of the compound. The structure also served as the schoolhouse for the children and was the largest building constructed by the internees. Shortly thereafter, during a terrific windstorm, the building was blown over. The kids, thinking they would have a long vacation from studies, were disappointed when the "schoolhouse" was pushed right back up. The Catholic *padres* constructed living quarters and a space for services directly across the compound from the Protestant church and close to the guardhouse. Along the east side, Del Monte Plantation employees constructed "shanties" for their families. Along the south side, individuals built eight shanties that housed twelve people, three women and nine men including Pat and Sam.

Shanties were a luxury, offering a sense of privacy in the crowded camp. The floor of the cabaret was crowded with families, makeshift bedding, possessions, and mosquito netting. Individuals who had local Filipino contacts could arrange with the Japanese guards for Filipino friends to deliver bamboo, nipa, building materials, and enough money to engage a fellow internee who had building experience to construct a shelter. Sam and Pat each constructed a ten-by-twelve shanty made of nipa, bamboo, and bejuco. The Protestant missionaries built a shanty enabling individuals and families, on a scheduled basis, some sanctuary away from the noisy, crowded cabaret. The *Gunseibu* made no protest about Pat and Sam's previous employees bringing them building supplies, even cots and mosquito netting.

In the center of the camp adjacent to the cabaret was the camp kitchen and a line of eight cooking shacks. The green coconut embers of the cooking fires put off an acrid, eye burning smoke. Maintaining privacy at the latrines was impossible. For concealment, prisoners hung worn fragments of cloth and palm fronds, but usually people maintained a sense of nonobservance in order to preserve a modicum of decency for one another.

§

A young woman named Boots Ryder worked in the modest camp infirmary. Boots had followed her fiancé, a naval commander, to the Philippines where they were married. He had shipped out on a destroyer about three weeks before Pearl Harbor, and when the Japanese came into Manila, the Navy evacuated Boots to Corregidor. She was among ten navy nurses and dependents that on April 29, 1942, were evacuated on two PBY seaplanes to Australia. The planes landed at Lake Lanao on Mindanao for refueling. As they taxied to take off, the PBY Boots was on hit a submerged rock. The plane was then unable to take off because one of the pontoons had sprung a leak. All of those on the seaplane including Boots, two other dependents, a naval officer, several nurses, and an army colonel tried unsuccessfully to evade the Japanese before capture. The officers were sent to military prison camps, the nurses were sent to Santo Tomas Internment Camp, but Boots and the two other dependents were sent to the Davao Internment Camp where she, Sam, and Pat became fast friends. The two brothers then built a nipa shanty for her and the two other navy dependents in a space between their own shanties.

Occasionally, the Japanese guards allowed the Davao prisoners a pass to fetch coconuts from the jungle surrounding the camp. On one such occasion, Boots and Sam came upon a native home containing a concert piano. They were invited in, gloriously fed, and Boots played well beyond the time allotted for coconut scavenging. Leaving to return to camp, the Filipino family handed them a generous bag of food. The guards at the gate were unhappy with them but were mollified when they found a live rooster for themselves at the bottom of the sack and let them pass. Few from the camp ever forgot the interlude of Chopin nocturnes wafting through the towering growth of Philippine vegetation that late afternoon.

Then there were the chicken coops against the fence and "Bud's Barber Shop" between the men's and women's showers. The latrines were quickly filled, covered over and new ones dug by Pat Frank and the mining crew from Davao Gold Mines.

For all of these various groups who came together at Davao, the expense of maintenance was borne by the internees themselves from the time they were taken prisoner. This Japanese policy continued at Happy Life Blues. The Japanese informed the executive committee of the camp that a per capita cash allowance of twenty-five centavos a day would be deposited by the International Red Cross in the Davao Branch of the Bank of Taiwan. Out of the twenty-five centavo allowance, the camp was required to pay for food, firewood, electricity, medical fees and supplies, water, the telephone in the guardhouse, and "rent" on the camp. Not only was the allowance insufficient to maintain life, but also Red Cross deposits were typically two to four months in arrears. Internees who had stashed away extra money before coming into camp accepted I.O.U.'s from the executive committee which used the funds for purchasing additional food from the Filipinos.

Sam, Pat, and other Davao businessmen in the camp also formed a committee to raise private funds from former employees and local Filipino businessmen and friends. Pat and Sam wrote I.O.U.'s using Davao Light & Power and Mindanao Sales & Services as collateral. Filipinos accepted these chits even though the companies had been taken over by Japanese. The executive committee received a total of 12,750 pesos in American Red Cross funds deposited in the Bank of Taiwan, all of which the camp committee used for the purchase of food. No internees in the Davao camp ever received Red Cross packages, but Sam and Pat both saw such packages in the Japanese *bodegas* when they picked up the periodic rations of rice and corn. Filipino friends also informed them that the Japanese were selling American cigarettes from Red Cross packages. The internees settled into a long period of semi-starvation. There were six deaths all of them elderly men over the sixteen months of internment at the Happy Life Blues Cabaret. Some had Filipino wives living outside the camp who picked up the bodies for burial. For others, the Catholic priests arranged burial in a parish cemetery.

The corn supplied for purchase from the Japanese was field corn, rough stuff, the type fed to cattle. The cooking crew ground up the maize and boiled the hard, splintered kernels in water for a few hours until they became gruel. Heads of cattle butchered by the Japanese were sometimes given to the prisoners, which they boiled in 55 gallon drums of water to make soup. "The Japanese cut out the tongues for themselves, but there was meat around the lips and neck and the prisoner's drank the water, too," Pat remembered, "Of course, it all tasted terrible, but we were hungry—starving actually."

An English couple, Elsie and Harold Baker, had a pet cat which was slowly famishing. The couple had a little five-year old son who loved the cat. Elsie and Harold approached Pat and plotted with him to kill the cat and have a dinner party, keeping the plans from the child. Elsie wanted no part in the actual dispatching or any part in the cooking but she looked forward to the feast, though quite conscience-stricken; Harold slew the cat and Pat skinned and cleaned it. They boiled the feline for three hours, removed the meat from the bones, chopped it up, sautéed it with onions, garlic, and added a little curry powder. They poured it over their rice ration, and the four had a dinner party, washed down with tea made from dry weeds. The next day they cracked the bones up, boiled them for about four hours, and served the broth to their little boy. Harold was an Oxford graduate and Elsie a baronet educated in Switzerland. Both adjusted to camp, making light of the hardships, which Pat considered admirable for the British, who, for the most part, he considered the worst gripers in the camp and the poorest sports. "They can't do this to a British subject," was a pet expression, Pat recalled.[1]

The Japanese guard unit, consisting of a sergeant and seven men, changed every week. Orders were written by Lt. Hosaka and were maintained in the guardhouse. The sergeant and his men usually interpreted the orders loosely in favor of the internees. However, there was a frightening night-potty incident.

Lacking toilet facilities in the cabaret building, at night mothers had to resort to old-fashioned chamber pots for their children, made from whatever was handy. One night a tired mother decided to empty her children's "potty" out the window. Unfortunately, a Japanese sentry was passing under the window at the time she made her decision, and he was the recipient of the contents. The corporal of the guard ordered everyone up and began an immediate investigation. The internees presented a solid front, everyone disclaiming the honor of the deed. Finally, the guards retired from the scene, with warnings of unhappy consequences if the incident occurred again.

Food was constantly on the internees' minds, and the monotony of what they had available to eat was wearing on morale. "Gulay" was the staple item on the menu, consisting of vegetables, mostly weedy greens, mixed in rice. Most internees had a spoon and a plate or bowl fashioned from a coconut shell. Occasionally there would be a few scraps of meat. Peanuts, when available, would be crushed to make an oily peanut butter which Sam would spread between halved bananas when they were obtainable.

The internees made toothbrushes from pig bristles imbedded in pieces of old truck tires, and shoes were woven from strips of hemp. Sam and Pat had grown up in the Philippines and knew how to process the poisonous Cassava plant into flour, cook it in coconut oil, and make tapioca, a source of carbohydrate. To the delight of the children, the brothers would drip the tapioca paste onto roof tin stretched over a hot fire, where it popped into small kernels. To preserve their increasingly worn clothes, the men fashioned *fundoshi*, Japanese loincloths, to cover their fronts and rears. Communication with Filipino friends outside was easily managed and special details of internees were allowed to roam near the camp for purchasing of supplies and picking up coconuts. The harshest discipline experienced by the internees during this time was cuffing and slaps by the guards for failing to bow in their presence. However, such interludes and treatment by the Japanese guards seemed to follow the course of the war. Sam explained, "If there was a setback for the Japanese, then the prisoners suffered. There would be more slapping, and the guards would not let Filipinos bring in fresh food or let the men, women, and older children out to scavenge."[2]

243

§ § §

In June 1943, after a year in Washington, desiring to reunite the children with her, Fran moved to St. Louis where she landed a job with the Red Cross. Housing was expensive and hard to find, and owners who would rent to families with children were rare. Finally, Fran found a rental and reunited with her children and mother in a small St. Louis house. Fran's sister Jean was now an invalid and with her husband, had moved to St. Louis. Jean and Fran rented houses close together so their mother could help in both places. Fran moved twice before finally buying a home in Webster Groves, with an F.H.A loan in September 1944. She received help with the down payment from her mother and one of Sam's engineering professors at Washington University. The price of the house was twenty-percent higher than pre-war cost.

In July 1943, General MacArthur launched a major Allied offensive in the Pacific. Australian-American forces landed on Rendova Island. Japanese and American navies clashed near Bougainville Island. In August Americans took another island in the Solomons, Vella Lavella, and fighting intensified on New Guinea. Ensign John F. Kennedy was able to save his crew after a Japanese destroyer split his PT boat in two. American troops were on Bougainville and Tarawa in the Gilbert Islands by November. Then in December United States forces invaded New Britain. The westward drive toward Tokyo had made a major dent in Japanese strongholds.

§ § §

Every morning and afternoon, all 279 children, women, and men lined up for Roll Call and counted off—"*ichi, ni, sar, shi, go, roku, shichi, hachi, cu, ju.*" The camp would bow as a group to the Japanese sergeant, who then bowed to the camp; then followed the camp president Father Ewing who made a final bow to the guards. Every work detail, both leaving camp and returning, would count and bow in the same way.

Filipino employees and friends of Sam and Pat were loyal to them; they would bring vegetables, bananas, papayas, and coconuts when they could. They also brought money that the two brothers used to buy food near the camp. Pat and Sam made up their minds early on that they would survive. They would keep what extra food they needed and share the rest with others, especially families with children. "But even though I shared, people were human," Pat recalled, and they would grumble about his store of food. "One man complained that I had papayas and his children needed the fruit. I told him that when the fruit was ripe, I was going to eat them. I was not going to share them. I established that very early on. I cared about the children and others, and I shared when I could, but I was going to survive." A woman bore a baby in camp and petitioned the camp executive committee for the child's ration but was denied. As camp secretary, Sam recorded in the minutes the consensus of the committee. The woman and her husband had known the rules about camp celibacy and had broken them. Now they would have to share their ration, as meager as it might be, with their new baby. Later Sam gave her husband a can of Carnation milk from his private food cache as did Pat.[3]

Japanese civilians were prohibited from bringing food to the internees, but some persisted in smuggling. Sam and Pat learned that the Japanese authorities executed Mr. Takekawa because he had smuggled food to the prisoners.

As the prisoners lined up for morning roll call on December 23, 1943, Lt. Hosaka gave them twenty-four hours notice that they were being transported to Manila to be interned with thousands of other civilians at Santo Tomas Internment Camp. In the camp was a water buffalo that pulled a small cart for gathering coconuts. The prisoners were hungry and they decided that the *carabao* would not stay behind. So they killed it. None of the internees were butchers, but they managed the task, then took sticks, stuck them through the meat, built a bunch of fires, and broiled steaks. The meat was dark and a little on the tough side, "but we really feasted. That *carabao* must have weighed 1,200 pounds," Pat recalled. Following the feast, the prisoners prepared to leave, packing their possessions in boxes and bags, but still leaving much behind.

The internees were fearful. American air squadrons were bombing Davao regularly. They also knew that American submarines were operating in the Davao Gulf and routinely sinking Japanese cargo ships, but the prisoners also held out hope that in Manila there might be some relief from their suffering. For Walter Tong there was anticipation of reunion with his wife and children. Sam and Pat had recently received money smuggled to them by a Japanese boy. The money had come from their father, so they knew he was alive.

Sam Frank's "shanty" built from materials supplied by Filipino friends was a luxury compared to the inadequate, crowded, and noisy conditions endured by the 250 prisoners living in the Happy Life Blues Cabaret building at the Davao Internment Camp. *(Courtesy of Emory University MARBL, Frank Family Collection)*

Filipino employees of Davao Light & Power Co brought Sam Frank a cot, mosquito netting, and other supplies that eased many of the stresses of internment. *(Courtesy of Emory University MARBL, Frank Family Collection)*

---- CHAPTER 33 ----

"We boarded the *Shinsei Maru* on Christmas Eve"

Samuel Boone Frank, Remembrances, 1990

On Christmas Eve, 1943, all 279 Davao internees were loaded on trucks, driven to the pier, and herded into the hold of the 7,000-ton ship, *Shinsei Maru*. It was an unmarked Japanese transport converted from an old, rusted, filthy ship that previously had taken troops to New Guinea and on its return to the Philippines had carried a smelly cargo of green animal hides and copra. Lt. Hosaka had told the internees that once on board they would receive plenty of good food. Instead, the guards packed them tight together in the rat-infested hold and provided only rations of steamed rice and seaweed as their Christmas Eve dinner.

That night the ship remained anchored in the harbor. For the prisoners, it was extremely hot, with not a breath of fresh air and no lights. Screams split the silence as rats scrambled over bodies and limbs, nibbling some and biting others. With no latrines in the hold, the men, women, and children felt around, whispered for privacy, and relieved themselves. Out of the dark someone began "Silent Night," and all joined in.

The passage to Manila was usually a three-day trip, but not this voyage. The internees spent the next ten days cramped and jammed together as the ship zigzagged to avoid American torpedoes. Blackouts were strictly enforced so all 279 continued to lie in complete darkness in the hold at night. During daylight hours, the prisoners were allowed on deck where there was barely standing room. Worry about American submarines and possible torpedoing of their unmarked ship was a constant source of anxiety and rumor. Through it all, Mother Clare, a Catholic nun, calmly kept her clinic going even as rainwater poured through the hatch boards and disgusting excrements flowed over prisoners cramped in lower cargo decks.

Because of the danger of American submarines, the ship traveled close to shore, sometimes dropping anchor during daylight and traveling at night. There were four other ships in the convoy, none of which carried prisoners. One day, as the internees aired and sunned on deck, they watched as one of the convoy ships took a torpedo from an American submarine and blew up. A nervous silence overtook the group. There was a small pile of life belts in a corner, and the prisoners had organized their own drill. However, neither the life belts nor the drill would have done much good if it had been there ship hit. The remaining ships completed the voyage around the Moro Gulf, stopped at Zamboanga for two days, and took on coal at Cebu; at both stops, the prisoners remained in the ship's suffocating hold.

When allowed out of the hold during the day for deck privileges, both the men and the women used with little privacy the latrine built out over the ship's scuppers; the trough was flushed with salt water which washed down the ship's sides. Salt water was also available for washing during a half-hour period after meals. Rice, fermented bean curd, radish, and dried seaweed mixture cooked in a large vat on deck were made available in small portions three times a day. Meager as the fare was, it was an improvement in quantity compared to the food that the prisoners had been given at Happy Life Blues Cabaret; for the first two days at sea it was good chow; after that, it palled. Drinking water was dingy and salty.

Among all the other smells was the odor of dead rats. The ship's infestation of the rodents was through-and-through, and the vermin constantly scurried about, day and night. Few of the prisoners escaped rat bites. Fleas were also a problem and led immediately to fear of typhus and bubonic plague. The fear with respect to typhus was well founded; five of the internees fell ill with the disease which doctors at Santo Tomas later successfully treated. One man, E.C. Clement, 81 years old, died on the trip. The Japanese sewed his body in a ballast weighted canvas shroud and buried him at sea close to Zamboanga following a somber ceremony conducted by one of the missionaries.

The *Shinsei Maru* arrived at Pier 7 in Manila during the black of night on Sunday, January 2, 1943. The prisoners were confined to the hold until trucks and busses arrived during the late afternoon; the internees were loaded on the conveyances and taken to Santo Tomas where, as dusk arrived, they lined up for processing in a roped off area in front of the commandant's office. There had been alarming rumors at Santo Tomas that the internees from Davao had been lost at sea. One diary described the Davao group as "dirty, tired, and starved looking men, women, and children. All Santo Tomas was there to welcome them, but no greetings were permitted until the new arrivals had passed through one door of the office, registered, answered various questions and had come out through another door—an exasperatingly slow business." It was nine o'clock at night before all the Davao internees were fed, ravenously eating the crude Santo Tomas supper of the day— peanut-loaf and green tea.[1]

The third and final period of internment had begun for Sam and Pat.

CHAPTER 34

"Santo Tomas looked like a summer resort but it didn't last long"

Samuel Boone Frank, Remembrances, 1990

Life at Happy Life Blues Cabaret and Santo Tomas was incongruous. Sam could not believe that people were so well dressed. Music played over loud speakers. Everybody looked happy.

When MacArthur declared Manila an open city on Christmas Eve, 1941, and the American and Filipino army retreated to Bataan, the American civilians had several days to prepare before Japanese entry and their imprisonment at Santo Tomas. When the Americans went into internment, they brought clothes, and many brought food and money. At first, the prisoners were under Japanese civilian rule. The Japanese authorities in charge of the camp allowed the Filipinos to come up to the fence, bring gifts of food, and sell whatever the internees needed. It was just the opposite in Davao where the men were caught with whatever clothes they had on and money they happened to have in their pockets.

Sam and Pat immediately looked for their father in the camp and learned that he was gravely ill at Philippine General Hospital. In January 1941, the Japanese had interned P.H. with other Manila Americans at Santo Tomas. He was soon paroled along with other "Old Timers," most of who were Spanish-American War veterans, to live at his Taft Avenue home. Soon the Japanese took over his house for use by a senior officer, and P.H. and Annie moved to a Filipino friend's home. The Japanese brought P.H. and other parolees back into camp after a year and a half, but P.H. after becoming seriously ill with tuberculosis and was sent to Philippine General Hospital. Reunion would have to wait.

§

Santo Tomas had developed its own internee organization, just as Davao had. Therefore, there was no need to maintain the organizational particularity of the Davao camp or of any of the groups who had surrendered in isolated geographical locations and eventually sent to Davao for internment. In Davao, the Cebu, IloIlo, and other groups maintained some of their identity when brought into Happy Life Blues Cabaret in late 1942. Each group had its own organization and finances and worked within the larger camp organization in which Sam remained the secretary-treasurer. Now that the camp was in Santo Tomas, the extant administrative committee managed things. The committee welcomed the Davao groups, integrated them into the camp organization, and split up the groups, blending them into the various camp living arrangements. Older prisoners went to live in the gymnasium; single women went to another area, and married families had their accommodations. Many of the Davao prisoners had worked for Manila companies and congregated in their own areas. Just as in Davao, the Japanese permitted internees who had resources to build shanties in a designated area of the camp.

Coming into Santo Tomas, the Davao prisoners looked terrible. Sam and Pat arrived wearing essentially the same clothes as when captured. The women wore the same dresses in which they went into camp, the colors faded, the cloth mended in several places, and clothes filthy from the hellish transport. They were a sorry spectacle contrasted with the many Manila women who had come into Santo Tomas with their practical, clean day dresses which made it easy to spot the bedraggled prisoners taken in the frontier provinces of the Philippines. A prison camp tailor outfitted the men with khaki shorts and some shirts as gifts from the Santo Tomas camp. The women received some simple spring-colored dresses that wrapped around the waist and tied.

Also awaiting the prisoners were Red Cross packages handed out by the civilian administration. Sam sat, opened his package, and studied the powdered milk and dehydrated rations packaged like candy bars. He had never seen this kind of food before. Beside the Red Cross package, there was a personal parcel from Fran sent through the International Red Cross via the American Red Cross and Japanese Red Cross. Fran had a limited amount of space for her package. She included nail clippers, scissors, needles, thread, buttons, toothbrushes, razor and blades, shaving soap, medicated soap, emery boards, combs, belt, knit shirt, socks, handkerchiefs, cap, two bars of soap, vitamins, chewing gum, prunes, sugar, cocoa, salt tablets, pepper, and a can of Spam which Sam promised himself to stash away. She had also included playing cards and dice. An old friend, Dan Tracy, had given Fran a pipe, tobacco, and pipe cleaners to include in the package. By this time, Sam had stopped smoking, and as food became increasingly scarce, he used many of Fran's items, including the pipe and tobacco, as valuable barter for nourishment.

The center for camp administration was the first floor of Main building, the oldest and largest building on the campus. Women and children were assigned to the second floor and men to the third and fourth floors. The camp committee assigned Sam and Pat to what had been the physical chemistry classroom on the fourth floor of Main. Twenty men lived in the room. Sam and Pat were among the lucky ones able to bring their folding cots with them from Davao. Their thin bamboo pads further softened sleep.

There was no problem with sanitary accommodations. Each floor had multiple showers and toilets. The university received Manila city water that remained on the entire period of internment.

Santo Tomas had a school for the children, plays, lectures, a fine library, and its own police force to maintain order and enforce camp rules. There was a music committee to select pieces for play over the camp loudspeakers and to announce the selections which were sometimes classical and other times popular. Sam soon became involved with a minstrel show produced by the prisoners, in which he sang in a quartet with three other men. The quartet gave a small program held under a starlit tropical night on the lighted quadrangle stage before thousands of appreciatively applauding prisoners. The group sang several numbers and "Lazy Bones" was the big hit of the evening,

At that time, the camp was still under the administration of the Japanese *Gunseibu*, and it was possible for Pat and Sam to receive passes to visit their father and be taken, under guard, by bus to the hospital. There were a limited number of visits a week, so Pat would go one time and Sam the next. By this time the boys were about broke, and their father gave them 500 pesos each. The Japanese mandated currency rolled off the presses, inflation was taking its toll, and the "Mickey Mouse" money, as it was known, would not buy much.

The early favorable impressions of Santo Tomas and the privilege of visiting their father did not last long. Shortly after Pat and Sam reached Santo Tomas, the camp came under the supervision of the *Kempetai*, the dreaded Japanese equivalent of a secret police, much like the German *Gestapo*.

The arrival of the *Kempetai* ended many privileges, and P.H. and a dozen other desperately sick prisoners were returned to Santo Tomas where P.H. was immediately placed back in the camp hospital. Shingles, tuberculosis, and his chronic malaria eventually returned him to the Philippine General Hospital at the insistence of the camp doctors. There he stayed until liberation. In all, he spent no more than three or four months at Santo Tomas during internment. Annie did have access to the hospital and spent most of her time nursing her husband while he was there.

As 1944 progressed, things got worse fast. The *Kempetai* clamped down on any communication or connection with the outside. Guards kept Filipinos back from the fence, and with no more food gifts or purchases, the prisoners had to live on what they had in camp. Any food getting to the prisoners came through the efforts of the internee committee. People began to barter, buy, and sell using any money they had left. Sam and Pat had almost used up their Red Cross packages. Sam had a pack of cigarettes left which he sold for $40. He also had a package of powdered milk that he sold for $100. Outside in the streets Filipinos were also suffering from inflation—a dozen eggs, $18; a pound of fish, $50; a pound of meat, $100.

A cash payment was not always part of the arrangement. There was a vice-president and sales manager for Manila Trading Company in the camp. He was sick and gave Sam a Mantrade-backed $100 IOU for milk. Sam then used the IOU as collateral to back his own IOU's to buy other food he needed; Sam and other prisoners were gambling on eventual liberation to collect on their IOU's. The sick man died in camp. Following the war, Sam sent his $100 IOU to Julius Reece, who was the founder and owner of Mantrade, and Reece sent him a check for the hundred dollars. Men, women and children could hear food vendors outside the camp crying their produce. Due to the lack of proper nutrition, people's joints were swollen, and incidences of stumbling and collapse were routine.

§

The camp executive committee assigned jobs to the prisoners. Once in Santo Tomas, Boots Rider reunited with American nurses who had not made it off Corregidor. They were all sent to the camp hospital which had its own kitchen. Boots arranged with the nurse dietician for Sam to have a cooking job there. He worked with three other men, all pre-war meteorologists in the weather department of Pan American airlines, which operated the Clipper Ships that flew the Pacific. The assignment was a choice job because it came with an extra ration of food.

However, work in the kitchen was hard. The men cooked with enormous *cawas*, wok like vats, heated over hot fires. Through a small window, tin plates were served to the prisoners confined to the infirmary and to the hospital staff. The cooks had little food to work with, mostly dirty rice. When corn was available, they made hominy. As 1944 wore on, matters worsened by the week, slowly at first, but then they accelerated. Rations became so sparse that the cooks would have about a pound of some unidentifiable kind of meat to feed twenty people. The best solution was to cut the meat into little pieces and put it into a watery soup. There was a little vegetable garden for the patients. The garden produced a lot of eggplant which tasted terrible in a soup, but Sam sliced it into small pieces, and it would help fill people up. Trying to find ingredients to put in the soup to give it some body was the cooks' goal. Sam took banana stalks from the banana plants and cut them into puny portions. Weeds would grow up between the vegetables and around the edges of the garden. Internee guards, not Japanese guards, were posted at the hospital garden to keep people out, not because they were picking the vegetables, which were soon gone, but because they were picking the weeds. The weeds had a little value, and Sam would add them to the soup.

There were also internee guards posted in both the infirmary and main kitchens to keep an eye on the cooks. They were all so hungry. A point came when the kitchen crew became too weak to cook and wash the huge pots, so an extra bowl of rice was authorized for them. Sam and the crew also shared the burned rice at the bottom and edges of the iron pots. Four could usually manage to get half a cup each after scraping the pots clean of burned rice. One of the Pan American men had children in the camp and made the most of that rice for his family. Three months after arriving at Santo Tomas, Sam and Pat were down to the last of any food that had come in the Red Cross packages. Soon even that was disappearing.

Sam and Pat always remembered September 21, 1944. Hundreds of American bombers and fighter escorts roared over Manila, simultaneously turning on their flashing lights. It was like a Biblical sign, given as fulfillment of General MacArthur's words, "I shall return." Other air raids followed, but hopes of a speedy release were not realized, and the *Kempetai* guards increased their arrogance and harsh treatment of the internees. The guards vented their feeling in acts designed to humiliate and degrade the prisoners—browbeating, slapping, and increasingly irritating rules and regulations.

On October 20, 1944, the United States army landed on the island of Leyte in the Philippines. Things were now desperate at Santo Tomas. The Davao poker group went shy of players willing to gamble for food, and Pat was out of money. By December 1944, people were dying of starvation.

In those days, parents made their children stay in bed to conserve energy. The adults did the same when they could. Sam would go from the hospital kitchen to his room and plop down, exhausted. Bathroom and shower calls were the only reason he left his bed, only rising again in the early dawn to walk through the camp to the hospital. The men he worked with in the kitchen were all younger than he, fresh out of college, in their early twenties, and in good shape. Sam was forty-one, and two years in Davao did not leave him a strong man at all. He had to do his share, and if he slowed down, he feared replacement and going without the extra ration that went with the job. "I had to fight my way through to hold onto that job, and I hung onto it, I'll tell you."[1]

Chris A. Larsen was one of four men who, along with Carroll Grinnell, E.E. Johnson, and A.F. Duggleby, operated in Santo Tomas an underground radio that communicated with Filipino guerrillas in the hills. On December 23, the *Kempetai* seized Grinnell, Johnson and Duggleby. A "Cliff" Larson roomed with Sam, Pat, and thirty-seven other men in Main. The Japanese guards called out what sounded like "Cliff" instead of "Chris" Larson. Cliff innocently responded and the guards seized and hustled him away, a case of mistaken identity. The reason for the arrests and location of the detention could not be determined; the four men were not seen again.

Christmas 1944 was celebrated meagerly. All children in camp received a single piece of candy. Boots Ryder and other nurses decided to have a party; and each nurse would invite a man. Boots invited Sam. The party became an exemplar of the *Stone Soup* story. They each had saved something from their Red Cross boxes delivered a year earlier. Sam had held back a small tin of pork and beans in addition to his Spam. Pork and beans was his contribution; he held onto the Spam. The men and women put together all the contributions of food for the party. Someone sneaked into the hospital garden, harvested some weeds, and they had a Christmas luncheon. From the clouds, there came a message of hope as American planes dropped thousands of leaflets saying, "The commander-in-chief and men of the United States Army of Liberation in the Pacific wish all their gallant allies, the people of the Philippines all the blessings of Christmas and the realization of their fervent hopes for the New Year."[2]

On January 9, 1945, American forces landed north of Manila at Lingayen and began their drive toward Manila. Soon there were landings to the south.

§

There was no dog, cat, mouse, rat, bird, or any kind of insect or worm that was safe in that camp. Anything that moved was food. An older couple had kept their cat in camp for three years. The cat died, and a friend of Pat promised burial, but the remains instead ended up in a pot and quickly eaten—Pat's second involvement in a cat feast. Weight surveys made by Dr. Ted Stevenson, the camp's chief medical officer, had shown that the average weight loss amongst the male internees was fifty-three pounds of which twenty-seven pounds had been lost since August 1944. By February 1, Sam was down to eighty-four pounds; Pat to one-hundred-ten pounds. Many of the Davao internees starved to death at this time—Betty Lou Gewald, Henry Sterling Peabody, Grace Sage Rigby, Samuel Wiley Thompson, and Henry Umstad. Dr. Stevenson, refusing to change the death certificates listing "starvation" as the cause of death, was arrested and placed in the camp jail. Pat, like his brother, stayed in bed to conserve energy. In those desperate days, he who slept ate.

A group of young boys from the camp broke into the Japanese kitchen and stole kitchen oil, and, as a result, the commandant gave orders for the sentries to shoot anyone coming near the area. Rumors were thick. Those on the hospital kitchen crew had a reliable source of news from the nuns who had given part of their Convent for the camp infirmary. The kitchen where Sam worked connected with both the Convent side and the infirmary side. The nuns had access to a radio. That meant they were receiving the news directly from American armed forces radio and Treasure Island in San Francisco, which had a transmitting tower powerful and high enough to get messages to the Philippines. Each morning, a nun would pass along the news to one of the kitchen crew sweeping the floor or the sidewalk outside the Convent. There were other covert radios in the camp, but the news was kept so compartmentalized that Sam and Pat did not always have good access. But prisoners knew about the landing of American troops at Leyte and Lingayen and about the heavy fighting.

Even before the landing at Leyte, American planes would fly over Manila. One day, Sam was returning from the kitchen. He looked high in the sky observing the usual daily activity of Japanese warplanes. He watched another plane approach, flying out of the sun, shooting one of the Japanese planes down. Then another plane came and shot another Zero down. Soon there was a ferocious dogfight as more and more American planes engaged. Word spread fast in hushed whispers. There was no cheering, only subdued acknowledgements among themselves and private thoughts of an ending to their near and present danger. The prisoners did not want to provoke the guards, and Sam walked on.

American planes were soon coming in waves into Manila. Pat, Sam, and other prisoners on the top floor of Main could see the aircraft in the distance, approaching like a storm, wave after wave. The men watched the planes descend to the horizon edge, saw the bombs released, flashes appear, and seconds later heard the sound of the explosions.

§

General MacArthur and his staff were processing December 14 intelligence of an atrocity on Palawan, an elongated island in the southwest Philippines abutting British Borneo. There Japanese guards had herded 150 American war prisoners living in a stockade into two air raid bunkers, doused the men with gasoline, and set them afire. Machine guns mowed down those able to climb out of the hellish inferno. Only three had escaped. Aided by Filipino guerrillas, the three men emerged from the jungle to report the atrocity. Fearing mass extermination of prisoners of war, MacArthur ordered the daring liberation of Japanese internment camps, thus sending troops on heroic rescue operations to Cabanatuan, Santo Tomas, Los Banos, Bilibid, and Davao Penal Colony.

In Santo Tomas, there were rumors that the *Kempetai* might kill everyone in the camp before the American troops could get to them. Early one evening, Japanese staff from the commandant's office, with a large force of guards armed with guns and fixed bayonets clamored up the steps of Main building, closed all the exits, and stationed guards on all the corridors. Screams mixed with the thunder of boots on the wooden floors preceded three soldiers' pushing into Sam and Pat's fourth floor room. The forty prisoners in the room flinched in anticipation of the worst. Following a ransacking search, the guards gave the men a half-hour's drill in bowing to the Japanese, interspersed with hard slaps to the face. The nearer the American and Filipino forces came, the more such acts of violence increased, and the more bitter and harsh they became.

§

An American fighter came in low over Santo Tomas, dipped its wings to both sides, and near the camp infirmary, the pilot threw down a pair of goggles with a scribbled message attached. Sam did not see the plane, but he received a vivid description from one of the Pan American weathermen on his kitchen crew. The message read, "Roll out the barrel."[3]

CHAPTER 35

"The boys smashed through and what a day it was"

Samuel Boone Frank, February 5, 1945

Sam was napping when he heard firing and explosions close to Santo Tomas. It was Saturday, close to nine o'clock on the evening of February 3, 1945. He heard a rumble and crash as an American tank broke through the double iron gate of Santo Tomas University. He ran to the window. There was a crescendo of cries, "They're here! They're here!" He heard machine guns, rifle fire, and grenades exploding. More tanks came through followed by infantry. Fighting with the Japanese guards started up immediately. The tanks ground to a stop in front of Main. Inside, there was hysterical joy. By that time, Sam had moved down the wide wooden stairs of the building to the ground level. The tall, ponderous front doors were closed, and internee monitors were trying to keep people inside. "There was shooting, but still people wanted to get out and jostled at the heavy doors. It was dangerous out there, but there was no stopping them, especially the kids. The doors burst open, and the children started out. I went through the door with the kids."[1]

Healthy looking American soldiers were sitting on armored machinery, tanks of a design Sam had never seen, throwing candy and chocolate bars. Kids were running around everywhere. Sam felt a moment of dissonance as he took in the sight of healthy American boys wearing steel helmets and combat utilities he did not recognize, looking as if they had come from another planet. The last American rifle he had seen was a single shot, bolt action Springfield. These American soldiers carried M-1 Garand rifles, M-1 carbines, M1A1 Thompson submachine guns, and Browning automatic rifles. Starved prisoners looked at K-Rations hitting the ground and did not know what they were. The M-4 tanks coughed and belched exhaust while troops spread out over the camp. As darkness fell, heavier firing flared, and the loud cacophony of rifle and machine gun fire was accompanied by bright streaks of tracer bullets. A large number of the Japanese guards had retreated to the Education Building where several hundred prisoners lived. With all the shooting going on, Sam helped get people, especially the children, back into Main and then stayed outside a little longer, thinking it would be safe. There was a GI strolling along with his rifle at the ready. Sam walked maybe a half step behind and to the side of him. There was a rustle in some bushes. The soldier swung around, fired and out rolled a Japanese soldier. Sam returned to Main. That was enough action for him.

§

In its race to Santo Tomas through Japanese lines, the First Cavalry Division, a Texas unit, had taken many casualties. Trucks and jeeps carrying the wounded sped through the mangled university gate and braked at the front steps of Main. Sam took a position at the door where a medic was directing the litter bearers saying, "This way" or "That way." If the bearer went "this way," Sam could tell that the wounded were taken for medical aid in a big room to his left. If the bearer went "that way," the stretchers were carried into a room designated the mortuary. Sam walked into the makeshift mortuary. Quietly, respectfully, the Catholic priests removed the uniforms of the dead, bathed their bodies, and gave last rites. "The bodies were laid side by side on a wide platform and I could see the mark where the bullets had hit–maybe one or two marks there. They looked so healthy. They were in such fine physical health, but they were dead." Sam stood among those men, his presence acknowledging their sacrifice in the midst of the exuberance of liberation, his respects paid to those dead soldiers and guerrillas, irregular Filipino fighters that had brought him freedom to rejoin his wife and children.[2]

Sam walked across the hall to the other room were the wounded were lying on cots. He went from one to the next. There were quite a few Filipino guerrillas, fine looking fellows. He stopped and talked for quite awhile to one who had been badly shot. He found out where he was from and who his parents were. They were prominent people on one of the islands. The soldier talked about his family and his guerrilla band coming to Manila to help with the fighting. Sam must have spent thirty or forty minutes communicating with him, the guerrilla fighter relaxing into easy conversation with someone who spoke his language flawlessly. At times their voices approached a whisper. Finally, the boy drifted into heavily sedated sleep, and Sam eased out of the room.

§

Later that night Sam and some of the Davao prisoners broke out the remaining food they had saved for the worst that, thankfully, never came. To the astonishment of the group, Sam brought out his can of Spam and, fishing around in his suitcase, low-and-behold, he revealed a bottle of scotch whiskey. The stuff was green, but it had "Scotch Whiskey" written on it. The whiskey had come into Sam's possession when a Filipino employee sneaked the brew and some mangos to him beneath the wire of the Davao camp, a dangerous generosity extended by the Filipino. Each person had a tin cup or can, and Sam poured. The women and men went out on the veranda that surrounded the interior courtyard of Main, and anyone who wanted a refill poured another drink. The bottle did not last long, Sam remembered. "It could put a buzz on you if it didn't make you sick. It was awful scotch." Outside, liberated prisoners continued their cheering and broke into "America the Beautiful."[3]

While all of that was happening around Main, fearful news was spreading that the Japanese officers and guards had barricaded themselves in the Education Building and were holding hostage over 200 prisoners. American troops began sending the liberated internees back into their quarters for safety, and Sam made his way to his room where he watched events unfold as American searchlights and flares lighted the dark night.

Near the entrance to the Education Building, Pat looked on as several internees came out the door to meet the American commanding officer and negotiate for the safe-conduct of the Japanese staff and guards out of the camp. Accompanying the American hostages were two Japanese civilian administrators, two Lieutenants, and the detested Lt. Abiko, who commanded the guards, oversaw the hated roll calls and forced labor, and required the deepest, longest bows. Abiko was also loathed by the prisoners for his cruelty and brutal slaps. Pat saw Abiko reach his hand toward a pouch. An American soldier's carbine roared, and Abiko fell. A revenge-seeking mob of prisoners dragged Abiko toward Main, kicking, slashing him with knives, and spitting on him. He died that night while under the care of Dr. Stevenson who had been released from the camp jail by American soldiers.

Meanwhile, the Japanese commandant refused surrender, and American tanks began a cannonade of the Education Building following shouted warnings to the hostages to take cover in rear rooms. Sam and Pat watched from the fourth floor of Main as the sharp, hard explosions and rattle of machine guns and rifle fire riddled holes in the building. Tracer bullets ricocheted off the tile walls and careened into the black sky. Later, the brothers learned that the fusillade killed one guard and wounded several hostages and guards; one American internee died in the firefight.

Negotiations continued through the night. Sunday morning the campus of Santo Tomas was crowded by more tanks, howitzers, trucks, jeeps the internees had never seen before and 1,300 additional troops. Fourteen army trucks bringing in food supplies arrived from Lingayen. The American troops began setting up tents and a field kitchen, and began cooking for the liberated prisoners. Sam and Pat's first meal was a rich stew made of mongo beans and canned corn beef, supplemented by food from the Japanese stores, including two cows. The meal proved too heavy, and Pat and Sam, having joined with other emaciated prisoners gobbling down the rich food, paid the price with painful cramps and vomiting

By evening, agreement was reached between the Japanese in the Education Building and the American officials on the outside that there would be no further firing. Early the next morning on Monday, February 5, forty-seven Japanese officers and men were escorted by

262

American soldiers out of Santo Tomas and released. The hostages in the Education Building poured out to the cheers of their friends. Eight of the Japanese soldiers who survived the enraged Filipinos in the city later returned to Santo Tomas to surrender unconditionally.

The entire camp was freed. Anxious to learn about their father's safety, Sam and Pat made inquiries of the American officers but could only learn that Philippine General Hospital was still behind Japanese lines and that all over Manila, fighting was ferocious. Walking across the campus quadrangle, Sam stopped in front of an army cameraman who recorded the scene of an American flag being unfurled by emaciated children, women, and men from the second floor of Main. The camera clicked catching Sam in profile, hand raised in salute as were many others singing, "God Bless America." The occasion was impromptu. A United States Navy commander, Sam Williamson, whose wife and two children were among the internees, had brought in the flag. There was no military ceremony, no speeches, no pomp and circumstance. Many of the thin and ragged internees, soldiers, and newsmen openly shed tears. Sam then went back to the makeshift infirmary to see the wounded Filipino guerrilla—he had died during the night.

By Wednesday, February 7, Japanese artillery shells, responding to the fire of American howitzers set up on the campus, began falling on the camp. Manila was ablaze and heavy explosions shook the ground. A little before nine o'clock, a big crowd of freed Americans gathered in the plaza in front of Main in anticipation of a visit by General MacArthur. Pat pressed in as the General left his car, followed by a group of officers and newspapermen. There was uproarious cheering as Pat struggled to approach MacArthur and, if possible, grasp his hand. Inside Main, Pat was part of the streaming crowd. There was little MacArthur could do but move with his entourage, pausing to greet and talk with old friends and the massive crowd which included Pat and the freed prisoners, jostling and cheering wildly. An Army Signals photographer captured a picture of Pat in the throng nearest to McArthur. Then the General disappeared from view, got into his car, and the entourage drove away. The camp's greeting of its liberator was disorderly, but there was no mistaking the freed Americans' admiration and gratitude. MacArthur remembered the moment in his *Reminiscences*: "One man through his arms around me and cried unashamedly. A once-beautiful woman in tatters laboriously lifted her son over the heads of the crowd and asked me to touch him. I took the boy momentarily and was shocked by the uncomprehending look of deprivation in his eyes. They wept and laughed hysterically, and all of them at once tried to tell me "Thank you." I was grabbed by the jacket. I was kissed. I was hugged. It was a wonderful and never-to-be-forgotten-moment—to be a life-saver, not a life-taker."[4]

Japanese shells raining down on Santo Thomas that night killed twenty-two former internees and wounded thirty-nine. Just before McArthur's arrival in the earlier part of the day, a shell had exploded in the women's wing of Main, killing three and wounding one. One man was killed in the shower room down the hall from Sam and Pat's room. Having survived the suffering of imprisonment for so long, ironically and tragically, dozens more were killed or wounded in shelling that lasted for days. And streams of wounded Filipinos caught in the Manila crossfire came into Santo Tomas.

The International Red Cross brought undelivered mail to the internees, held for years by the Japanese in Manila warehouses. The Red Cross also established expedited communications, and Sam was able to send off to his family a penciled message on tissue thin Red Cross stationery, the organization's bold red symbol printed top center.

§ § §

In St. Louis, Gen and Fran went through anxious days and hours of uncertainty. Headlines in the St. Louis newspapers carried the hopeful progress of MacArthur's troops moving on Manila and the liberation of Santo Tomas. They did not know whether Pat, Sam, and P.H. were among those released. On the same pages were stories of starvation, death, and the fear that civilian internees held hostage in the Education Building had been massacred. At work, Fran used every available network of the Red Cross for information, relaying what she learned to Gen.

Days later, Sam's letter arrived.

Santo Tomas
Manila—February 6, 1945

Dearest Sweetheart, Sammy, P.H., Rusty, "Grandma,"
and everybody—

The boys smashed thru and what a day it was! The best
bunch of fellows in the world—and then FOOD! I will
not attempt a story of what we have gone thru, but as you
have not heard from me, although I've written at least
forty letters and cards and cables—here are the headlines

I was in Davao in charge of the Ice Plant, Telephones,
and Electric Service for the army from December 8 to 20,
1941. All the Americans did something to help. I had
to keep the Plant going till the last minute so the phones
and radios could keep going till the army could evacuate.
That was where they got Pat and me. We were interned
in Davao for two years, then shipped to Santo Tomas in
Manila, arriving here on January 3, 1944. Here I had my
first letters from you. I have received at least twenty from
you and more from family and friends. They were most
reassuring.

Pat and I are both whole and well. Dad has been in an
outside hospital most of the time although the first year
he lived at home on a pass due to age. Annie was never
interned because she was able to revive her Portuguese
Passport. She has been a very great help to Dad. Dad was
in Santo Tomas with us for about six weeks then taken to
Philippine General Hospital. Last I heard he was doing
fine but so far we have not established contact with that
side of town and I've been worried because the Japs have
been blowing up the big buildings the last two days and
they stop at nothing low and dirty.

I have to have a talk and plan with Dad before I can make
plans. So far no news from Davao, although the Plant was
not scratched when we left it. What has pained me often is

that our house and Pats in Davao were completely looted. All our personal belongings are gone. I was caught with clothes we had on and all we got in Davao was due to the fine loyalty of our employees and Filipino friends.

I just got the Red Cross letters today. Heard from you, the boys, Mother (Bessie Russell), Sis, Stu Britt, Aunt Duece, Aunt Edna, Mabel Reed. I'm proud of you all and thankful for all Mother (Bessie Russell) has done. You will hear my plans soon. It will be for the best interests of all, but I wish I could see you all as soon as possible. I love you Frannie, and it'll be fun starting all over again.

Love to all,

Sam, (DADDY)[5]

Across town, Gen opened Pat's letter.

February 6, 1945

Dearest Gen,

Dad, Sam and I have come through it O.K. We were interned (Sam and I) in Davao for two years, then shipped to Manila, where we were liberated by our forces three days ago. We have been badly treated and almost starved, and the first year Sam and I had to do forced labor. But it's all over now, and soon we can make definite plans. For the present, we have been promised transportation to the U.S., and unless I join up, I hope to see you and the children within the next three months.

God bless all of you, and tell Denny, Mike and Paddy that I have seen some real bombing and fighting, and will tell them all about it when I see them. Love to the family—I'm so excited, I think I've done a rotten job with this letter, but all my love goes with it to you and our three boys.

My love,

Pat[6]

§ § §

The brothers' reassurances of their father's condition were premature. Miles away, behind Japanese lines, P.H. was at Philippine General Hospital, Annie assisting with his care. Everywhere American and Filipino forces were moving in on most of Manila's old landmarks, the Intramuros, walled city, large government office buildings, Manila Hotel, and dozens of buildings that were the core of Frank family remembrances over the previous forty-seven years. The Thirty-Seventh Division started crossing the Pasig River on February 7 and moved on the hospital where P.H. and Annie, cut off from Pat and Sam at Santo Tomas, were in a desperate struggle to survive.

The Japanese had converted the hospital, together with the nearby buildings of the University of the Philippines, the Bureau of Science, and the college of Medicine, into a fortress, mounting five-inch naval cannons and machine guns in the hospital corridors in entire disregard for the helpless patients.

MacArthur had forbidden the use of artillery in order to save Filipino lives, but American casualties became so heavy in the fierce street fighting that the order had to be altered. Artillery, however, was not to be aimed at churches and hospitals known to contain Filipino civilians. But even that restriction had to be lifted at Philippine General Hospital. The fighting around P.H and Annie became horrific. The Japanese took up positions in the hospital wards, constructed entrenchments around the three-story hospital, and held out to the last man. P.H. and Annie, along with other patients, took refuge in a four-foot crawl space on the ground under the first floor. Shells slammed into the building above them as they sought what protection they could from the thin mattress they had dragged from P.H.'s bed.

On and on the misery trailed, the P.H. and Annie holding out for ten days, the last three days of which they had no food, little water, and no sleep. The floors above turned to rubble and dust as the Japanese soldiers held out. Patients too sick to be moved along with medical staff were slaughtered by the Japanese or died from bombardments by both American and Japanese forces. On February 17, American tanks and infantry pulverized the Japanese defenses, taking the grounds around the hospital. Within hours, the Japanese retook the hospital grounds, and back and forth the ferocious fighting continued. Finally, P.H. felt strong American arms picking him up and dragging him behind a shield of American tanks.

P.H. was driven across the Pasig River into American lines to the safety of Santo Tomas. Annie became separated from him during the escape, and he was in frenzy from illness and worry, lying on a stretcher tied to a Jeep, feverish, hallucinating, and dressed in filthy pajamas. All of Santo Tomas was abuzz about the liberation of fifty Americans at Philippine General Hospital, and Pat and Sam were present when their father was brought in. Delirious, he questioned, "Where is Annie? Where is Annie?" He wanted Sam and Pat to find her, but it was impossible. Manila lay in ruins and on fire. Black smoke in an inky cloak streaked the sky.[7]

Annie, separated from her husband in the desperate break from Philippine General Hospital, made her way to Santo Tomas the next day. She had survived the previous night in Manila rubble.

§

Sam and Pat walked the several miles to their father's Taft Avenue home. They worked themselves slowly through the debris-strewn streets and barely recognizable landmarks. Japanese snipers were active, but the brothers wanted to find out if anything remained. There was not much. The entire house was gone, as were other houses all along the street. As far as their eyes could see, broken and burned rubble was strewn everywhere and there was no way of escaping the stench. P.H. and Annie had an iron fence surrounding the house. Large cement stanchions supported the wide gate. The Japanese had fortified with sandbags around the gates and mounted a machine gun through the mail slot. The bodies of three Japanese soldiers lay sweltering and bloated in the tropical sun. There were no trees or shrubs, nothing recognizable from the pre-war manicured gardens that were now scorched stubble. What remained was a cement slab. Their father's reinforced walk-in concrete safe rose from the center. Inside the safe were incinerated bodies of Japanese soldiers. The teakwood box crafted by their father in 1916 to hold surviving treasures of their sister Laura's life was gone. There was nothing but a small pile of ashes lifting and bowing with the breeze.

Following liberation, young American internees at Santo Tomas University prisoner of war camp, swarm over an American M-5 tank in the university courtyard. *(Courtesy of MacArthur Memorial Archives, U.S. Army Signal Corps)*

Sam Frank *(circled)* joins in *God Bless America* as the flag was unfurled over the front entrance of the Santo Tomas Main Building on Monday, February 5, 1945, at 9:15 in the morning. *(Courtesy of MacArthur Memorial Archives, U.S. Army Signal Corps)*

Pat Frank *(circled)* among freed prisoners of war who cheer General Douglas MacArthur when he visits Santo Tomas Internment Camp on February 5, 1945. *(Courtesy of MacArthur Archives, U.S. Army Signal Corps)*

CHAPTER 36

"Rejoice—it won't be long now"

Frances Russell Frank April 4, 1945

Having been freed from their hellish lives in Santo Tomas, Sam and Pat felt that the war was over. But, in reality, it continued to rage on. The allies in Europe were crossing the Rhine, and Churchill, Roosevelt and Stalin were meeting at Yalta. During the next two weeks, Sam and Pat followed the news of MacArthur's troops' landing on Corregidor and United States Marines' assaulting Iwo Jima. The brothers wanted to go home; they had no way to get home, and their father was critically ill. Fighting in the Philippines was continuing, and Mindanao was still under Japanese control, making it impossible to find out the condition of the family businesses in Davao.

Following the experience of their first meals when the army took over the camp, Sam and Pat learned to take it easy on the food. They were regulating themselves now, gaining strength and weight fast eating plenty of meat, potatoes, bread and butter, milk, and spooning all the ice cream they could handle. Soon they were feeling much better. Some of the prisoners were too far gone to benefit from medical attention and food. By February 5, seven former internees had died, malnutrition the chief cause of death; more followed.

Sam closed out the Davao Internment Camp financial records and handed them over to Walter Tong for auditing. Sam additionally gave Walter the balance of camp funds he had held as secretary-treasurer.

Within months of repatriation to the United States, Sam and Walter had the satisfaction of knowing that all internees within the Davao group had settled their accounts with one another and with the Filipino friends who had smuggled money to them in the camp. Filipino engagement in this dangerous business was sure proof of their love and loyalty to all the Davao Americans; Sam never forgot the generosity of his Japanese friends in Davao.

On February 21, the beheaded body of Cliff Larson was found next to Carroll Grinnell, A.F. Duggleby, and E.E. Johnston—all bound together by wire with a fifth person, an unknown nun—Cliff's death a case of his mistaken identity two days before Christmas, 1944.

§

Pete Grimm, a good friend of Pat and Gen in pre-war Manila, was a member of MacArthur's staff and was placed in charge of Santo Tomas as acting commandant. By February 26, Grimm had scheduled the first group of Americans for repatriation to the United States and had made sure that Pat and Sam were on the first list. But the boys hesitated to leave their father alone in Santo Tomas. They pow-wowed with Annie and came up with a plan for Annie to find housing in the less damaged outskirts of Manila. Pat would go to the States first and Sam would follow as soon as their father was recovered enough to be moved. P.H. gave Pat and Sam $5,000 notes drawn on Crocker National Bank in San Francisco where he had made pre-war deposits resulting from his sale of Cotabato Light & Power Company.

On Monday morning, February 22, Pat's name was called on the camp loud speaker, and by two o'clock he and thirty other men and boys as well as forty-one women and children boarded army trucks to be taken to an airfield newly carved into a Manila highway. He tucked himself into a twin-engine C-47 that circled over the battle-scared city, twice spotting the sixty-four acre prison camp where the death rate had been so high in the last weeks of his internment. The flight continued to Tacloban on Leyte where Pat, following additional recuperation, boarded a transport for the United States.

Several days following Pat's repatriation, P.H. prematurely left the camp, against the advice of the army doctors, to stay with his Filipino attorney with whom he had left many of his important business papers.

P.H. was anxious to find out conditions in Davao and begin again. That left Sam free to go home, and Pete Grimm put Sam's name on the March 2 list of the next group to leave. At Nichols Field, Sam scrambled up the ladder of a C-47 that followed his brother's route to Tacloban where he bunked in a large canvas army tent and took long strolls on the beach where General MacArthur had wadded ashore months earlier.

On March 8, Sam boarded an LST (Landing Ship Tanks) that ferried him to the *USS Admiral Capps* where he joined 844 former internees including 250 women and children. The transport took a thirty-six day, wide-ranging southern route, zigzagging to avoid enemy submarines.

§

On April 5, Sam landed at a cold, windy San Francisco wharf, still wearing the army utilities issued him at Santo Tomas liberation. Major Burk Dresher, a fraternity brother from Washington University days, met him. Burk carried a letter from Fran as well as a warm jacket he had brought along for his friend. The Red Cross had called Fran days earlier advising that her husband would be arriving on the next boat. She shot off a telegram and then a letter through Burk.[1]

> *Darling,*
>
> *I'm so excited and nervous I can hardly write…Oh, darling—can hardly believe it…so welcome home, darling…call us as soon as possible, I will be hugging the telephone, and oh, come to us soon…so darling—rejoice, it won't be long now.*
>
> *Frances*

Fran, like Gen, wanted to meet her husband at the pier, but the State Department discouraged her. The War Department was moving men and material from the European theatre of war to the Pacific. Thus, for Fran, arranging transportation was nearly impossible. Additionally, Fran did not know when to expect Sam. Ship convoy movements were top secret, and places to stay in San Francisco were extremely limited.

At the Dresher's home that night, Sam enjoyed slumber in luxuriating silence and privacy, his first in over three years. There were no camp noises, smells, or discomforts of nagging hunger to keep him from sleeping. Late in the morning, he awakened to the aroma of coffee and the serene view of the Big Sur out his bedroom window.

Working with the Red Cross, Sam was able to secure a single room in the quiet, old Cecil Hotel, just a block from the St. Francis where he and Fran had honeymooned in 1931 before leaving for the Philippines. He was lucky because most internees had to double up with strangers.

Fran wired $500 that enabled her husband to turn in his utilities for a new gray suit, topcoat, shoes, robe, some socks and ties, and a suitcase. The Red Cross was going to take care of his transportation to St. Louis. He loosened the purse strings just a little, but said he "should arrive in St. Louis with $400." Sam closed, "I can't wait to see you and the swell family you've kept together all these years." Nine days later, he held a Red Cross issued ticket for a seat on the Missouri-Pacific Railroad. News of the death of President Franklin Delano Roosevelt in Warm Springs, Georgia, came on April 12, as his train thundered across the plains.[2]

CHAPTER 37

"I found the family all well after some trying years"

Samuel Boone Frank, May 11, 1945

§ § §

My father arrived at Delmar Station in St. Louis on a cold April 14, 1945, afternoon. I was wearing navy wool shorts and coat, knee socks, a wool cap, and Buster Brown shoes. I remember standing at the head of the stairs leading down to the train platform. A handrail of polished brass was cold to my touch. My mind's eye still sees a man dressed in a suit at the bottom of the steps. He was carrying everything he owned in a suitcase. We all stood for a moment not quite knowing what to do. Mother got down the steps first. My brothers and I were soon behind her. I remember being in the man's arms; I remember his whiskers against my cheek, and wetness.

That evening, my mother's family shared the dining room table with us. I went upstairs and brought down a pair of my freshly washed, faded blue socks, placing them in front of my father's dinner plate. I remember the warm appreciative laughter and applause of the adults. My father had found his way home.

§ § §

A few days following his arrival, getting his bearings, assimilating the changes in his children, wife, and himself, and continuing to nurse his health, Sam wrote to his father, "I found my family all well after some trying years. I have some catching up to do…Fran was underweight from working and looking after the boys, but in good health. Sammy is twelve years old, doing well in school, is a fine strong boy, a little too serious sometimes, but a natural leader. He is well liked by his schoolmates, is often chosen captain of teams, and excels in all the games and sports the boys play. He is in a good Boy Scout troop, and has been taking piano lessons for three years. He has some talent and plays well, but like all boys, hates to practice, and would rather work on model aero planes, which he also does." [1]

Pat had an eighth birthday coming up, and Sam observed, "He is a deep thinker, and has an amiable disposition, doing well in school, but no particular tendencies showing up yet, except the one outstanding thing—he is thinking when most people are just listening. He has a keen sense of humor, full of wit, and gets along well with other children."[2]

Sam noted that Russell, not yet in school, would be five on the Fourth of July. He also wrote that Russell was full of good sense and loved to help around the house. "He is very bright and full of fun. He loves to tease and tries to keep up with Pat and Sammy." He noted that "none of the boys show signs of being large men," but adding only as a father might, "they will all be strong and way above average intelligence."[3]

Washington University provided Sam the opportunity to have free work done on his teeth by dental students. The years of internment had taken its toll, and Sam required a dozen fillings and three extractions that left a vacant space that showed until he received a new tooth. He also had a complete medical examination. His blood count, hemoglobin, heart and lungs were all in excellent shape. His only troubles were a stress ulcer and stomach acidity that he would have to watch with proper diet and anti-acid preparations. In 1952, while attending a meeting in Jacksonville, Florida, one of those ulcers gave way, and he came close to bleeding to death.

Sam began to consider the future, and, while he remained open, he sensed there was a strong likelihood he would never return to the Philippines. He decided to provide his father with a fair picture of his and his family's situation. He wrote even as P.H. and Annie were on the Pacific Ocean aboard a hospital ship.

§

Back in Manila, there had been frequent warnings to the former internees that they should take advantage of transportation offered by the U.S. government for their return to the United States. P.H. was reluctant to go before he had straightened out his affairs and, at times, did not want to go at all. The Philippines had been his home for forty-seven years. His Eugenia and Laura were buried in Zamboanga. In addition, even though his credit was solid, his lack of funds handicapped him, for no banks had yet been allowed to reopen their doors in the Philippines. Moreover, his business records were destroyed, except for a few left with a friend in an outlying province where there was continuing heavy fighting that kept him from retrieving them. He was eager to get to Davao to see what was left of his businesses, but Davao had not been retaken from the Japanese. There was still heavy fighting there, and getting permission from the area commander to travel on Mindanao was impossible. Manila lacked means of communication, and transportation in the city was difficult; Annie had to walk for hours to get anywhere in the sprawling ruins. P.H. was seriously ill, weak, and in no shape to get to Davao even if he could.

The British, Dutch, Swedes and other civilian nationals, intent on remaining in the islands and rebuilding their businesses and lives, were receiving help from their governments—but not the Americans. Through the Bell Act passed by Congress in 1944, the United States was providing aid to the Philippine Commonwealth government for rebuilding, and the State Department felt it politically undesirable to provide financial assistance to U.S. citizens to rebuild from relief funds given to the Philippine Government. MacArthur wrote all Americans on March 23, saying, "Such individuals who decline to accept repatriation (to the United States)…when transportation is made available to them should be informed that…transportation may not be available at a later date." P.H. Frank was shocked, disappointed, and angry.[4]

P.H. and many Old Timers looked upon the Philippine government much as a citizen in the United States looked upon the U.S. government. Many of these Americans had helped to build the Philippines, supported the commonwealth government, and while there had paid taxes every year. Were not the islands still the Commonwealth of the Philippines? Why should they not share in any relief extended by the United States?

Right as they might have been, any voice they had was subordinate to the clamor of fighting the war. P.H. reluctantly and sadly accepted the "transportation offered," even though it meant abandoning everything he had left and the possibility that he might not be able to return for a long time.

P.H. could hardly walk when he was once again admitted to the hospital at Santo Tomas. Then on April 10, leaving for the transport ship, he and Annie rode in one of several jungle green army ambulances that led a long line of big trucks. At one of the Manila piers, corpsman carried him by stretcher onto the hospital ship, *SS Pennant*. He twisted his head just enough to see Manila Bay littered with some 500 ships that had been sunk there, sixty-two of them over 2,000 tons each. The scene he witnessed was the biggest ship-salvaging job undertaken at any harbor in the world.

§

P.H. and Annie and Sam and Pat had gone through an experience in the Philippines that for anyone not there was difficult, if not impossible, to comprehend. Terror had often seized hold of them and death had stalked near. P.H. had spent forty-seven years on the islands and made enormous contributions advancing America's noble purposes. His children were native-born *mestizo* sons of the Filipino-American experience. His grandchildren were born in the islands, scions of his investments in transportation and utilities on the Philippine frontier. Commenting on the departure of so many American residents in the Philippines, the *Free Philippines* newspaper observed poignantly, "With them passes an era."[5]

Eugenia, Laura, and Don Fermin Garcia lay in the Old Catholic Cemetery in Zamboanga. In Cotabato lay the indigenous ancestors of Sam and Pat. Their native grandmother was still living, but they did not know that.

In the *Pennant*'s tuberculosis ward where P.H. lay, three TB patients died, all Old Timers, and their bodies committed to the sea. Annie, in a separate part of the ship, spent much of her time dancing and playing cards, the young soldiers bringing her cokes and cigarettes.

The Franks were reuniting in Saint Louis, and P.H. and Annie were on the Pacific, the *SS Pennant* threading its way through the Caroline Islands, zigzagging to avoid enemy submarines. P.H. and Annie arrived in San Francisco May 14, 1945. He was transferred directly to Marine Hospital where doctors confirmed his diagnosis of tuberculosis that had spread to both lungs. He was then sent to Letterman Army Hospital where he began an unpredictable convalescence. The doctors were hopeful that within three months he might show enough improvement to recuperate in eighteen to twenty-four months. Nevertheless, if after three months, there were no improvement, "I will just be a case of lingering on," he wrote. His heart was weak and circulation bad. His legs turned blue when he stood and trembled so that it was difficult for him to stand. He was seventy years old. Three more of his friends died in the wards.[6]

§

America had turned its attention to the battle for Okinawa and Roosevelt's death in April. Germany surrendered in May, and final preparations were underway for the invasion of Japan. Australian troops invaded Borneo, and the Chinese were launching drives against the Japanese invaders. Ex-colonialists were old news—especially in San Francisco, which was then getting ready to host the conference that would establish the United Nations, set up by the United States to lead the world into a post-colonial era.

Part 7
Return to the Philippines
1946 to 1950

"With them passes an era"

Manila Free Press, April 1945

CHAPTER 38

"I know how to start from scratch.
That's about all I do know"

Patrick Henry Frank, July 4, 1945

The Japanese troops in the southern Philippines were now completely isolated and no longer posed a threat to the progress of MacArthur's prosecution of the war against Japan. Lt. General Robert Eichelberger and the American Eighth Army launched its campaign April 17, 1945, against the 43,000 Japanese forces remaining on Mindanao. The operation on Mindanao and Sulu was to liberate Filipinos and destroy Japanese forces. The primary target was Davao, headquarters of the Japanese One-Hundredth Division that was protected by an extensive naval and air base built up the last three and a half years. The task went to the U.S. Twenty-Fourth Division which commenced landings at Cotabato, taking ten days of hard eastward fighting to arrive at the outskirts of Davao. On May 3, the Nineteenth Infantry Regiment was at the Davao River looking across at the ruined and smoldering city, a shambles from American bombing and naval guns powered from the Davao Gulf. Mines at each end of the Davao River Bridge were defused, and the American infantrymen moved unopposed into town. The Japanese had left the town, erecting strong fortifications in the hills west of Davao. All the 13,000 Japanese civilians remaining in Davao had fled with them. At last, Japan's last urban stronghold in the Philippines was back in American and Filipino hands.

With the capture of Davao, General MacArthur announced victory in Mindanao even though American soldiers continued slugging it out with Japanese soldiers in what history has named the "Battle of the Abaca Fields." Fields cleared from the jungle during the early century were now overgrown with impenetrable hemp plants and razor-edged cogon. Men could see no further than ten feet within that interwoven welter of green. What had been poignantly beautiful fields, cleared and nurtured by the early American pioneers and Filipino workers in 1905 and nurtured by giant Japanese corporations in the 1920's and 30's, now lay in ruins. Where abaca had once been harvested by P.H.'s hemp-stripper, there was now no more than a gloomy expanse of tangled green killing fields. Throughout this unearthly battlefield, the Japanese had built a network of hidden fortifications. Fighting had been close range. Often point troops received fire just yards before locating enemy positions. Not until June 10 did the last organized resistance in the Davao area end. Mop up operations continued for weeks.

The campaign through the abaca fields and into the foothills around Davao took 820 American soldiers' lives and wounded 3,000 more. The Japanese refused to surrender, lost 13,000 troops, and reportedly killed their own civilians.

§

In Manila, Billy Gohn, one of the earliest Davao pioneers and lifelong friend of P.H., was now seventy-one years old, recovering from internment and ill health. He pressed Lt. General Bob Eichelberger, area commander on Mindanao, for permission to return to Davao for salvaging company property and restoring electric service even as fighting continued. Gohn wanted desperately to learn what had survived of his own home and life's work in Davao. That work had been tied largely to his friend P.H. Frank's companies, in which he was the second largest stockholder. What Gohn found and reported to P.H. was devastating. Davao Light and Power Company had suffered 80 percent losses, and nothing was left of Mindanao Sales and Services—offices, showrooms, shops were absolutely destroyed. A large bomb had hit on the south side of the power company offices and store, blowing off the roof and ceiling and severely damaging one complete sidewall. Other walls were badly cracked and full of shell holes. The shop building was blown to pieces. Not a single piece of vital equipment remained. The powerhouse was a complete loss. Five of the enormous Fairbanks-Morris generators that had once hummed life into the Davao economy lay torn apart from their moorings, burned or destroyed by bombs. Two of the engines were at the bottom of a twelve-foot bomb crater in the powerhouse floor. Even if replaced, no new floor could hold the engine tonnage on inevitably settling fill dirt. The small barrio generating plants had disappeared. Most of the transmission and distribution system were gone. Long stretches of wire were missing and, in other places, cut between posts. The Japanese had removed transformers and other materials and supplies and hidden them in caves and on hemp plantations. In some cases, the equipment was simply strewn along roads, trails, and grass fields. Gohn reported that his own old residence as well and those of Sam and Pat were completely gone—nothing, absolutely nothing, remained.

The worst news of all was that Pedro Lat, a Filipino collaborator, and other local Filipino politicians who had cooperated with the Japanese had filed an affidavit with the city council for a franchise to light the city. Gohn was trying to get a small army auxiliary generator turned over to him until he could get one of the company's generating units up and running, but Lat and others wanted the army's generator turned over to them. Gohn was fighting to protect Davao Light and Power's fifty-year franchise, the one asset left with remaining value.

The Philippines was slated to gain full independence in less than a year. Corruption was solidly imbedding itself within the Philippine culture, and P.H. and his sons were out of the country. All that P.H., Sam, and Pat had built was ingloriously dissolving. Someone with capital was backing Lat and the politicians, and with ample grease, they could steal the franchise.

Gohn appealed for assistance from Major Woodruff, the Davao sector commander, to intercede in the attempted takeover by Lat. Woodruff did this immediately, and Gohn received a promise that the army would assist in construction of a provisional plant. What Billy Gohn desperately needed were P.H.'s proxies to hold a stockholders meeting, put him in charge, meet payrolls, and begin enough construction to hold the franchise. There was no time to discuss options at such great distance and under the conditions existing in Davao. So Gohn wrote P.H. about the proposed deal, the last sentence doing nothing to hide the urgency, "Writing paper costs ten centavos a sheet, take it or leave it," Fortunately for Gohn, an army captain was willing to send the letter and future mail through priority channels. The news reached P.H. within eight days, and he replied from Letterman Army Hospital, authorizing Gohn to take charge.[1]

On May 3, 1945, the 19th Infantry Regiment entered a ruined Davao.
(MacArthur Memorial Archives, U.S. Army Signal Corps)

American bombs and naval gunfire reduced Davao Light & Power Co to ruins. *(Courtesy of Emory University MARBL, Frank Family Collection)*

Davao Light & Power Company's Fairbanks-Morris engines and generators were unsalvageable. *(Courtesy of Emory University MARBL, Frank Family Collection)*

Twisted remains of Mindanao Sales and Services Company's shops and show rooms, Davao, 1945. *(Courtesy of Emory University MARBL, Frank Family Collection)*

CHAPTER 39

"I built castles in the air...
but it all came tumbling down"

Patrick Henry Frank, February 13, 1946

The vultures were more than circling. P.H. knew it, and he had to know what support he could expect from the American government. Sick and fragile, he dictated a letter through Annie to Richard Ely, Executive Assistant to the United States High Commissioner in the Philippines. Ely responded: "...I doubt very much the United States government does very much to help private firms in the Philippines." The war was still going. The Philippines was to receive its independence in a year. "I hate to be so discouraging."[1]

P.H. and his sons began analyzing their options even as Billy Gohn was trying to hold together the franchise. First, the men would require large amounts of capital to rebuild. Provisions of the Bell Act, passed by Congress while American civilians languished in the internment camps, authorized payments to companies like P.H.'s only for "repairs and replacements." The intent of Congress was to prevent business people like P.H. from collecting large damage claims and then leave the Philippines with their money rather than rebuilding infrastructure and investing in the islands. Any money the family might receive for war damages had to remain in the Philippines and be used specifically for rebuilding their utilities.

The Bell Act also prevented the family from claiming damages from American military action. They could claim for Japanese action, but only for damages before January 2, 1942. For the Franks, the provision was madness. The Japanese had done no harm to the family's utilities and businesses when they entered Davao. It was American action that had brought about their destruction in 1944-45. It was also becoming clear that reparations from Japan would also be impossible to collect. Leaving Germany, Italy, and Japan open to war reparations was counter to the prevailing view of the Marshall Plan for rebuilding those countries into peaceful, prosperous economies.

Additionally, the Philippines would be sovereign under provisions of the 1935 Tydings-McDuffie Act granting the islands full independence in 1946. Under amendments to those provisions, the Franks would have to give up sixty-percent ownership of their utilities to Filipinos following independence. Therefore, even if the family could have raised the capital to rebuild independent of war-damage compensation, they would loose control of their ownership.

There was one loophole available to them. Sam, Pat and their sons were born in the Philippines. Under the Tydings-McDuffie Act, they had civil parity with the Filipinos. They were qualified for sixty-percent ownership of the family businesses by claiming their rightful Philippine citizenship. It was quite literally as simple as filling out a form. The family knew this, but P.H. never asked his sons or his grandsons to give up the American citizenship and cultural identity for which he himself had always sought for them.

For Sam and Pat, there were also issues of leaving their families again after so much suffering and separation. There were children to raise and educate, pressing needs for jobs and cash flow, and the ever-present question of inheritance—where did the boys fit into their father's plans after the years it would take to rebuild? The wellbeing of Annie, so close to the boys in age, was also on P.H.'s mind..

The complexity of the whole issue was an insufferable Catch 22. Sam and Pat mounted job searches while keeping open their Philippine options—because opportunities to rebuild were highly lucrative under certain conditions and because of their desire to please their father.

For a year, P.H. fretted over his options, corresponding with his sons and trying to sort it all out. Many of P.H.'s business friends came to visit him at Letterman, sharing their plans to return to Manila and rebuild. P.H. was seventy-one years old now, seriously ill and still recovering when he left with Annie for the islands with an almost delusional goal, "Perhaps a generating unit can be put back together out of the wreck and a start from scratch made. And I know how to start from scratch, that's about all I do know."[2]

§

P.H. and Annie boarded a Swedish freighter in April 1946, with twelve other passengers, all wanting desperately to return to the islands to assess matters for themselves, and all willing to accept less than commodious accommodations—six men in one cabin and six wives in another. They saw land only once when they passed Saipan and enjoyed warm weather several days before arriving in Manila. The Swedish captain, chief engineer, stewards, and Annie played cards for pennies, competed in deck golf, and wagered on a daily mileage pool.

The six couples stood at the freighter's rail astonished at the sight of over 100 cargo ships lying inside and outside the breakwater waiting to get to the Manila docks for unloading. They saw many more hundreds of wrecks of Japanese warships sunk by American bombers and still awaiting salvage. Because of the backup, it took all day for the twelve to get to shore on a Navy LST; it was a month before their heavy steamer trunks made it to the wharfs.

Friends managed to arrange a small apartment for P.H. and Annie. It was Vito Cruz only three blocks from the ruins of their old home on Taft Avenue. The apartment was terribly hot, dusty, and the rent was inflated. There was little privacy because of two additional apartments in the building. Meals for fifteen pesos a day enabled them to avoid the dirty, bromidic restaurants which would cost them more. The Manila P.H. returned to was in ruins. The greater part of the city was a shack-town of rickety structures perched on toppled buildings. The tired looking people were poorly dressed. Blasts of raucous music filled the air. Manila, once Gen's Pearl of the Orient, was ravaged and ruined.

Billy Gohn found P.H. in Manila on May 17 and came straight to the point. Davao Light & Power and Mindanao Sales and Services were destroyed. Gohn had sold the salvage, drawn his prewar salary and expenses, sold his minority shares to the Dacudao family, and claimed the company owed him 6,000 pesos. He had made a fortune working for the army and said he now owned and operated his own power plant at the Furakawa Plantation for the U.S. government. Things could not have been bleaker for P.H. He felt betrayed by Gohn to whom he had entrusted his proxies. His only chance would be the return of his sons to rebuild his franchise.

§

A month later in June 1946, Patrick Henry Frank stood numbed in the ruins of Davao and saw the situation for himself. The immense Fairbanks-Morse generators that had once hummed life into the Davao economy lay torn apart from their moorings; the streets of Davao were unrecognizable. The Davao Mission Hospital where his grandsons Mike and Russell were born still stood amongst the utter destruction, one wall of the hospital obliquely angled. The hemp plantations lay fallow; the Frank hemp-strippers rusted in the overgrown tropical fields. The islands that had been P.H.'s home since 1898 were returning to chaos and a life that had changed drastically in his absence. He was in a world he could no longer comprehend. His thoughts may have been the same as expressed four months earlier to Bessie Russell, "When I think back over the years it all seems like a dream...I built many castles in the in the air and made many dream plans for the future, but it all came tumbling down."[3]

Before returning to Manila, P.H. was in Davao for three weeks, suffering from diarrhea, recurrent malaria, cough, and fever, unable to go through with any plans to resurrect his life in the Philippines. He had to have his sons.

A letter from Sam mailed to him on May 20, but delayed in transit, awaited him. Sam had joined Pat in deciding to make his and his family's lives in the United States. P.H. was devastated.

§

P.H. was in Manila but had no attraction for the ceremonies on July 4, 1946, when the flag of the Philippine Republic replaced the American flag on a white cord. It was a voluntary emancipation of a colony by its former sovereign. Still, there was a powerful lure, and P.H. Frank braved the torrential rains and crowds of jubilant Filipinos who packed the Luneta and heard the "Star Spangled Banner" followed by the "Marcha Nacional." He stood to the side, well away from the dignitaries protected by tenting. His focus was on the walls of the Intramuros where he had watched the American flag raised August 13, 1898. In Manila Bay, the U.S. Seventh Fleet fired a salvo of twenty-one guns, joined by Australian, Portuguese, and Siamese war ships. A great surge of nationalistic aspirations coursed through the body politic of the Far East. And later P.H. wrote his sons, "What we will do next, or where to go, and when, is the problem. It is a terrible thing that has happened to us, and is too long a story to tell now."[4]

§

Ramon Aboitiz came to see P.H. The Frank-Aboitiz contract of November 1941, selling Davao Light and Power before the war, was no longer extant, but Aboitiz valued the chance to purchase the fifty-year power company franchise to add to his power plants in Cebu, Jolo, and Cotabato. "I decided to sell Davao Light and Power shares at 70 centavos per share," P.H. wrote Gen. He had sold his life's work for what he could get. A centavo is a hundredth of a peso, the same as a penny is to a dollar. "Aboitiz is to pay us whatever pro rata share of the War Damage Compensation amounts to. He paid cash, with the balance to be paid in twenty quarterly installments at 7 percent interest"—one fifth of the company's contract sale value to Aboitiz weeks before Pearl Harbor, 1941.[5]

On August 6, the United States dropped the atomic bomb on Hiroshima, and two days later on Okio Yamaguchi's home in Nagasaki.

§ § §

The Southern Crescent spirited down the track somewhere between St. Louis and Atlanta. It was the summer of 1946, after midnight, and hot enough to have the window cracked and smell the acrid mix of coal smoke and dusty cinders. I was on a Pullman train car, the lower bunk, turned on my side facing the window. Mother was next to me. My brother Pat was on the upper bunk. A curtain separated our private sleeping area from the public corridor periodically patrolled by a conductor, our comfort overseen by a white coated attendant.

Mother gave me the window side next to the webbed clothes hammock. The train hissed, the rails clicked and clacked. My senses absorbed the eerie sounds of the whistle and unearthly figures standing in the yellow light of loading platforms. I remember the clank, buckle, and heave-to of the train cars at switching time, the fried chicken lunch packed by my grandmother, supper in the dinning car with rattling dishes and utensils on a linen tablecloth, the streaming countryside, and the earth turning red as we entered Georgia. I was on a journey from uncertainty to certainty, a place that became home.

My parents, my brothers, and I arrived in Atlanta and moved into a small home on Hancock Drive just in time for us boys to enroll at Druid Hills School next to Emory University on the day following Labor Day, 1946. Sammy was in first year of high school; Pat in fourth grade; and I in first grade. My father had received an appointment as Chief Engineer and Sales Manager for the James R. Kearney Company's southeastern district, and Atlanta, with a population of 250,000, would be his headquarters. My uncle and his family remained for a time in St. Louis and then Pittsburgh in the automobile industry on a trajectory that led to a position in advertising with Young & Rubicam, managing the Plymouth automobile account in Detroit.

The war had not ended our lives, but it changed its trajectory.

§ § §

For the last time, Patrick Henry Frank, treading a requiem for a fallen cause, a broken and nerve-shattered soldier, made his final crossing of the Pacific and entered his country through the Golden Gate. They were the same Golden Gate hills through which he had passed on the way to the Philippines in 1898.

P.H. immediately entered Ross General Hospital, with recurring tuberculosis, neuritis, and shingles. Ross was a rather scattered residential village for long-term care eighteen miles from San Francisco on the road crossing the Golden Gate Bridge. The valley was small and seemed to P.H. to widen at the ends, but it was almost a gorge in the center where the hospital was located. High sloping, heavily wooded hills were on either side of the narrow valley. The main part of the complex was a three story terraced sanatorium on the side of the mountain overlooking the hospital. Beyond the mountain enclosing the opposite side of the valley, Mt. Tamalpai loomed south in the background. "It is a splendid view with gorgeous autumn colors," he wrote from the hospital in November 1946, a stoical, even serene, small masterpiece of unsentimental dignity—a soldier's letter.[6]

The hospital from which P.H. wrote was nothing special, but he had known worse. His room was on the top floor. Only seven rooms occupied that floor, with one patient to a room. Forty-two other rooms occupied the three terraces. Doors on the south side remained open to the fresh, cool air. He found creature comforts sufficient: food good enough, nurses efficient, and everything clean. He lived under strict rules—bed rest, no medicine except vitamins, no smoking, and no visiting. His doctor said he should be well in five months. P.H. mused, "Come spring we will see what we see. Nothing to do now but hole up for the winter...in the meantime with my little radio and the daily paper, I will see what goes on—and there seems to be plenty.[7]

P.H. also spent quiet, drifting time on the south side patio in the sunshine, reading and connecting with memories that reflected an earlier period of his life and centering his eyes on the distant knoll anchoring Golden Gate Park and the Presidio. Those grounds, which had encompassed Camp Merritt, were where Private Frank encamped with the 23rd Infantry in 1898 before departing for the Philippines. He was letting go of his life in the islands, "I think the Philippines is in for a long siege of turmoil and I do not expect to go there to live permanently, but may go to attend to some things."[8]

P.H. Frank had survived a horrible year and the disheartening end of his life's work, but he did not look back. Annie came and went on the bus to Vallejo, while he holed up for the winter and waited for spring. If getting back his health was not easy, at least it was a task with some clarity to it, a task that was not hopeless. The gains and losses of a long and eventful life seem put behind him, and he vowed to leave the future to take care of itself. "This is a perfect day after the rain," he concludes. "Love to everyone."—He was alert, but at peace, a version of the final man.[9]

§

P.H. and Annie moved into a two-bedroom house in a suburb of Benicia called West Manor built in the early 1940's. All the streets had Spanish names. Theirs was Buena Vista, the house being "on an outside street, no houses in back of them, nice view of the west hills, trees and the Coquinas Straits and hills beyond." He purchased a used 1946 Packard from a man who had just bought it and decided he could not afford the payments. The motor vehicle department issued P.H. an "Instruction Permit" after he had applied for a driver's license and been turned down. For all of P.H.'s years in the transportation business, he had never learned to drive. He rationalized that because of his age, seventy-three, "No auto insurance company will permit me to drive a car...I could take the risk without the insurance but there are so many reckless drivers on the roads." He missed old Pantar, his chauffeur for all those years, executed by the Japanese in the waning years of the war.[10]

CHAPTER 40

"A special favor I would ask of you…"

P.H. Frank, April 1947

In April 1947, P.H. wrote his friend James Wilson in Zamboanga. It had been in Wilson's machine shop that P.H. had developed his prototype hemp-stripper during the early years. It was in Wilson's shop that he fashioned a box that held remembrances of his daughter's life. "A special favor I would ask of you. In the Catholic Cemetery near the chapel, my wife and child are buried in an enclosed lot, concrete blocks with concrete cross about six feet high standing in the center. I would like to know the condition of the graves."[1]

Wilson replied to his favored friend, "I went out and looked them over. Yours are covered over with grass, vines and brush. The cross was the only thing visible. I will have it cleaned up…" The men kept up that exchange for the next three years, P.H. always ending his letters, "I will thank you to give about 20 pesos to the almoner kitty at Mt. Alpo Lodge." This kitty was a fund maintained by the Masons for the distribution of alms. His last letter to Wilson was written just before Decoration Day in May 1950, "I don't want you to go out of your way, but it would be a great favor to…" Wilson responded, "I took flowers out and placed them on the graves of your plot in the cemetery. I don't want you to send any money next year, but send me a reminder so I will not forget…" It was their last correspondence. [2]

§ § §

On Christmas Day 1950, Patrick Henry Frank died at the age of seventy-five at his small cottage in Benicia, California. I remember the arrival of a Western Union telegram sent by Annie to my family's North Decatur Road home two doors up from Springdale Road, close by Emory University. I was working graphite into the wheels of my new Flexi-flyer and took off down the hill to Emory Village. I was astride, stomach down, holding both steering bars with naive confidence. My father was on the telephone when I returned. He was talking serious talk in a way and in a language I had never heard before. Mother told me grandfather had died and that my father was talking to his brother. Mixed Spanish and Cebuano was the best way for them at that moment, reverting to their mother's native tongue. I rode with my parents to Union Station where my father took the long train ride cross country—remembering, reflecting, and writing notes to himself.

§ § §

Patrick Henry Frank's service was Masonic and his burial military at the Golden Gate National Cemetery, in the same ground on which he had encamped with the 23rd Infantry before shipping out to the Philippines in 1898. One automobile pulled up late. An elderly man stepped out. At an earlier time, he bartended P.H. Frank's First and Last Chance Saloon, managed the spirited soldiers, and helped P.H. roll H. M. Dennison's beer kegs back to the Red House. Dick Thrasher gathered himself, leaned forward into the hill, and led the young soldiers carrying the flag draped coffin up the rise to the gravesite. An Army chaplain led the service, and the military honors ended with a melancholy bugle sounding beyond the Pacific oaks at the crest.

John Russell Frank, Ph.D.

The Gospel of Zamboanga

Away back in the memory of every America-born lad, there was a time when a misty-haze of romance penetrated and engraved itself upon his mind. It may have been the oriental splendor of barbarian trappings; lost treasures of gold plate, sunken chests of rare old Spanish coins; or only that uncertain "something-we-have-never-seen;" but it was there when we first sailed westward from the Golden Gate. The majority of us, on reaching our destination, were in time convinced of our delusion; but a few there were who drifted down toward the equator to the islands called the Moro group, and there found paradise.

"Moro Province Mindanao: The Pioneer's Paradise,"
Philippine Magazine (October 1908) pg. 82

Dick Thrasher leads honor guard carrying P. H Frank's casket. Golden Gate National Cemetery, December 29, 1950.

EPILOGUE

Manila, 1996

The Philippine airliner settled into a glide path toward Manila Airport. The flight from Zamboanga had taken only a few hours. This was the second time I had made a landing in the islands as I followed my family's pivotal years in this corner of America's past. Below me was the blue-green South China Sea, every manner of ship and transport making way to the Boca Chica, the narrow channel into the Manila harbor. The left wing dipped, revealing a perfect view of the island of Corregidor rising steeply out of the sea, masking in its tropical growth the remnants of rusted naval guns, giant mortars, and innumerable bullet and bomb fragments from another time, my family's time—"The Rock" it was called, from the Spanish "*Correggio*." This was the place where the remnants of an American and Filipino army surrendered to Japanese forces in March 1942. In the distance, the massive bluffs of Bataan and the mountain ranges beyond dipped into the sea. I was looking at the place where the Bataan Death March began.

Off to my right, there was a glimpse of the salt beds of Las Penas just south of Manila, where salt water flows into great pools and where the crystal is raked out as the water evaporates. Small rafts transported the salt in white bags just as my mother had described in her letters home in 1931.

The airport lay within the low, flat lands of Cavite. Outside the terminal, I entered a cocoon of tropical heat. It was here, in 1570, that Spanish troops landed, initiated a devastating raid on Manila, and established a permanent Spanish colony. In this same place, my grandfather landed in July 1898, and encamped with his regiment in a peanut field close by Manila.

My taxi drove along Roxas Boulevard, with the waters of Manila Bay to the left, past the American Embassy to the Manila Hotel. My parents, aunt, and uncle danced into the evenings in this fashionable hostelry in the 1930's. My grandfather and Annie Simoes took high tea and drinks in the salon. A Filipino orchestra was playing a Mozart violin sonata, a favorite of my father.

A brief explanation to the manager of my reasons for being in Manila and staying in the Manila Hotel resulted in his solicitous showing of the fourth floor suite where General Douglas MacArthur, his wife Jean Faircloth, and their son Arthur lived while he was the U.S. Army Commander in the Far East. The General's famous gold-embroidered military hat, tall-bowled corncob pipe, and Field Marshall's baton lay in the open on a desk. It was there at 3:40 on Sunday morning, December 8, 1941, that a communication from Washington informed MacArthur of the Japanese attack on Pearl Harbor.

The following morning I climbed the ramparts of the ancient Intramuros fortress across the boulevard from the Manila Hotel and looked back toward Cavite, trying to envision the lines of the American march into Manila. Then I drove out to Santo Tomas University.

There was Main, and there were the iron gates that fell to the American tanks. The wide wooden stairway that my father had descended that liberation eve in February 1945, ascended to the fourth floor room he shared with his brother and forty prisoners. I saw the two rooms, one for the dead and the other for the wounded where he spent much of his first night of liberation. I stood at the university gate where my grandfather, supine on a litter, dehydrated, delirious, wearing filthy pajamas, found deliverance and safety from the Japanese holdout at Philippine General Hospital.

Filipino students walked on the long green lawns that once held 5,000 American and Allied prisoners. I observed warm, welcoming glances and sensed their knowing that I came to connect with the prison camp that had once occupied their campus—part of a never failing succession of guests.

Returning to the hotel, I walked the oval to the waterfront. Dusk was coming and a tropical sunset was underway. A stunning afterglow of oranges and purples silhouetted Corregidor in the distance. A million electric lights of Manila sparkled in the darkness.

The moon rose in the early dark. There were two shadows—my grandfather's and mine. Then the shadows merged. The ebb tide had retreated; the seawall remained strong. There were two shallow heartbeats, and then there was one. I felt the pull that must happen inside all migrating birds. That evening I flew out of Manila—on the road home.

Author John Russell Frank holds the tombstone of Laura Frank in the
Frank-Garcia plot, Old Catholic Cemetery, Zamboanga, 1996.

ACKNOWLEDGEMENTS

D. Michael Parker, a colleague, historian, and now Provost of Anderson University, South Carolina, first recognized the significance of our family's papers, assisted my research and writing, and encouraged the family to consider a permanent depository of its historical records. Without his interest and encouragement, this work would never have begun.

Special appreciation to Janice Wilson, Truett-McConnell College librarian, for her assistance in locating sources and processing the earliest inter-library loans required of this work. I also extend appreciation to research librarians Debra Gross of Duke University, two unknown Filipino researchers at the Lopez Library in Manila who were brought into service by Lewis Gleek, Nolan Hatcher of the DeKalb County (Georgia) Library, Elizabeth McBride and Nancy Rhinehart of Emory University, and Leith Tate at the University of North Carolina–Asheville. John J. Slonaker, Chief of Historical Reference, U.S. Army Military History Institute, provided invaluable service in locating microfilmed regimental returns of the 23rd, 9th, and 10th regiments. Charles Reeves, Assistant Director of the S.E. Regional Branch of the National Archives tracked down valuable enlistment and medical records of my grandfather. Originals were lost in a fire, but he found copies preserved in records of the Veteran's Administration. Morton Netzorg, Cellar Book Store, Detroit, Michigan provided excellent bibliographical resources and copies of rare publications. James Zobel, Archivist at the General Douglas MacArthur Memorial and Center in Norfolk, Virginia, was instrumental with accessioning photographs and other primary and secondary sources. Catherine Williams was responsible for the Philippine map illustration, and processed photographs for the book. Marian Ward completed the final proofreading of the manuscript.

Lewis E. Gleeck, Jr., Editor and Curator of the American Historical Collection, Manila, reflected at long distance on many of my questions. He provided valuable leads, arranged for research assistance at the Lopez Library in Manila. In 1996, Lewis and his wife Fira provide me a glimpse of modern day Manila, and at the Army-Navy Club reflected on my family's place in the American period.

Frances R. Cruces, D.D., Archbishop of Zamboanga, researched the location of our family gravesites and found them in an enclosed area of the Old Catholic Cemetery where they were marked with a large cross with the names Frank and Garcia on either side. Bishop Cruces put me in touch with Josefina Garcia, a cousin who tended the tombs on All Souls Day. Josefina provided me with the remarkable information about my Philippine ancestors.

Naomi Nelson, Acting Director and Coordinator of Research Services, Manuscript, Archives, and Rare Book Library, Robert W. Woodruff Library, at Emory University was instrumental in the gifting of our family collection, organizing the exhibit, announcing the opening of the papers, and providing excellent reflections and suggestions on my writing. Susan Potts McDonald, Coordinator for Arrangement and Description, and Teresa Burke, Research Services Archivist processed collection and mounted the opening exhibit. Theresa Kaminski, Professor of History, University of Wisconsin–Stevens Point came a great distance to speak at the Emory symposium opening the Frank archives, awakened me to women's roles, viewpoints and contributions during the American period in the Philippines, read my book proposals, and offered welcome encouragement.

Steve Crytser and Jim Burchfield, sons of my parents' Davao friends have generously shared correspondence and photographs, and Jim allowed my use of the rich resource of his mother's unpublished memoirs of her Davao years. George Francis George, Annie Simoes Frank's second husband, graciously gifted to me all the remaining photographs, correspondences, memorabilia and relics of my grandfather's life which are now entrusted to Emory University. Historian Henry J. Copeland provided perspective and careful analysis of my proposal. Scholars

Richard A. Ray and Samuel Hill loaned their significant time and gentle criticism to the manuscript. Jean and Carl Franklin, owners of Black Mountain Books and Cases, were expeditious in ordering books.

And warm acknowledgement to John and Cinnamon Kennedy, proprietors of Our House Writers, Black Mountain, North Carolina, who have served as my editors, redirected my writing, offered up commentary, shared much of the writers art, and welcomed me to their weekly writers group. The Kennedy's left New York's 9/11 ash trail in 2001 and moved with their two young daughters to Last Resort Road, where they offer helpful, compassionate guidance to writers. For over a year Dick Ray, Gari Carter, Nat Justice and I were regulars at the Kennedy's home on Tuesday evenings. Knowing that I faced a group every week expecting to share their commentary on my previous week's submission and expecting to leave with them that evening another of my chapters, kept me focused on deadlines for fourteen months of my writing.

My brothers and cousins contributed substantially to this work. My cousin Pat Frank, Jr. reflected at long distance from Portland, Maine on the numerous questions about the materials I was working with. His brother Mike Frank in Detroit, shared the audio taped recordings of his father's life in the Philippines, and their brother Dennis suggested reading F. Sionil Jose's *Dusk* (originally published in the Philippines as *Po-on*), which led me into the literature of the Filipino experience. My brother Sam's video tapes which preserved much of our father's remembrances were invaluable. Together with my brother Pat, the two were always ready to help with chronologies, stories and reflections on the meaning of our family's experience.

To paraphrase T. S. Eliot, every ending has a beginning. Such a beginning was in and with my father Samuel Boone Frank who kept letters and documents, photographs and diaries of his and his father's family in the Philippines. He kept all this in his filing cabinets, boxes, on his bookshelves, safe-deposit box, and in his head, saying of the writing I was doing, "I don't know what to say; I'm just flattered that someone would take an interest." In addition, there was my grandfather who considered "details and incidentals to be the point of a letter and the very life of it, as by them one conveys a clearer picture of their life and surroundings," and my mother who in her letters accomplished exactly that. Her voice is clearly a part of this book.

My aunt and uncle, Gen and Pat Frank, Sr., generously shared their saved letters, photos, and remembrances—Gen writing this encouragement to me: "Your book could become the core flow from which the saga of the American experience in the Philippines springs."

On the thirty-fifth anniversary of the bombing of Pearl Harbor, Gen wrote a piece she called *Nostalgia*, in which she remembered her life in the Philippines in the 1930s and the horrors of the war that destroyed it. In her conclusion, she wondered, "Have we done all we can to make the record as clear, as precise, and as vivid as possible? Perhaps this is all we can do for both those who suffered so much and for our posterity so that history may not have to repeat itself."

GLOSSARY

amah. An oriental nurse or servant for children.

amuck. One who for some reason looses his head/goes crazy and runs through the streets killing everyone in sight until he is subdued or killed.

anting-anting. An amulet that is worn to shield from disease or danger.

baguio. Tropical cyclone or typhoon occurring in the Philippines or China Sea.

baksheesh. Tip or bribe to expedite service.

banca. Hollowed out log boat.

baniaga. Slaves captured or kidnapped from among non-Muslims.

barong. Thick-backed thin-edged knife or sword used by the Moros.

barrio. Neighborhood in a town or city.

bejuco. Woven rattan sleeping surface.

bodega. Storehouse or warehouse.

bolo. Long heavy single-edged knife of Philippine origin.

caminero. System of maintaining roads or common areas.

campilans. Head taking knives.

capis. Translucent shell.

carabao. Water buffalo.

carromatos. Small two or four-wheeled buggy.

casco. A storage area on a small launch.

cassava. Fleshly edible rootstock which yields a nutritious starch.

cawa. Giant wok-like cooking vat.

chop. A seal, official stamp or its imprint.

cota. Moro fortress.

datu. Muslim leader who presides over a group of followers/and or a territory.

despedida. A festive event.

fundoshi. A Japanese loincloth to cover front and rear.

guerrilla. One who engages in irregular warfare.

gunseibu. Japanese military government

illustrados. Wealthy landed and business elites of Spanish and Chinese ancestry.

jambangan. Land of flowers.

juramentado. One who swears an oath to kill the enemies of Islam.

kempetai. Military police of the Imperial Japanese Army.

kris. A wavy bladed Moro sword.

lantaka. A brass cannon.

lavandera. A woman who launders clothes.

mestizo/a. A person of mixed blood/ a woman who is a mestizo.

Moro. A member of any of several Muslim peoples of the Southern Philippines.

Muezzin. A Muslim crier who calls the daily hours for prayer.

nipa. A thatch made of a Malay or other palm.

olipon. Moro bond slave.

padres. Catholic priests.

pahagads. Sleds for moving objects (typically pulled by water buffalo).

pandita. Muslim religious leader.

petate. Woven mat for sleeping.

salle. A hall or room.

samurai. A Japanese warrior practicing the chivalric code of Bushido.

sarong. A loose skirt made of a long strip of cloth wrapped around the body.

shannala. A leather sandal.

shoji. Light weight Japanese shutters.

siesta. A midday nap.

sukiyaki. A dish consisting of thin slices if meat, bean curd, vegetables cooked in soy sauce, sake, and sugar.

tuxie. The tough sheath surrounding the petiole of the hemp(abaca) plant.

vinta. Small outrigger boat with multicolored sail.

SELECTED BIBLIOGRAPHY

Achenbach et al. v. The United States, 02-894C U.S. Court of Appeals (2003).

Adams, H.C. "Snapshot of Philippine America." *Worlds Work*, 28:31-42, May 1914.

Anderson, Isabel. *The Spell of the Hawaiian Islands and the Philippines.* Boston, MA: The Page Co, 1916.

Bailey, Thomas A. *A Diplomatic History of the American People*, 5th ed., New York: Appleton-Century-Crofts, 1950.

Bain, David H. *Sitting in Darkness, Americans in the Philippines.* Boston, MA: Houghton Mifflin Co, 1984.

"Battle with Moro Outlaws." *Outlook* 82:583-583; 625-626 (Mr 17, 24, 1906).

Bowden, Mark. "Jihadist in Paradise." *The Atlantic* (March 2007).

Bowles, Flora. *A History of Trinity County Texas.* Groveton, TX, 1966.

Brent, J.E. "Strenuous Vacation." *Outlook* 8: 233-237 (Je 3, 1905).

Breuer, William B. *Retaking the Philippines, America's Return to Corregidor and Bataan: October 1944-March 1945.* New York: St. Martin's Press, 1986.

Burchfield, Evelyn. "Twenty Years With the Filipinos." An account of the Davao women and children's escape from Davao in December, 1941, survival in the jungle and rescue aboard the

U.S. submarine *Narwhal,* unpublished typescript, 191pgs, copy in the possession of author.

Cary, Frank. *Letters from Internment Camp: Davao and Manila, 1942- 1945.* Ashland, Oregon: Independent Printing Co., 1993.

Climaco, R.C. *Zamboanga Vignettes, (A Sequel to Small-Town VIP's): A Collection of Stories of Old Zamboanga.* Zamboanga City, PI: Leader's Press, 1992.

Cloman, S.A. "Selungan and Sulu." *World's Work,* 46:306-315 (Jl, 1923).

Coats, Stephen T. *"Gathering at the Golden Gate: The U.S. Army and San Francisco, 1898"* dissertation (University of Kansas, 1998).

Cogan, Frances B. *Captured, The Internment of American Civilians in the Philippines, 1941- 1945.* Athens, GA: University of Georgia Press, 2000.

"Commercial Awakening of the Moro and Pagan." *North American Review* 197: 325-340 (Mr 1913).

Cook, W.B. "Pictures From the Philippines." *Missionary Review of the World.* 40: 598-601 (Ag, 1917).

Cosmas, Graham A. *An Army for Empire, The United States Army in the Spanish-American War.* College Station, TX, Texas A&M University Press 1994.

Crouter, Natalie. *Forbidden Diary, A Record of Wartime Internment,* 1941-1945. Edited with an introduction by Lynn Z Bloom. New York: Burt Franklin & Co, 1980.

Cushman, H. "War-Nourished Philippine Industries" *World Outlook.* 5:21 (Mr 1919).

Department of Mindanao and Sulu at the Second Philippine Exposition, January 31 to February 14, 1914, Zamboanga, P.I., (Perkins Library Pamphlet Collection, Duke University): The Mindanao Herald Pub. Co., 1914.

DioGuardi, Ralph. "Santo Tomas Testament" *EX-POW Bulletin: American Ex-Prisoners of War,* vol.45, no.9, September 1988.

Downey, Fairfax. *Indian Fighting Army*, (Valuable for its coverage of the various Indian wars and for its picture of the regular army which would fight the Spanish American War) New York: Charles Scribner Sons, 1941.

Dull, Paul S. *A Battle History: The Imperial Japanese Navy (1941-1945)*: Annapolis, MD (1978) 5th Printing 1989.

Egan, E.F. "Eliminating the American" *Saturday Evening Post*. 194 (Ag 27, 1921).

_____. "Chances in the Islands for Young Men" *Sunset Magazine* 18: 42-49 (N 1906).

_____. "Do the Filipinos Want Independence" *Saturday Evening Post*. 194: (O 15, 1921).

_____. "Philippines for the Filipinos" *Saturday Evening Post*. 194 (Sp 17, 1921).

_____. "Preserving the Philippines." *Saturday Evening Post*. 194 (O 1, 1921).

Faust, Karl I. Campaigning in the Philippines. 1899. Reprint, New York:Arno Press, 1970.

Frank Family Papers 1898-1992. Manuscript Collection No. 966: Manuscript, Archives & Rare Book Library, Robert W. Woodruff Library, Emory University, Atlanta. The collection consists of the papers of the Frank family from 1898-1992, arranged into six series: (1) Correspondence, (2) Internment Camps, (3) Other Papers (4) Photographs, (5) Printed Material, and (6) Audio-Visual Material.

Frank, Ellie "American Civilians in the Philippines in 1941: Why Did They Stay?" Senior Thesis, History 400S, Professor Weil, University of Georgia, (Winter, 1991).

Frank, Genevieve Quinlin. "A Beautiful City, A Tropical Paradise." *The Anchora of Delta Gamma* (March 1943).

Frank, J. Russell and D. Michael Parker. "'Boss:' A Philippine Legacy." Manila, PI: *Bulletin of the American Historical Collection*. 78: 7-23 (January-March 1992).

_____. "'Boss:' A Philippine Legacy (II)" 79 (April-June, 1992).

_____. "'Boss:' A Philippine Legacy (III)" 87 (April-June, 1994).

_____. "'Boss:' A Philippine Legacy (IV)" (88 July-September, 1994).

Freeman, L.R. "Philippines as a Business Proposition." *Engineering Magazine*, 45:649-663 (August 1913).

Fulton, Robert A. *Moroland 1899-1906: America's First Attempt to Transform an Islamic Society.* Bend, Oregon: Tumalo Creek Press, 2007.

Gates, John M. *Schoolbooks and Krags: The United Sates Army in the Philippines, 1899- 1902.* Westport CN: Greenwood Press, 1973.

Gleeck, Jr., Lewis E. *American Business and Philippine Economic Development.* Filipino- American Historical Studies, Manila, PI: Camelo & Bauermann, 1975.

_____. *American Institutions in the Philippines 1898-1941.* Filipino-American Historical Studies, Manila, PI: Camelo & Bauermann, 1976.

_____. *Americans on the Philippine Frontier.* Filipino-American Historical Studies, Manila, PI: Camelo & Bauermann, 1974.

_____. *General History of the Philippine: The American Half Century (1898-1946).*

Historical Conservation Society, Part V, Vol.1, Quezon City, PI: R.P. Garcia Publishing Co, 1984.

_____. *The Manila Americans.* Filipino-American Historical Studies, Manila, PI: Camelo & Bauermann, 1977.

Gopal, Lou and Bunn, Michelle, producers. *Victims of Circumstance, Santo Tomas Internment Camp.* CD audio-video recordings of survivors, Kawayan Productions, General Douglas MacArthur Archives, Norfolk, VA.

Gowing, Peter G. *Mandate in Moro Land, The American Government of Muslim Filipinos 1899-1920.* Quezon City, PI: New Day Publishers 1983.

_____.*Muslim Filipinos, Heritage and Horizon.* Quezon City, PI: New Day Publishers 1979.

Hahn, Emily. *The Islands, America's Imperial Adventures in the Philippines.* New York: Cowad, McCann & Geoghegan, 1981.

Halsema, James. *E. J. Halsema: Colonial Engineer: A Biography.* Quezon City, PI: New Day Publishers, 1991.

Hartendorp, A.V.H. *The Japanese Occupation of the Philippines, vol I,* Manila: Bookmark, 1967.

_____. *The Japanese Occupation of the Philippines, vol.II.* Manila: Bookmark, 1967.

_____. *The Santo Tomas Story,* ed. Frank H. Golay. New York: McGraw-Hill, 1964.

Hilsman, Roger. *American Guerrilla: My War Behind Japanese Lines.* Brasey Press, 1990.

Hoffman, Richard. E. *The Bamboo American.* Quezon City, PI: New Day Publishers 1988.

Holland, Robert B. *The Rescue of Santo Tomas: Manila WWII, The Flying Column: 100 Miles to Freedom.* Paducah, KY: Turner Publishing Co. 2003.

Ienaga, Saburo. *The Pacific War, World War II and the Japanese, 1931-1945.* First published by Iwanami Shoten: Tokyo. English translation, Random House, 1978

Japanese Operations in the South West Pacific Area, Vol. 2: Part 1 in Japanese and English. *Reports of General McArthur, Japanese Demobilization Bureau x Records,* Washington, DC 1966.

Jones, O.G. "Athletics Helping the Filipino" *Outing Magazine:* 64:585-592 (Ag 1914).

Jose, F. Sionil. *Dusk* (Po-on). Published in the United States by Random House, 1998.

Jurika, Blanche. "Housekeeping and Raising a Family in Zamboanga," *Bulletin of the American Historical Collection.* Vol. 6 No.3: 67-75 (Manila, 1978).

Kaminski, Theresa. *Prisoners in Paradise, American Women in the Wartime South Pacific.* Lawrence, KN: University Press of Kansas, 2000.

_____. "So Many Things Have Happened to Me": An American Woman in the Philippines." Symposium opening the Frank Family Papers, Special Collections and Archives, Robert W. Woodruff Library, Emory University, 2004 (copy in possession of author).

Kramer, Paul A. *The Blood of Government: Race, Empire, the United States and the Philippines.* Chapel Hill: University of North Carolina Press, 2006.

Lee, G.S., "Abaca (Manila Hemp); The Fiber Monopoly of the Philippine Islands." *Science Monthly,* (August 1920).

Lewis, Winnifred. *Islands of the Western Pacific.* New York: McMillan Co, 1950.

Lichauco, Marcial P. and Moorfield Storey. *The Conquest of the Philippines by the United States 1898-1925.* New York,: G.P. Putnam's Sons 1926.

Linn, Brian McAllister, *Philippine War 1899-1902.* Lawrence: University of Kansas Press, 2000.

MacArthur, Douglas. *Reminiscences.* New York: McGraw, 1964.

McGee, John H. *Rice and Salt: A History of the Defense and Occupation of Mindanao During WWII.* San Antonio, TX: Naylor Co, 1962.

Manchester, William. *American Caesar.* Boston: Little Brown and Company, 1978.

Marcial P. Lichauco. *Roxas, The Story of a Great Filipino and of the Political Era in Which he Lived.* Manila: Kiko Printing, 1952.

Marshall, Cecily Mattocks. *Happy Life Blues: A Memoir of Survival.* Clinton, MA: Agnus MacGregor Books, 2007.

Maynard, Mary McKay. *My Faraway Home, An American Families WWII Tale of Adventure and Survival in the Jungles of the Philippines.* Guilford, CT: Lyon Press, the Globe Pequot Press, 2001.

Miller, Stuart C. *Benevolent Assimilation, The American Conquest of the Philippines*. New Haven: Yale University Press, 1982.

Mills, Walter. *The Martial Spirit*. Boston: Houghton Mifflin. 1931.

Mindanao Herald (The). Microform, Serial: Zamboanga, Mindanao, Perkins News- Microfilm Collection, Duke University.

Morrison, Samuel E. *The Liberation of the Philippines, Luzon, Mindanao, the Visayas 1944- 45*. History of United States Military Operations in World War II, Volume xiii, Boston: Little Brown and Company, 1959.

Morton, Louis. *United States Army in World War II, The War in the Pacific: The Fall of the Philippines*. Washington, DC: Center of Military History, United States Army, 1989.

O'Toole, G.J.A. *The Spanish War, An American Epic – 1898*. New York: W.W. Norton & Co., 1984.

Park, Hugh. ——"The Day the First Cavalry Rescued American Prisoners." Based on the experiences of Sam B. Frank. *Around Town* a column by Hugh Park, *The Atlanta Journal*, September 25, 1957.

——"The Day the First Cavalry Rescued American Prisoners." Based on the experiences of Sam B. Frank. *Around Town* a column by Hugh Park, *The Atlanta Journal*, October 2, 1957.

Parsons, E.C. "American Snobbishness in the Philippines" *Independent* 60: 332-333 (F 8, 1906).

Petillo, Carol M. ed. *The Ordeal of Elizabeth Vaughn*. Athens: University of Georgia Press, 1985.

Pitcher, A.L. "Need of Good Men in the Philippines." *Independent*, 63:980-983, 24 October 1907.

Pitcher, A.L. "Need of Good Men in the Philippines" *Independent* 63: 980-983 (O 24, 1907).

Reports of Cases Decided by the Supreme Court of the Philippine Islands. Philippines Supreme Court. Manila, Bureau of Printing, 1908-1950.

Reports of the Philippine Commission, the Civil Governor, and the Heads of the Executive Departments of the Government of the Philippine Islands Philippine (1900-1903), Bureau of Insular Affairs, War Department. Washington: Government Printing Office, 1904.

Robb, Robert Yelton. "Nightmare in Santo Tomas" Collier's: 5 February 1949.

Rowan, William. *On the Spring Tide, A Special Kind of Courage*. Greenboro, NC: Cenographix Publishing, 1998.

Sam, Margaret, Sascha Jean Jansen, Jane S. Wills, and Karen K. Lewis. *Interrupted Lives: Four Women's Stories of Internment During World War II in the Philippines*. Introduction by Llly Nova, Edited by Lily Nova and Iven Lourie: Artemic Books 1995.

San Antonio Military Academy Record. San Antonio, TX, Vols. 1920, No. 2, Vol 1922, No.2, Vol.1923, No 1.

"Santo Tomas Internment Camp Internews: Campus Health," contains smuggled first hand accounts, diagrams of camp layout, and health statistics, *Relief for Americans in the Philippines*, New York, 1942.

Sawyer, Frederick H. *The Inhabitants of the Philippines: The Chinese in Mindanao*. New York: Scribner and Sons, 1900.

Shelpby, A. "Army's Songs of the Philippines" *Harper's Weekly* 40:12-17 (Mr 5 1920).

Steinberg, Raphael. *Return to the Philippines*. Alexandria, VA: World War II Time-Life Books, 1979.

Stevens, Frederic. *Santo Tomas Internment Camp*. New York: Stratford House, Limited Private Edition, 1946.

Tindall, George B. *America, A Narrative Story*. New York: W.W. Norton Co. 1988.

Tong, Walter and Margaret Papers. (Record Group No.189). Divinity Library Special Collections, Yale University Library. Margaret and Walter Tong were missionaries serving under the American Board of Commissioners for Foreign Missions in Davao, Philippines and close friends of the Frank family. Letters written to family and friends before and after WWII are helpful to understanding the pre and post WWII Davao.

Twain, Mark. *The Innocents Abroad, or The New Pilgrims' Progress, Being Some Account of the Steamship Quaker City's Excursion to Europe and the Holy Land.* George Macy Co. special edition, 1962.

U.S. Congress. *Enemy Property Commission, Hearings Before the Committee On Interstate and Foreign Commerce, House of Representatives, Eighth Congress, First session. A Bill To Provide A Commission To Adjudicate Claims Of American Nationals Who Were Prisoners Of War Of Japan, For Payments Of Its Awards, And For Other Purposes.* March 20, 21 and April 21, 1947. Washington: U.S. Government Printing Office, 1947.

U.S. Military Institute. Carlisle Barracks, Pennsylvania.

_____. Company Returns, 10th Infantry Roll 118: 1900-1901; Roll 119: 1902.

_____. Company Returns, 17th Infantry Roll 188:1901-1904.

_____. Company Returns: 23rd Infantry Roll 239:1891-1897; Roll 240:1898-1900; Roll 241:1901-1902.

_____. Registers of Enlistments in the U.S. Army: Roll 47. A-K 1893-1897.

_____. Returns from U.S. Military Posts 1800-1916: Includes monthly post returns, morning reports, field returns, and rosters of officers. Generally shows movements of troops, or detachments in the field from units stationed at the Post: Roll 256 Cotabato, Mindanao PI: 1900-1913.

Wetmore, Clio M. *Beyond Pearl Harbor: Civilians Imprisoned at Santo Tomas, Manila 1942-1945.* Haverford, PA: Infinity Publishing, 2001.

Whitt, W.L. "They Were Expendable." *Reader's Digest*, (September, 1942).

Wiley, Doreen G. *One Hundred Candles.* Haverford, PA: Infinity Press.

Wilson, Bessie Hackett. *Memories of the Philippines.* Interviewed by Michael P. Onorato. Fullerton, CA: Oral History Program, California State University, 1989.

Woodcock, Teedie C. *Behind the Sawali : Santo Tomas in Cartoons, 1942-1945.* Greensboro, NC, 2001.

Wright, H.M. "Development of the Philippines" *World's Work* 12: 8083-8090, 1906.

Wygle, Peter R. *Surviving a Japanese P.O.W. Camp: Father and Son Endure Internment in Manila During WWII.* Ventura, CA: Pathfinder Publishing of California, 1991.

REFERENCE WORKS

*Army Air Forces in World War II. Vo. I, Plans and Early Operations, January 1939-August 1942.*edited by W.F. Craven and J.L. Cate, Office of Air Force History, University of Chicago Press 1948.

Atlas of the Philippines. (*Observatorio de Manila*), published by the U.S. Coast and Geodetic Survey, Special Publication No. 3, Government Printing Office, Washington, DC, 1900.

Baum, Willa K. *Transcribing and Editing Oral History.* 3rd Edition,. Nashville, TN:American Association for State and Local History, 1985.

Britannica Encyclopedia. 15th edition, Chicago, 1998.

Chicago Manual of Style, The Essential Guide for Writers, Editors, and Publishers. 14th Edition.Chicago: University of Chicago Press, 1993.

Chronicle of the 20th Century. Clifton Daniel, Editor. American Booksellers Association. Mount Kisco, NY: Chronicle Publications, 1987.

Historical Atlas. William P. Shepherd. 9th edition, New York: Barnes & Noble Inc., 1964.

Inventing the Truth, The Art and Craft of Memoir. Russell Baker, Jill Ker Conway, Annie Dillard, Ian Frazier, Henry Louis Gates, Alfred Cazin, Frank McCourt, Toni Morrison. Edited by William Zinsser. Boston, MA: Houghton Mifflin, 1998.

McGraw Central Station Directory, 1941. New York, McGraw-Hill Publishing Co. 1941.

Speeches and Addresses of William McKinley From March 1, 1897 to May 30, 1900. New York, 1900.

Philippine Newspapers: An International Union List. Compiled by Shiro Saito and Alice W. Mak, Philippine Studies Occasional Papers, No. 7, Belinda A. Aquino, editor. Center for Asian and Pacific Studies. Honolulu: University of Hawaii. July 1984.

Philippine Rainforest(The), Vanishing Treasures. Foreword by Angel C. Alcala. Chicago: Field Museum, 2005.

Telling True Stories, A Nonfiction Writers' Guide, From the Nieman Foundation at Harvard University. Nora Ephron, David Halberstam, Tom Wolfe, et.al., Edited by Mark Kramer and Wendy Call. Penguin Group, 2007.

Polking, Kirk. *Writing Family Histories and Memoirs.* Cincinnati, OH: Betterway Books 1995.

Strunk, William. *The Elements of Style With Revisions, an Introduction, and a Chapter on Writing by E.B. White.* 4th edition, Allyn & Bacon, 2000.

END NOTES

Introduction

[1] Letter, Lewis Gleeck to J. Russell Frank, August 5, 1994, in possession of the author.

Chapter 1 "I am proud I am of an age and in this thing"

A problem with the whole period of American possession of the Philippines is that the period is a scholarly battlefield, especially the themes of American colonialism, made more quarrelsome since America's involvements in Iraq. There is a ton of literature from Halstead to Faust to Karnow, Miller, Cosmas, Gleeck, Fulton and Kramer. Reviewing those texts may leave one lost in a postmodern house of mirrors. I utilized these authors without apology, but I say as little as possible about anything that does not tell the story of P.H. Frank and his family.

[1] FFP: Series 1, Box 8, Folder 8, P.H. Frank to D.P. Quinlan, November 3, 1933.

[1] Frederick Jackson Turner, *Report of the American Historical Association for 1893*, 199-227.

[2] Flora Bowles, *A History of Trinity County Texas*, Groveton, Texas, 1966, p.81-84.

[3] P.H. Frank, U.S. Department of War enlistment and medical records in possession of author.

[4] Company Returns, 23rd Regiment, (July, 1896-December, 1897), U.S. Military History Institute, Carlisle Barracks, Pennsylvania.

[5] Many authors have treated the subject of America's early "accidental imperialism" in the Philippines. Stanley Karnow, *In Our Image*, 1989, is one of the more recent.

[6] Karnow, p.107; *San Francisco Chronicle*, May 17, 1898.

[7] FFP: Series 1, Box 1, Folder 1, P.H. Frank to his sisters, June 2, 1898.

[8] Ibid

⁹ *Ibid.*

¹⁰ *Ibid.*

¹¹ San Francisco Chronicle, June 16, 1898

Chapter 2 "They did not think we could shoot so well…but they got fooled"

¹ FFP: Series 6, Original cassette tapes [restricted]. Samuel B. Frank, January 26, 1990.

² K.J. Faust, *Campaigning in the Philippines*, New York: Arno Press, 1970: 86-87. *Harpers Weekly*, September 24, 1898.

³ FFP: Series 5, Box 6, Folder 30, P.H. Frank to his mother, September 18, 1898, printed in *Groveton Herald* (Texas).

⁴ Faust, *Campaigning in the Philippines*, 80

Chapter 3 "I for one do not want any more war"

¹ P.H. Frank to his mother, October 20, 1898, printed in *Groveton)* *Herald* (Texas). FFP: Series 5, Box 6, Folder 30.

² *Ibid.*

³ P.H. Frank's time in the stockade is revealed in a review of his 1935 application for a pension, Certificate 1-545-140, Veterans Administration.

⁴ Returns for Company F, 23rd Regiment, December-April 1898.

⁵ Letters, P.H. Frank to his mother, December, 1898, printed in Groveton Herald (Texas). FFP: Series 5, Box 6, Folder 30.

⁶ *Ibid.*

⁷ *Ibid.*

⁸ *Ibid.*

⁹ As quoted in Karnow, *In Our Image*, 109

¹⁰ Karnow, *In Our Image*, 127-128.

¹¹ Horace P. Hobbs, *Kris and Krag: Adventure Among the Moros of the Southern Philippines* (1962), 43; quoted in Peter Gordon Gowing, *Mandate in Moroland: The American Government of Muslim Filipinos 1899-1920*, 27.

Chapter 4 "Hence her love for the chap who wore Uncle's duds"

¹ Returns for Company C, March 1900.

² Returns for Company C, April 1900.

³ Peter Gordon Gowing, *Mandate in Moroland*, 82-84; Returns for Company C, April 1900; Samuel B. Frank, FFP: Series 6, Original Cassette tapes [restricted].

⁴ P.H. Frank to his sister Texanna Frank (Pike), November 5, 1905. FFP: Box 1, Folder 1.

⁵ Returns for Company A, 17th Infantry, Roll 188

⁶ Samuel B. Frank, FFP: Series 6, Original cassette tapes [restricted]. Reference to N.F. Duckworth in Lewis E. Gleeck, Jr., *The Manila Americans (1901-1964)*, 274 & 276.

7   As quoted in Peter Gordon Gowing, *Mandate in Moroland*, 85

8   Ibid, Gowing, 86.

9   Returns for Company A, 17th Infantry, June 1902.

10   Ibid, P.H. Frank to Texanna Frank.

Chapter 5 "Success of failure she has remained the same"

1   Chapter 3 *Encyclopedia Britannica*, 12th ed., s.v. "Cotabato City"; "Mindanao." Frederick Jackson Turner, *Report of the American Historical Association for 1893*, 199-227. Lewis E. Gleeck Jr. *Americans on the Philippine Frontier*, 106-109.

2   P.H. Frank to sister Texanna, November 5, 1905, FFP: Box 1, Folder 1.

3   Ibid

4   Ibid

5   Ibid. From President McKinley's "Benevolent Assimilation" proclamation, December 21, 1898.

6   Op. cit Frank to Texanna

7   Letter of Patrick J. Frank, Jr. to the author, July 2, 1999.

8   Marriage Certificate P.H. Frank and Eugenia Garcia (true copy Cotabato 26 de Abril de 1933) in possession of the author. P.H. Frank to sister Texanna, November 5, 1905, FFP: Box 1, Folder 1.

Chapter 6 "I came here to Zamboanga"

1   P.H. Frank to sister Texanna, November 5, 1905, FFP: Box 1, Folder 1.

2   Ibid

3   *Mindanao Herald*, December 9, 1905

4   Ibid

Chapter 7 "Mr. Frank named his plantation Frankfort"

1   P.H. Frank to sister Texanna, November 5, 1905, FFP: Box 1, Folder 1.

2   J.Russell Frank and D. Michael Parker. "*Boss: A Philippine Legacy (II)*", Bulletin of the American Historical Collection, Vol. XX, No. 2 (79), 56.

3   FFP: Series 6, Original cassette tapes 9 & 10 (restricted) Samuel Boone Frank, June 14 & 20, 1990.

4   *Mindanao Herald*, November 16, 1905

5   J. Russell Frank & D. Michael Parker, "Boss" A Philippine Legacy (II), Bulletin of the American Historical Collection, Vol. XX, No. 2, 61.

6   Frank and Parker, 61-62.

7   Frank & Parker, 62.

8   P.H. Frank to sister Texanna, November 5, 1905, FFP: Box 1, Folder 1.

Chapter 8 "It seems that Old Fate has marked out my path"

1   Frank & Parker, 65.

2   Frank & Parker, 65-66.

3   Frank & Parker, 66.

4 **Chapter 9** "The world is my home"

5 Photograph, Frank family reunion, 1908. FFP: Series 4, Box 6, Folder 1.

6 P.H. Frank to sister Cody. FFP: Series 1, Box 1, Folder 2.

Chapter 10 "If you know a bright enterprising young man"

1 J. Russell Frank, edited by D. Michael Parker. *"Boss" A Philippine Legacy (III)*, Journal of the American Historical Collection, Vol. XXII, No. 2(87), April-June 1994, 39-48. Also *"Boss" A Philippine Legacy (IV)*, Journal of the American Historical Collection, Manila, Vol. XXII, No. 3 (88), July-September 1994, 71-83.

2 Peter Gordon Gowing, *Muslim Filipinos-Heritage and Horizon*, 100-102, 117. *Mandate in Moroland, The American Government of Muslim Filipinos 1899-1920*, 98-99.

Chapter 11 "Following her recovery, Okio was looking for a job"

1 J. Russell Frank, edited by D. Michael Parker, *"Boss" A Philippine Legacy (III)*, Journal of the American Historical Collection , Vol. XXII. No. 2(87), April-June, 1994, 39-48.

2 Peter Gordon Gowing, *Mandate in Moroland, The American Government of Muslim Filipinos, 1899-1920*, 235.

3 Gowing, 257-314.

4 *Mindanao Herald*, Twenty-First Anniversary Edition, December 20, 1925.

5 Bessie Hackett Wilson, *Memories of the Philippines*, 2.

6 Isabel Anderson, The Spell of the Hawaiian Islands and the Philippines, 344-345.

7 D.M. Parker, in "Boss" A Philippine Legacy (III) Bulletin of the American Historical Collection, Vol. XXII, No.2(87) 45-46.

Chapter 12 "When death became inevitable, Laura was not denied"

1 Lewis E. Gleeck, Jr. *American Business and Philippine Economic Development*, 58, 74-75.

2 Peter Gordon Gowing, *Mandate in Moroland, The American Government of Muslim Filipinos, 1899-1920*, 276, 279-281.

Chapter 13 "Mr. Frank is taking his hemp striping machine to exhibit"

1 *Manila Times*, June 20, 1920.

2 FFP: Box 1, Folder 2

3 Ibid; FFP: Series 6, Box 6, Folder 41, CD3.

4 Ibid

5 As reported in *Mindanao Herald*, January 21, 1921

6 *Mindanao Herald*, January 28, 1921

Chapter 14 "I'm sending the boys' to that great country I've told them about"

1   Sources utilized in Chapter 14 included: FFP: Series 6, Folder 41, CD's 2-6; Biographical sketches from Lewis Gleeck, Jr., *The Manila Americans (1901-1964)*.

Chapter 15 "I have to build and deliver ten hemp machines…and it's some job"

1   FFP: Series 3, Box 5: Folder 18.
2   Quoted in *Bulletin of the American Historical Collection:* Lewis Gleeck, Jr., *Davao In American Times 1899-1948, 62-87*.
3   FFP: Series 6, Folder 41, CD's 16-19.
4   FFP: Series 1, Box 1: Folder 3.

Chapter 16 "I'll not ship any package off to the university unless I know its contents"

Sources utilized in Chapter 16 included oral histories of Sam B. Frank and Patrick J. Frank: FFP: Series 6, Box 6, Folder 41 CDs 1-36.

1   As quoted in FFP: Series 6, Box 6: Folder 41, CD's 5-6.

Chapter 17 "I'm a little scared — new land new people"

1   FFP: Series 6, Folder 41: CD 5
2   Patrick J. Frank, biographical sketch of Genevieve Quinlan (1911-1999), copy in possession of the author.
3   FFP: Series 1, Box 1, Folder 4.

Chapter 18 "Our boat got in at three o' clock and how excited I was"

1   FFB: Series 1, Box 1, Folder 4. Frances Frank to Bessie Russell, October 20, 1931.
2   Ibid: October 20, 1931.
3   Ibid: October 20, 1931.
4   Ibid: October 22, 1931.
5   Ibid: October 22, 1931.
6   Ibid: October 28, 1931.
7   FFB: Series 1, Box 1, Folder 5. Frances Frank to her mother, Bessie Russell , November 5, 1931.
8   Ibid: November 11, 1931.
9   Ibid: December 15, 1931.
10   Ibid: December 15, 1931.
11   Ibid: Frances Frank to her sister Elizabeth Russell, December 19, 1931.
12   Ibid: November 11, 1931.
13   Ibid: December 28, 1931.

[14]   Opcit: Frances Russell to sisters Elizabeth & Jeannie Russell, December 28, 1931.

Chapter 19 "I'm in a daze — absolutely — totally gone"

[1]   FFP: Series 1, Box 1, Folder 6. Frances Frank to "Everybody," February 5, 1932.
[2]   Ibid: February 5, 1932.
[3]   Ibid: February 5, 1932.
[4]   Ibid: February 10, 1932.
[5]   Ibid: February 10, 1932.
[6]   Ibid: March 4, 1932.
[7]   FFP: Series 1, Box 1, Folder 7 Frances Frank to Bessie Russell , October 14, 1932.
[8]   FFP: Series 1, Box 1, Folder 6 Sam Frank to Bessie Russell, March 7, 1932.
[9]   Ibid: Frances Frank to Bessie Tucker, March 15, 1932.
[10]   Ibid: Frances Frank to "Family," April 1, 1932.
[11]   Ibid: April 1, 1932.
[12]   Ibid: April 1, 1932.
[13]   Ibid: April 30, 1932.
[14]   Ibid: May 4, 1932.
[15]   Ibid: May 5, 1932.
[16]   Ibid: May 5, 1932.
[17]   Ibid: May 7, 1932.
[18]   Ibid: August 3, 11, 12, 13, 1932.
[19]   Ibid: Sam Frank to Bessie Russell, September 4, 1932.
[20]   Stanley Karnow, In Our Image, 250-256.
[21]   Op.cit.: Frances Frank to Bessie Russell, September 23, 1932.
[22]   FFP: Series 1, Box 1, Folder 8 Frances Frank to Bessie Russell, October 30, 1933.

Chapter 20 "You know what a big 'fraidy cat' I usually am"

[1]   FFP: Series 3, Box 5, Folder 15, Genevieve Frank writing, *Anchora of Delta Gamma*. March 1943.
[2]   Ibid: Genevieve Frank, March 1943.
[3]   Genevieve Frank, letter to the author, circa 1992.
[4]   FFP: Series 6, Pat Frank Memories, CD's 23-32.

Chapter 21 "So many things have happened to me"

[1]   FFP: Series 1, Box 2, Folder2.
[2]   FFP: Series 3, Box 5 Folder 15, Genevieve Frank writings.
[3]   Letter: Pat Frank, Jr. to author, circa, 1999.

4   FFP: Series 1, Box 2, Folder 1. Frances Frank to Bessie Russell, September 9, 1936; Series 1,Box 4, Folder 1, Genevieve Frank to Mother, September 19, 1937.

5   Ibid: Folder 2 Frances Frank to Bessie Russell.

Chapter 22 "Don't worry about the Japanese trouble"

1   FFP: Series 6, Box 6 CDs 3-6, Frank interviews.

2   Ibid.

3   Ibid.

4   FFP: Series 1, Box 2, Folder 2, Sam Frank to Bessie Russell, October 7, 1939.

5   Ibid: Frances Frank to Bessie Russell, July 16, 1939.

6   Ibid.

7   Ibid: P.H. Frank to Sam Frank.

8   Ibid: Frances Frank to Bessie Russell, October 28, 1940

9   Ibid: Folder 2, November 29,1940. Folder 3, January 7, 1941.

10 Ibid: Box 2, Folder 3, January 12, 1941

11 FFP: Series 6, Box 6 CD's 5-6.

Chapter 23 "Frances Children Leaving End March Proceed Tucker"

1   Sam Frank, Jr. to author, E-mail May 15, 2002.

2   Genevieve Frank, *"When Manila was Young"* Anchora of Delta Gamma, March 1943.

3   FFP: Series 1, Box 2, Folder 3, Sam Frank to Frances Frank, April 1 1941.

4   Op.Cit. Sam Frank, Jr.

5   FFP: Series 1, Box 4, Folder 1, Patrick J. Frank to Grandpa Quinlin, April 16, 1941. Op.Cit. Sam Frank to Frances Frank, April 17, 1941.

6   Ibid: Peg Tong to Frances Frank, June 9, 1941. Sam Frank to Frances Frank, July 18, 1941.

7   Ibid: Sam Frank to Frances Frank, April 27, May 3, June 4, 1941. Par Frank to Genevieve Frank , July 14, 1941.

8   Ibid: Sam Frank to Frances Frank, June 8, 1941.

9   Ibid: July 1, 1941.

10 Ibid: Sam Frank to Frances Frank, July 28, 1941.

11 Ibid: August 23, 1941.

12 Ibis: August 23, 1941.

13 Ibid: August 23, 1941.

14 Ibid: August 23, 1941.

15 Ibid: September 23, 1941.

16 Ibid: October 21, 1941.

17 Ibid: November 25, 1941.

18 Ibid: November 19, 1941.

19 FFP: Series 1, Box 2, Folder 3, Genevieve Frank to Pat Frank, December 2, 1941.

20 Op.Cit.: Sam Frank to Frances Frank, November 25, 1941.

[21]   Ibid: Frances Frank to Sam Frank, December 1, 1941.

Chapter 24 "Those were Japanese planes bombing our airfield"

Helpful sources for establishing chronology and scenes: MacArthur Reports, *Japanese Operations in the South West Pacific Area* (in Japanese and English); John H. McGhee, *Rice and Salt*, A.V.H. Hartendorp, *The Japanese Occupation of the Philippines*, Vol.1; James Halsema, *The Santo Tomas Story*; FFP: Series 6, CD 7-15 & 23-32; and historical weather reports for Pine Bluff, Arkansas.

[1]   Evelyn Burchfield, unpublished manuscript, p.42-43.
[2]   E-mail: Sam Frank, Jr. to author, February 27, 2000.
[3]   FFP: Series 1, Box 2, Folder 4, Frances Frank to Sam Frank, December 9, 1941.
[4]   FFP: Series 1, Box 4, Folder 2, Genevieve Frank to Pat Frank, December 9, 1941.

Chapter 25 "Situation Normal All Well Love Sam"

[1]   FFP: Series 6, Box 6, CD 7, Sam Frank Interviews.
[2]   Ibid: Pat Frank memories, Sam Frank interviews.
[3]   Bob Cryster, typescript: events of the fall of Davao, December 8 – December 20, 1941 (dated July 13, 1959).
[4]   Op.Cit.: Sam Frank.
[5]   Op.Cit. Evelyn Burchfield.
[6]   Op.Cit.: Sam Frank
[7]   FFP: Series 1, Box 2, Folder 3, Sam Frank to Frances Frank, Radio Telegram; Ibid. Frances Frank to Sam Frank, December 13, 1941.

Chapter 26 "How helpless and forsaken we felt"

Helpful sources for establishing chronology and scenes: FFP: Series 6, Sam Frank Interviews, CDs 7-8; Ibid: Pat Frank memories, CDs 23-32; Evelyn Burchfield, unpublished manuscript; MacArthur Reports, *Japanese Operations in the South West Pacific Area* (in Japanese and English); John H. McGhee, *Rice and Salt*; A.V.H. Hartendorp, *The Japanese Occupation of the Philippines*, Vol.1.

[1]   FFP: Series 6, Pat Frank memories, CDs 23-32.
[2]   John H. McGee, *Rice and Salt*.
[3]   Evelyn Burchfield, unpublished manuscript, p.48.

Chapter 27 "We surrendered at the Club"

Primary source material FFP: Series 2, Internment Camps, 1941-1945, Box 4: Folder 6-Box 5, Folder 11; OP1-2; BV1-4. Series 6, Audio-Visual Materials, 1964-1990, Box 6: Folder 41; CD1-44;DVD1-2.

1   FFP: Series 2, BV1, Camp Diary maintained by Samuel B. Frank; Series 2, Box 4, Folder 9, letter of surrender.
2   FFP: Series 6 Original cassette tapes (restricted) Samuel B. Frank, February 3, 1990, Japanese invade the Philippines, first year of internment at Davao, December 1941-December 1942.
3   FFP: Series 1, Box 2, Folder 4, Frances Frank to Sam Frank, December 21, 1941.

Chapter 28 "We volunteered to go beyond the Japanese lines"

Primary source material FFP: Series 2, Internment Camps, 1941-1945, Box 4: Folder 6-Box 5, Folder 11; OP1-2; BV1-4. Series 6, Audio-Visual Materials, 1964-1990, Box 6: Folder 41; CD1-44;DVD1-2.

1   FFP: Series 6, Sam Frank interviews, CD's 7-8.
2   Ibid.
3   FFP: Series 6, Pat Frank memories, CD's 23-32. *Charlottesville* (Virginia) *Daily Progress*, February 27, 1994.
4   Op.Cit.: Sam Frank interviews.
5   Ibid: Sam Frank interviews.
6   Ibid: Sam Frank interviews.
7   FFP: Series 2, BV1, Davao Internment Camp Diary, December 25, 1941.

Chapter 29 " Somehow I have made myself believe you are still alive"

Primary source material FFP: Series 2, Internment Camps, 1941-1945, Box 4: Folder 6-Box 5, Folder 11; OP1-2; BV1-4. Series 6, Audio-Visual Materials, 1964-1990, Box 6: Folder 41; CD1-44; DVD1-2. Scenes of P.H. and Annie Frank in Manila and P.H.'s initial internment augmented by A.V.H. Hartendorp, *The Japanese Occupation of the Philippines, Vol.2*; James E. Halsema, *The Santo Tomas Story*; Theresa Kaminski, *Prisoners in Paradise: American Women in the Wartime South Pacific*; Frances B. Cogan, *Captured, The Internment of American Civilians in the Philippines, 1941-1945*.

1   FFP: Series 6, Sam Frank interviews, CDs 7-8.
2   FFP: Series 1, Box 2, Folder 4, Frances Frank to Sam Frank, December 27, 28, and P.H. and Annie Frank, December 28, 1941.
3   Op.Cit.: Sam Frank Interviews; Pat Frank memories.
4   FFP: Series 2, BV1, Davao Internment Camp Diary, January 14, 1942.

Chapter 30 "Lt. Hosaka advised that that the internees would be used for labor"

Scenes of Tucker augmented by the authors return to Tucker, Arkansas in Spring, 2001.

1   FFP: Series 2, BV1, Davao Internment Camp Diary, May 14.
2   Ibid. Diary, April 29, 1942. FFP: Series 6, Sam Frank interviews, CDs 7-8.

Chapter 31 "They shot him in the back of the head"

1   FFP: Series 2, Box 4, Folder 18, Executive Committee Minutes, 1942-1943.
2   FFP: Series 6, Sam Frank interviews, CD's 7-8.
3   FFP: Series 6, Pat Frank memories, CD's 23-32. *Charlottesville* (Virginia) *Daily Progress*, February 27, 1994.
4   Ibid.
5   FFP: Series 2, Box 4, Folder 12, Correspondence of Ack Brown, Honorary British Vice-Consul at Davao.

Chapter 32 "Fourteen men were driven to the former Happy Life Blues Cabaret"

1   FFP: Series 3, Box 5, Folder 23, "Patrick James Frank writings.
2   FFP; SERIES 6, Pat Frank Memories, CD's 23-32.
3   Ibid.: Pat Frank memories. FFP: Series 6, Box 6, CDs 9-11, Sam Frank interviews. Series 2, Box 4, Folders 18-19, Executive Committee minutes and notes.

Chapter 33 "We boarded the *Shinsei Maru* on Christmas Eve"

Primary source material FFP: Series 2, Internment Camps, 1941-1945, Box 4: Folder 6-Box 5, Folder 11; OP1-2; BV1-4. Series 6, Audio-Visual Materials, 1964-1990, Box 6: Folder 41; CD1-44; DVD1-2. Scenes of P.H. and Annie Frank in Manila and P.H.'s initial internment augmented by A.V.H. Hartendorp, *The Japanese Occupation of the Philippines,Vol.2*; James E. Halsema, *The Santo Tomas Story*; Frederick H. Stevens, Santo Tomas Internment Camp 281-294. Theresa Kaminski, *Prisoners in Paradise: American Women in the Wartime South Pacific*; Frances B. Cogan, *Captured, The Internment of American Civilians in the Philippines, 1941-1945*.

4   A.V.H. Hartendorp, The Japanese Occupation of the Philippines, 79-85;

Chapter 34 "Santo Tomas looked like a summer resort, but it didn't last long"

Primary source material FFP: Series 2, Internment Camps, 1941-1945, Box 4: Folder 6-Box 5, Folder 11; OP1-2; BV1-4. Series 6, Audio-Visual Materials, 1964-1990, Box 6: Folder 41; CD1-44; DVD1-2. Scenes of P.H. and Annie Frank in Manila and P.H.'s initial internment augmented by A.V.H. Hartendorp, *The Japanese Occupation of the Philippines,Vol.2*; James E. Halsema, *The Santo Tomas Story*; Frederick H. Stevens, Santo Tomas Internment Camp 281-294. Theresa Kaminski, *Prisoners in Paradise: American Women in the Wartime South Pacific*; Frances B. Cogan, *Captured, The Internment of American Civilians in the Philippines, 1941-1945*.

1   FFP: Series 6, Box 6, CDs 13-14, Sam Frank interviews.
2   Ibid. A.V.H. Hartendorp, The Japanese Occupation of the Philippines, Vol.2, p. 462.
3   Op.Cit.: Sam Frank interviews. Numerous accounts of this event abound in the literature of Santo Tomas Internment Camp.

Chapter 35 "The boys broke through and what a day it was"

1   FFP: Series 6, Box 6, CD 13, Sam Frank interviews.
2   Ibid: Sam Frank interviews.
3   Ibid: Sam Frank interviews.
4   Douglas MacArthur, *Reminiscences*, 247.
5   FFP: Series 1, Box 2, Folder 8, Sam Frank to Frances Frank, February 6, 1945.
6   FFP: Series 4, Box 4, Folder 4, Pat Frank to Gen Frank, February 6, 1945.
7   Op.Cit: Sam Frank interviews.

Chapter 36 "Rejoice—it won't be long now"

1   FFP: Series 1, Box 2, Folder 8, Frances Frank to Sam Frank, April 5, 1945.
2   Ibid: Sam Frank to Frances Frank, April 10, 1945.

Chapter 37 "I found the family all well after some trying years"

1   FFP: Series 1, Box 2, Folder 8, Sam Frank to P.H. Frank., May 11, 1945.
2   Ibid: Sam Frank, May 11, 1945.
3   Ibid: Sam Frank, May 11, 1945.
4   Quoted in A.V.H. Hartendorp, *The Japanese Occupation of the Philippines, Vol.2*, p. 614.
5   *Manila Free Press*, as quoted in Hartendorp, Ibid, p. 618.
6   FFP: Series 1, Box 4, Folder 4, P.H. Frank to Genevieve Frank, June 10, 1945.

Chapter 38 "I know how to start from scratch. That's about all I do know"

Scenes of retaking of Mindanao and Davao drawn from Samuel E. Morrison, *The Liberation of the Philippines: Luzon, Mindanao, the Visayas, 1944 -1945*; Raphael Steinberg, Return to the Philippines: World War II Time-Life Books; Louis Morton, *The U.S. Army in WW II, The War in the Pacific, The Fall of the Philippines*.

1   FFP: Series 1, Box 4, Folder 4, Billy Gohn to P.H. Frank, August 20, 1945.

Chapter 39 "I built Sandcastles in the air…and they all came tumbling down"

1   FFP: Series 1, Box 3, Folder 11, Richard R. Ely to Sam Frank, June 2, 1945.
2   FFP: Series 1, Box 4, Folder 4, P.H. Frank to Genevieve Frank, July 4, 1945.
3   FFP: Series1, Box 3, Folder 1, P.H. Frank to Bessie Russell, February 13, 1946.
4   P.H. Frank to Genevieve Frank, August 1, 1946.
5   Ibid: P.H. Frank to Genevieve Frank, August 1, 1946.
6   Ibid: P.H. Frank to Genevieve Frank, and family, November 25, 1946.
7   Ibid: P.H. Frank to Genevieve Frank and family, November 25, 1946.
8   FFP: Series 1, Box 3, Folder 1, P.H. Frank to Sam, Frances and boys, December 16, 1946.
9   Op.Cit.: P.H. Frank to Genevieve Frank and family, November 25, 1946.
10   FFP: Series 1, Box 3, Folder 2, P.H. Frank to Frances Frank, August 15, 1947.

Chapter 40 "A special favor I would ask of you"

1   FFP: Series 1, Box 3, Folder 2, P.H. Frank to James Wilson, April, 1947.
2   Ibid: James Wilson to P.H. Frank, April 28, 1947; Ibid: Folder 3, P.H. Frank to James Wilson, April 1950; Wilson to P.H. Frank, May 9, 1950.

LaVergne, TN USA
19 January 2010
170542LV00002B/27/P